CONTENTS

—INTRODUCTION—

Aim of this book

The aim of this book is to offer you the opportunity to improve your command of Spanish by focusing on one aspect of language learning that invariably causes difficulties – verbs and the way they behave. Whether you are a complete beginner or a relatively advanced learner, you can consult this book when you need to know the form of a certain verb, or you can increase your command of Spanish by browsing through. Whatever your approach, you should find *Teach Yourself Spanish Verbs* a valuable support to your language learning.

How to use this book

Read the section on verbs and how they work. This starts on page 2.

Look up the verb you want to use in the verb list at the back of the book. You will need what is known as the *infinitive*, the equivalent to the *to* . . . form in English (e.g. **venir** *to come*).

The verbs have been allocated a number or numbers between 1 and 202. If the number is in **bold print**, the verb is one of the 202 presented in the verb tables; if it is not among the 202, the reference numbers (in ordinary print) will direct you to a verb that behaves in the same way as the verb you want to use.

Turn to the verb(s) referred to for details of your verb. If you are not sure which verb form to use in a given context, turn to the relevant section of 'What are verbs and how do they work?'

The examples of verbs in use are divided into three categories:

The 'nuts and bolts' of the verb in use. This section deals with basic uses of the verb and gives full-sentence examples of the verb in various tenses.

The second category contains well-known phrases and idiomatic expressions based on the verb in question.

The third category contains important words sharing the same origin as the verb.

WHAT ARE VERBS AND HOW DO THEY WORK?

1 What is a verb?

It is difficult to define precisely what a verb *is*. Definitions usually include the concepts of actions, states and sensations. For instance, *to play* expresses an action, *to exist* expresses a state and *to see* expresses a sensation. A verb may also be defined by its role in the sentence or clause. It is in general the key to the meaning of the sentence and the element that can least afford to be omitted. Examine the sentence:

My neighbour works excessively hard every day of the week.

The elements *excessively hard* and/or *every day of the week* can be omitted with no problem whatsoever. In an informal conversation even *My neighbour* could, with a nod in the direction of the neighbour in question, be omitted. It would, however, not be possible to omit the verb *work*. The same is true of the verb in Spanish sentences – you could not take **trabaja** out of the following sentence.

Mi vecino trabaja mucho todos los días de la semana.	*My neighbour works hard every day of the week.*

2 I, you, he, she, it . . .: person

You will recall that the form of the verb given in dictionaries, the *to* . . . form in English, or the **-ar**, **-er**, or **ir** form in Spanish, is called the infinitive. In English, the verb is normally used in connection with a given person or persons known as personal pronouns (e.g. *I work*, *she works*). Traditionally, these persons are numbered as follows:

First person singular	**yo**	*I*
Second person singular	**tú**	*you* (familiar form)
	usted, Vd	*you* (polite form)
Third person singular	**él, ella**	*he, she*
First person plural	**nosotros, nosotras**	*we* (masc./fem.)

Second person plural	**vosotros, vosotras**	*you* (familiar, masc./fem.)
	ustedes, Vds	*you* (polite form)
Third person plural	**ellos, ellas**	*they* (masc./fem.)

In Spanish the verb is normally used without the personal pronouns:

Creo que es difícil.	*I think that it is difficult.*
¿En qué piensas?	*What are you thinking about?*

The ending of each verb form indicates who is performing the action:

le**o**	*I read*	le**emos**	*we read*
le**es**	*you read*	le**éis**	*you read*
le**e**	*he/she reads*	le**en**	*they read*

Personal pronouns are used only for emphasis in Spanish:

Yo creo que es difícil. ¿Y qué crees **tú**?	*I think that it is difficult. And what do* ***you*** *think?*

Tú is the informal form used mainly to address a member of the family, a child, a friend or an animal. It is becoming increasingly used even among people who do not know each other.

Vosotros, **vosotras** is the informal form used for addressing more than one person. If all the persons addressed are female, **vosotras** is used; otherwise it is **vosotros**, even if there is only one male present in a predominantly female group. Again the informal form is widely used in Spanish.

Usted, **ustedes** are the formal forms, singular and plural. Although the informal forms are in widespread use, it pays to be a bit cautious and to use the polite form when you first start conversing with complete strangers, especially in business contexts. Be guided by what the Spanish themselves use to address you. **Usted** and **ustedes** are normally written in their abbreviated forms: **Vd.** and **Vds**.

South American usage

The **vosotros, vosotras** forms are not used in South America. **Ustedes** is used both formally and informally. However, the distinction between **tú** and **usted** is made in South America. The written abbreviations for **usted** and **ustedes** are **Ud.** and **Uds**.

3 Past, present, future . . .: tense

(*a*) What is tense?

Most languages change the verb form to indicate an aspect of time. These changes in the verb are traditionally referred to as *tense*, which may be *present*, *past* or *future*. It is, of course, perfectly possible to convey a sense of time without applying the concept of tense to the verb. Nobody would have any trouble understanding:

Yesterday I work all day.
Today I work hard.
Tomorrow I work for only one hour.

Here the sense of time is indicated by the words *yesterday*, *today* and *tomorrow* rather than by changes to the verb *work*. But on the whole, you should change the verb form (making use of *tense*) to convey a sense of time:

*He work**s** hard as a rule.*	= Present tense
*I work**ed** for eight hours non-stop.*	= Past tense

In most languages, this involves adding different endings to what is called the *stem* of the verb. In the examples above, the stem is *work*. You add *-s* to make the third person singular present form of the verb; *-ed* is added to make the past tense, whatever the person. In Spanish, the same principle applies. To form the stem, you remove the **-ar**, **-er** or **-ir** from the infinitive, for example, the stem of **hablar** is **habl-**. You then add the appropriate endings.

(*b*) Auxiliary verbs

A verb used to support the main verb, for example, *I **am** working*, *you **are** working* is called an *auxiliary* verb. *Working* tells us what activity is going on; *am/are* tell us that it is continuous.

The most important auxiliary verbs in English are *to be*, *to have* and *to do*. You use *do*, for example, to ask questions and to negate statements:

***Do** you work on Saturdays?*
*Yes, but I **do** not work on Sundays.*

Spanish does not use **hacer** (*to make, do*) as an auxiliary for asking questions or for negating statements, but **haber** (*to have*) is used to form compound tenses, as you shall see below.

(*c*) Simple and compound tenses

Tenses formed by adding endings to the verb stem are called *simple* tenses, for example:

I worked in a factory last summer.

The ending *-ed* has been added to the stem *work* to form the simple past tense.

English and Spanish also have *compound* tenses where an auxiliary verb is used as well as the main verb, for example:

I have worked in a factory every summer for five years.

The auxiliary verb *to have* has been introduced to form what is known as the perfect tense.

(*d*) Participles

In the above examples of compound tenses, the auxiliary verbs *to have* or *to be* are used with a form of the main verb known as a *participle*. The *past participle* is used to form the perfect tense in both Spanish and English:

he estudiado	*I have studied*
he comido	*I have eaten*
he salido	*I have gone out*

In English, the *present participle* is used to form the continous tenses:

*I am **working, eating** and **sleeping**.*
*I was **working, eating** and **sleeping**.*

The present participle **(participio de presente)** or gerund **(gerundio)** is used in Spanish, too, to form the present and past continuous tenses:

correr

Estoy corriendo	*I am running*
Iba corriendo	*I was running*

It is also used in constructions such as these.

trabajar

Le vi trabajando.	*I saw him working.*

andar

Siguieron andando.	*They went on walking.*

4 Regular and irregular verbs

All European languages have verbs which do not behave according to a set pattern and which are referred to as *irregular* verbs.

In English, the verb *to work* is regular because it conforms to a set pattern. The verb *to be*, however, does not.

Fortunately, most Spanish verbs are regular, forming their tenses according to a set pattern. There are three groups of verb which are identified by their type of conjugation and endings. Here they are with the model verb for regular verbs in each type:

- **-ar** trabajar
- **-er** comer
- **-ir** partir

Irregular verbs (ones which do not behave like those in the three groups listed above) have to be learned individually. But many of the so-called irregular verbs are more or less regular in their behaviour. Sometimes the irregularity is merely a change in spelling to maintain consistency of pronunciation. These verbs present an abnormality that recurs constantly and persistently, creating a pattern:

cerrar	*to close*
costar	*to cost*
sentir	*to feel*
pedir	*to ask*

Other verbs are totally irregular. They simply present no logical explanations for their forms:

ir	*to go*
decir	*to say*
caer	*to fall*

5 Formation and use of tenses

(*a*) The present

To form the present tense, simply take off the **-ar**, **-er** or **-ir** part of the infinitive to find the stem; then add the endings:

-ar verbs	**-er** verbs	**-ir** verbs
trabaj**o**	com**o**	viv**o**
trabaj**as**	com**es**	viv**es**
trabaj**a**	com**e**	viv**e**
trabaj**amos**	com**emos**	viv**imos**
trabaj**áis**	com**éis**	viv**ís**
trabaj**an**	com**en**	viv**en**

The present tense (**presente**) is used:

- to indicate an action that occurs at a present time.

  Veo un pájaro. *I see a bird.*

- to refer to regular activities or ongoing states.

  Toco el piano todas las tardes. *I play the piano every evening.*

- in certain circumstances, to refer to the future, or to the past.

  Mañana voy a Londres. *I go / am going to London tomorrow.*

In Spanish, there is also a present continuous tense which is formed with the verb **estar** + present participle.

Estoy trabajando. *I am* (at this moment) *working.*

(*b*) The imperfect

-ar verbs	**-er** verbs	**-ir** verbs
trabaj**aba**	com**ía**	viv**ía**
trabaj**abas**	com**ías**	viv**ías**
trabaj**aba**	com**ía**	viv**ía**
trabaj**ábamos**	com**íamos**	viv**íamos**
trabaj**abais**	com**íais**	viv**íais**
trabaj**aban**	com**ían**	viv**ían**

The imperfect (**pretérito imperfecto**) is used:

- to refer to an ongoing state, or a repeated or continuous action in the past:

Comía a las dos.	*I used to eat at 2 p.m.*
Vivíamos en Madrid.	*We lived in Madrid.*

- to refer to an action which was in progress when something else happened. In this case, the verb referring to the new action is in the past definite tense:

Hablaban de tí cuando llegué.	*They were talking about you when I arrived.*

The verbs **ser** (*to be*), **estar** (*to be*), **tener** (*to have*) and the impersonal form of **haber** (*to have*) (**había** *there was*), are those most frequently used when describing the past:

El hotel estaba enfrente de la iglesia.	*The hotel was opposite the church.*
Había muy pocos turistas.	*There were very few tourists.*

(*c*) The perfect and past definite

The perfect (**preterito perfecto**) is a compound tense formed by the relevant form of the present tense of the auxiliary verb **haber** with the past participle of the main verb.

-ar verbs	**-er** verbs	**-ir** verbs
he trabaj**ado**	**he** com**ido**	**he** viv**ido**
has trabaj**ado**	**has** com**ido**	**has** viv**ido**
ha trabaj**ado**	**ha** com**ido**	**ha** viv**ido**
hemos trabaj**ado**	**hemos** com**ido**	**hemos** viv**ido**
habéis trabaj**ado**	**habéis** com**ido**	**habéis** viv**ido**
han trabaj**ado**	**han** com**ido**	**han** viv**ido**

The perfect tense is used to refer to completed actions carried out in the past, but associated in some way with the present.

El no ha comido todavía.	*He has not eaten yet.*
No he estado nunca en Francia.	*I have never been to France.*

The use of the perfect tense does sometimes overlap with the use of the past definite (**preterito indefinido**), generally used to refer to actions in the past separated from the present.

Hemos dicho que no.	*We have said no.*
Dijimos que no.	*We said no.*

(*d*) The pluperfect

The pluperfect (**pretérito pluscuamperfecto**) is a compound tense and is formed by the relevant form of the imperfect tense of the auxiliary verb **haber** with the past participle of the main verb.

-ar verbs	**-er** verbs	**-ir** verbs
había trabajado	**había** comido	**había** vivido
habías trabajado	**habías** comido	**habías** vivido
había trabajado	**había** comido	**había** vivido
habíamos trabajado	**habíamos** comido	**habíamos** vivido
habíais trabajado	**habíais** comido	**habíais** vivido
habían trabajado	**habían** comido	**habían** vivido

It is used as in English to express an action in the past that was completed before another one was started.

Cuando llegó ya te habías ido.	*When he arrived you had already left.*

(*e*) The past perfect

The past perfect (**pretérito anterior**) is a compound tense formed by the relevant form of the past definite tense of the auxiliary verb **haber** with the past participle of the main verb.

-ar verbs	**-er** verbs	**-ir** verbs
hube trabajado	**hube** comido	**hube** vivido
hubiste trabajado	**hubiste** comido	**hubiste** vivido
hubo trabajado	**hubo** comido	**hubo** vivido
hubimos trajado	**hubimos** comido	**hubimos** vivido
hubisteis trajado	**hubisteis** comido	**hubisteis** vivido
hubieron trabajado	**hubieron** comido	**hubieron** vivido

The past perfect indicates a past action that has occurred before another past action:

Apenas hubo cenado se acostó.	*As soon as he had had his supper he went to bed.*

(*f*) The future

The future tense (**futuro imperfecto**) is formed by adding the appropriate endings to the full verb.

-ar verbs	**-er** verbs	**-ir** verbs
trabajar**é**	comer**é**	vivir**é**
trabajar**ás**	comer**ás**	vivir**ás**
trabajar**á**	comer**á**	vivir**á**
trabajar**emos**	comer**emos**	vivir**emos**
trabajar**éis**	comer**éis**	vivir**éis**
trabajar**án**	comer**án**	vivir**án**

The future tense has three main uses:

- to express an action or state which will occur in the future.

Estaré hasta que cierren.	*I shall stay until closing time.*

- to express probability.

Tendrás hambre.	*You will* (no doubt) *be hungry.*

- in the second person it can be used as an imperative or as an obligatory order.

Irás a casa.	*You'll go home.*

(*g*) The future perfect

The future perfect tense (**futuro perfecto**) is a compound tense formed by the relevant form of the future tense of the auxiliary verb **haber**, and the past participle of the main verb.

-ar verbs	**-er** verbs	**-ir** verbs
habré trabajado	**habré** comido	**habré** vivido
habrás trabajado	**habrás** comido	**habrás** vivido
habrá trabajado	**habrá** comido	**habrá** vivido
habremos trabajado	**habremos** comido	**habremos** vivido
habréis trabajado	**habréis** comido	**habréis** vivido
habrán trabajado	**habrán** comido	**habrán** vivido

The future perfect indicates a future action that will have been completed by a certain time in the future:

Cuando llegues ya habré acabado.	*I will have finished by the time you arrive.*

Note that the verb in the **cuando** clause is in the subjunctive (see below). It can also indicate probability, surprise or even hesitation:

Habrá salido ya.	*He must have left already.*

6 Indicative, subjunctive, imperative . . .: mood

The term *mood* is used to group verb phrases into broad categories according to the general kind of meaning they convey.

(*a*) The indicative mood

This is used for making statements or asking questions of a factual kind.

We are not going today.
Does he work here?
Crime does not pay.

All the tenses we have just been looking at are in the indicative mood.

(*b*) The conditional

This is sometimes regarded as a tense and sometimes as a mood in its own right. It is often closely linked with the subjunctive and is used to express conditions or possibilities:

I would accept her offer, if . . .

In Spanish, the present conditional (**potencial simple**) is formed by adding the appropriate endings to the full verb.

-**ar** verbs	-**er** verbs	-**ir** verbs
trabajar**ía**	comer**ía**	vivir**ía**
trabajar**ías**	comer**ías**	vivir**ías**
trabajar**ía**	comer**ía**	vivir**ía**
trabajar**íamos**	comer**íamos**	vivir**íamos**
trabajar**íais**	comer**íais**	vivir**íais**
trabajar**ían**	comer**ían**	vivir**ían**

The present conditional indicates a future or present action as advice, a suggestion, aspiration, politeness, possible or impossible wishes:

Deberías estudiar más.	*You should study more.*
Podríamos ir mañana.	*We could go tomorrow.*

If the verb in the main clause is in the past, and the verb in the subordinate clause refers to the future, you must use the conditional.

Me dijiste que vendrías.	*You told me that you would come.*

The conditional perfect (**potencial compuesto**) is formed with the conditional of **haber** and the past participle.

-ar verbs	**-er** verbs	**-ir** verbs
habría trabajado	**habría** comido	**habría** vivido
habrías trabajado	**habrías** comido	**habrías** vivido
habría trabajado	**habría** comido	**habría** vivido
habríamos trabajado	**habríamos** comido	**habríamos** vivido
habríais trabajado	**habríais** comido	**habríais** vivido
habrían trabajado	**habrían** comido	**habrían** vivido

The conditional perfect is used to express what might have happened or what might have been done.

Me habría gustado cenar con ellos.	*I would have liked to have dinner with them.*

(*c*) The subjunctive mood

This is used for expressing wishes, conditions and non-factual matters:

*It is my wish that John **be** allowed to come.*
*If I **were** you . . .*

The use of the subjunctive in English is rare nowadays, but it is still frequently used in Spanish. There is a subjunctive form for all the tenses, many of which are given on the next page.

-ar verbs	**-er** verbs	**-ir** verbs
Present		
trabaj**e**	com**a**	viv**a**
trabaj**es**	com**as**	viv**as**
trabaj**e**	com**a**	viv**a**
trabaj**emos**	com**amos**	viv**amos**
trabaj**éis**	com**áis**	viv**áis**
trabaj**en**	com**an**	viv**an**
Imperfect		
trabaj-**ara/ase**	com-**iera/iese**	viv-**iera/iese**
trabaj-**aras/ases**	com-**ieras/ieses**	viv-**ieras/ieses**
trabaj-**ara/ase**	com-**iera/iese**	viv-**iera/iese**
trabaj-**áramos/ ásemos**	com-**iéramos/ iésemos**	viv-**iéramos/ iésemos**
trabaj-**arais/aseis**	com-**ierais/ieseis**	viv-**ierais/ieseis**
trabaj-**aran/asen**	com-**ieran/iesen**	viv-**ieran/iesen**
Perfect		
haya trabajado	haya comido	haya vivido
hayas trabajado	hayas comido	hayas vivido
haya trabajado	haya comido	haya vivido
hayamos trabajado	hayamos comido	hayamos vivido
hayáis trabajado	hayáis comido	hayáis vivido
hayan trabajado	hayan comido	hayan vivido
Pluperfect		
hub-iera/iese trabajado	hub-iera/iese comido	hub-iera/iese vivido
hub-ieras/ieses trabajado	hub-ieras/ieses comido	hub-ieras/ieses vivido
hub-iera/iese trabajado	hub-iera/iese comido	hub-iera/iese vivido
hub-iéramos/iésemos trabajado	hub-iéramos/iésemos comido	hub-iéramos/iésemos vivido
hub-ierais/ieseis trabajado	hub-ierais/ieseis comido	hub-ierais/ieseis vivido
hub-ieran/iesen trabajado	hub-ieran/iesen comido	hub-ieran/iesen vivido

The present subjunctive is often introduced by verbs of hoping and doubting, together with **que** (*that*):

Espero que te guste.	*I hope* (that) *you like it.*
Dudo que ellos vengan.	*I doubt* (whether) *they will come.*

It is also used in negative expressions indicating doubt or uncertainty.

No creo que sea necessario.	*I don't think it is necessary.*
but	
Creo que **es** necessario.	*I think it is necessary.*

The imperfect and pluperfect subjunctive have two forms which are used interchangeably. The imperfect is frequently dependent on a clause which contains a verb in the conditional.

Nos gustaría que vinieses.	*We would like you to come.*

It is used after **si** (*if*) to introduce an idea which is unlikely to occur.

Si hubiese algún problema te llamaría.	*If there were any problem I would call you.*

Certain verbs indicating advice, suggestion or command require the subjunctive:

Te sugiero que no salgas.	*I suggest you don't go out.*

The subjunctive is often used after **antes** (*before*), **cuando** (*when*), **en cuanto** (*as soon as*), **después** (*after*), etc.

En cuanto vuelvas.	*As soon as you get back.*

(*d*) The imperative mood

This is used to give directives or commands:

Give *me a hand.*
Help *Sharon with her homework.*

Because we have only one version of the second person (you) in English, we have only one form of the second person imperative. However, as Spanish has polite and informal forms of the second person, the imperative is more complex. It is further complicated by the fact that the negative version is quite different from the affirmative version. This means that there are *eight* versions for giving someone a command in Spanish (familiar singular, polite singular, familiar plural, polite plural – and all these again in the negative!).

There are actually only two forms of the imperative, those relating to the second person (**tu** or **vosotros/vosotras**). The rest, including the negative forms, are expressed by using the appropriate form of the subjunctive:

habla	*do speak*	no hables	*do not speak*
hablad	*speak, all of you*	no habléis	*do not speak*
¡Que lo hagan ellos mismos!		*Let them do it themselves!*	

7 The active and passive voice

Most actions can be viewed in one of two ways:

The dog bit the postman.
The postman was bitten by the dog.

In the first example the dog is clearly the initiator of the action and the postman receives or suffers the action. This type of sentence is referred to as the *active voice*.

In the second example, the postman occupies first position in the sentence even though he is the object of the action. The subject, the dog, has been relegated to third position (after the verb) and could even be omitted. This type of sentence is referred to as the *passive voice*.

In Spanish the passive voice is formed by the appropriate tense of the verb **ser** and the past participle of the verb concerned.

La canción ha sido cantada.	*The song has been sung.*
Peter ha sido besado.	*Peter has been kissed.*
El agua ha sido bebida.	*The water has been drunk.*

Note that the past participle must agree in number and gender with the subject of the verb:

Don Juan es amado.	*Don Juan is loved.*
Carmen es amada.	*Carmen is loved.*

A model of a verb in the passive is given on the next page.

8 Transitive and intransitive verbs

To a large extent the verb we choose determines what other elements are used with it. With the verb *to occur*, for instance, you say what occurred but you do not have to provide any further information.

The accident occurred.

ser amado *to be loved*

INDICATIVE

Present
soy amado/a
eres amado/a
es amado/a
somos amados/as
sois amados/as
son amados/as

Imperfect
era amado/a
eras amado/a
era amado/a
éramos amados/as
erais amados/as
eran amados/as

Perfect
he sido amado/a
has sido amado/a
ha sido amado/a
hemos sido amados/as
habéis sido amados/as
han sido amados/as

Future
seré amado/a
serás amado/a
será amado/a
seremos amados/as
seréis amados/as
serán amados/as

Pluperfect
había sido amado/a
habías sido amado/a
había sido amado/a
habíamos sido amados/as
habíais sido amados/as
habían sido amados/as

Past Definite
fui amado/a
fuiste amado/a
fue amado/a
fuimos amados/as
fuisteis amados/as
fueron amados/as

Future Perfect
habré sido amado/a
habrás sido amado/a
habrá sido amado/a
habremos sido amados/as
habréis sido amados/as
habrán sido amados/as

Past Perfect
hube sido amado/a
hubiste sido amado/a
hubo sido amado/a
hubimos sido amados/as
hubisteis sido amados/as
hubieron sido amados/as

CONDITIONAL

Present
sería amado/a
serías amado/a
sería amado/a
seríamos amados/as
seríais amados/as
serían amados/as

Perfect
habría sido amado/a
habrías sido amado/a
habría sido amado/a
habríamos sido amados/as
habríais sido amados/as
habrían sido amados/as

SUBJUNCTIVE

Present
sea amado/a
seas amado/a
sea amado/a
seamos amados/as
seáis amados/as
sean amados/as

Imperfect
fu-era/ese amado/a
fu-eras/eses amado/a
fu-era/ese amado/a
fu-éramos/ésemos amados/as
fu-erais/eseis amados/as
fu-eran/esen amados/as

Perfect
haya sido amado/a
hayas sido amado/a
haya sido amado/a
hayamos sido amados/as
hayáis sido amados/as
hayan sido amados/as

Pluperfect
hub-iera/iese sido amado/a
hub-ieras/ieses sido amado/a
hub-iera/iese sido amado/a
hub-iéramos/iésemos sido amados/as
hub-ierais/ieseis sido amados/as
hub-ieran/iesen sido amados/as

GERUND

siendo amado/a

PAST PARTICIPLE

ser amado/a

IMPERATIVE

sé amado, sé amada
sed amados, sed amadas

With a verb like *to give*, on the other hand, you state *who* or *what* did the giving and also have to state *who* or *what* was given:

Darren gave a compact disc.

It is admittedly just possible to say *Darren gave* in the sense that he made a donation, but this is a very special use of *to give*. With this verb it would also be very common to state the recipient of the giving:

Darren gave a compact disc to Tracey.

or even better:

Darren gave Tracey a compact disc.

In the above examples *a compact disc* is said to be the *direct object* of the verb *to give* because it is what is actually given. *To Tracey* or *Tracey* is said to be the *indirect object*, since this element indicates who the compact disc was given to.

Verbs which do not require a direct object are said to be *intransitive*.

to die	The old man died.
to wait	I waited.

Verbs which *do* require a direct object are said to be *transitive*.

to enjoy	Noeline enjoys **a swim**.
to need	Gary needs **some help**.

Because many verbs can be used either with or without a direct object, depending on the precise meaning of the verb, it is safer to talk of transitive and intransitive uses of verbs:

Intransitive	**Transitive**
He's sleeping.	He's sleeping a deep sleep.
I'm eating.	I'm eating my dinner.
She's writing.	She's writing an essay.

9 Reflexive verbs

The term *reflexive* is used when the initiator of an action (or *subject*) and the sufferer of the action (or *object*) are one and the same:

She washed herself.

Spanish has many more reflexive verbs than English, so it is important to understand the concept. For instance, Spanish says the equivalent of *The door opened itself* where English simply says *The door opened.*

Spanish often uses a reflexive verb where English would use the passive. The equivalent of *Here Spanish speaks itself* is used instead of *Spanish spoken here.*

Se habla español.	*Spanish spoken here.*

Reflexive verbs are also used in Spanish in impersonal constructions where *one* might be used in English:

¿Se puede entrar?	*Can one enter? / Is it possible to enter?*
Aquí no se puede fumar.	*One cannot smoke here. / It is not possible to smoke here.*

In the above examples, the reflexive pronoun is also the direct object. In Spanish it is also possible to find the reflexive pronoun used as an indirect object; for instance in sentences which would in English be the equivalent of:

I have cleaned ***to myself*** *the teeth.*
He has broken ***to himself*** *the arm.*

Me lavo las manos.	*I wash my hands.*
Carlos se ha hecho daño.	*Carlos has hurt himself.*
Pedro se afeita.	*Pedro shaves himself.*

Reflexive verbs are the only ones that can end in **-se** after the obligatory **ar**, **-er**, **-ir**: **lavarse** (*to wash oneself*), **caerse** (*to fall*). The reflexive pronouns are: **me**, **te**, **se**, **nos**, **os**, **se**.

10 Modal verbs

Verbs which are used to express concepts such as permission, obligation, possibility, etc. (*can*, *must*, *may*) are referred to as *modal verbs*. Verbs in this category cannot in general stand on their own and therefore also fall under the general heading of auxiliary verbs. Because modal verbs tend to behave differently from other verbs, they need your special attention. Here are some examples:

No pueden comprenderte.	*They cannot understand you.*

¿Puedo guardármelo?	*May I keep it?*
No pudimos verlo.	*We could not see it.*
Podía escuchar la música.	*I could hear the music.*

oír = *to hear*; escuchar = *to listen*

Abbreviations used in this book

aux.	auxiliary	m.	masculine
fem.	feminine	r.	reflexive
imp.	impersonal	tr.	transitive
intr.	intransitive		

VERB TABLES

On the following pages you will find the various tenses of 202 Spanish verbs presented in full, with examples of how to use them.

Sometimes only the first person singular form is given. These tenses are given in full in the section on verbs and how they work (pp. 2–19). You should also check back to this section if you are not sure when to use the different tenses.

1 acertar *to guess, be right* tr./intr.

INDICATIVE

Present	Imperfect	Perfect
acierto	acertaba	he acertado
aciertas	acertabas	has acertado
acierta	acertaba	ha acertado
acertamos	acertábamos	hemos acertado
acertáis	acertabais	habéis acertado
aciertan	acertaban	han acertado

Future	Pluperfect	Past Definite
acertaré	había acertado	acerté
acertarás	habías acertado	acertaste
acertará	había acertado	acertó
acertaremos	habíamos acertado	acertamos
acertaréis	habíais acertado	acertasteis
acertarán	habían acertado	acertaron

Future Perfect	Past Perfect
habré acertado	hube acertado

CONDITIONAL / SUBJUNCTIVE

Conditional Present	Subjunctive Present	Subjunctive Imperfect
acertaría	acierte	acert-ara/ase
acertarías	aciertes	acert-aras/ases
acertaría	acierte	acert-ara/ase
acertaríamos	acertemos	acert-áramos/ásemos
acertaríais	acertéis	acert-arais/aseis
acertarían	acierten	acert-aran/asen

Perfect	Perfect	Pluperfect
habría acertado	haya acertado	hub-iera/iese acertado

GERUND	PAST PARTICIPLE	IMPERATIVE
acertando	acertado	acierta, acertad acierte (Vd), acierten (Vds)

Has acertado la respuesta correcta. *You've guessed right.*
Tenemos que acertar. *We must guess.*
No sé si acertaremos. *I wonder if we'll guess.*
Si acierta ganará el premio. *He'll win the prize if he guesses.*

Acertó a la primera. *He guessed right first time.*
Acertamos por casualidad. *We were right by pure chance.*
Acerté a lo tonto. *I guessed without intending to.*
No aciertas la manera de hacerlo. *You don't seem to know how to do it.*

un acertijo *a riddle*
acertadamente *correctly*
un acierto *good shot, success*
acertante *one who guesses*
con acierto *successfully*
acertado/a *correct, right, sensible*
acertador(a) *good guesser*

acordar *to agree* tr. 2

INDICATIVE

Present	Imperfect	Perfect
acuerdo	acordaba	he acordado
acuerdas	acordabas	has acordado
acuerda	acordaba	ha acordado
acordamos	acordábamos	hemos acordado
acordáis	acordabais	habéis acordado
acuerdan	acordaban	han acordado
Future	**Pluperfect**	**Past Definite**
acordaré	había acordado	acordé
acordarás	habías acordado	acordaste
acordará	había acordado	acordó
acordaremos	habíamos acordado	acordamos
acordaréis	habíais acordado	acordasteis
acordarán	habían acordado	acordaron
Future Perfect	**Past Perfect**	
habré acordado	hube acordado	

CONDITIONAL	SUBJUNCTIVE	
Present	**Present**	**Imperfect**
acordaría	acuerde	acord-ara/ase
acordarías	acuerdes	acord-aras/ases
acordaría	acuerde	acord-ara/ase
acordaríamos	acordemos	acord-áramos/ásemos
acordaríais	acordéis	acord-arais/aseis
acordarían	acuerden	acord-aran/asen
Perfect	**Perfect**	**Pluperfect**
habría acordado	haya acordado	hub-iera/iese acordado

GERUND	PAST PARTICIPLE	IMPERATIVE
acordando	acordado	acuerda, acordad acuerde (Vd), acuerden (Vds)

Han acordado firmar el tratado. *They have agreed to sign the treaty.*
Los colores acuerdan. *The colours match.*
Se acordó hacerlo. *It was agreed to do it.*
Acordaron salir temprano. *They agreed to leave early.*

No me acuerdo. *I don't remember.*
Si mal no me acuerdo . . . *If my memory serves me right . . .*
¿Te acuerdas de Juan? *Do you remember Juan?*
No se acuerda ni del santo de su nombre. *He can't even remember his own name.*

un acuerdo *an agreement, accord*
Estoy de acuerdo contigo. *I agree with you.*
acordado/a *agreed*
acordadamente *unanimously*
llegar a un acuerdo *to reach an agreement*
ponerse de acuerdo *to agree*
tomar un acuerdo *to pass a resolution*

3 acostarse *to go to bed, lie down* r.

INDICATIVE

Present	Imperfect	Perfect
me acuesto	me acostaba	me he acostado
te acuestas	te acostabas	te has acostado
se acuesta	se acostaba	se ha acostado
nos acostamos	nos acostábamos	nos hemos acostado
os acostáis	os acostabais	os habéis acostado
se acuestan	se acostaban	se han acostado
Future	**Pluperfect**	**Past Definite**
me acostaré	me había acostado	me acosté
te acostarás	te habías acostado	te acostaste
se acostará	se había acostado	se acostó
nos acostaremos	nos habíamos acostado	nos acostamos
os acostaréis	os habíais acostado	os acostasteis
se acostarán	se habían acostado	se acostaron
Future Perfect	**Past Perfect**	
me habré acostado	me hube acostado	

CONDITIONAL	SUBJUNCTIVE	
Present	**Present**	**Imperfect**
me acostaría	me acueste	me acost-ara/ase
te acostarías	te acuestes	te acost-aras/ases
se acostaría	se acueste	se acost-ara/ase
nos acostaríamos	nos acostemos	nos acost-áramos/ásemos
os acostaríais	os acostéis	os acost-arais/aseis
se acostarían	se acuesten	se acost-aran/asen
Perfect	**Perfect**	**Pluperfect**
me habría acostado	me haya acostado	me hub-iera/iese acostado

GERUND	PAST PARTICIPLE	IMPERATIVE
acostándose	acostado	acuéstate, acostáos acuéstes (Vd), acuéstense (Vds)

Leonor se acuesta a las 3. *Leonor goes to bed at 3.*
¿Te acuestas tarde? *Do you go to bed late?*
Es hora de acostar al niño. *It is time to put the child to bed.*
Nos acostamos boca abajo. *We go to bed face down.*

Se acuesta con cualquiera. *She goes to bed with anyone.*
Nos acostamos juntos desde hace tres años. *We have been living together for three years.*
Me acuesto por los palestinos. *I support the Palestinians.*
Nos acostamos contra la pared. *We leaned against the wall.*

una acostada *a sleep, lie down*
acostarse boca arriba *to lay down face up*
acostado/a *lying down, stretched out*
acostar el barco *to bring the ship alongside*

acrecentar *to increase* tr. 4

INDICATIVE

Present	Imperfect	Perfect
acreciento	acrecentaba	he acrecentado
acrecientas	acrecentabas	has acrecentado
acrecienta	acrecentaba	ha acrecentado
acrecentamos	acrecentábamos	hemos acrecentado
acrecentáis	acrecentabais	habéis acrecentado
acrecientan	acrecentaban	han acrecentado
Future	**Pluperfect**	**Past Definite**
acrecentaré	había acrecentado	acrecenté
acrecentarás	habías acrecentado	acrecentaste
acrecentará	había acrecentado	acrecentó
acrecentaremos	habíamos acrecentado	acrecentamos
acrecentaréis	habíais acrecentado	acrecentasteis
acrecentarán	habían acrecentado	acrecentaron
Future Perfect	**Past Perfect**	
habré acrecentado	hube acrecentado	

CONDITIONAL	SUBJUNCTIVE	
Present	**Present**	**Imperfect**
acrecentaría	acreciente	acrecent-ara/ase
acrecentarías	acrecientes	acrecent-aras/ases
acrecentaría	acreciente	acrecent-ara/ase
acrecentaríamos	acrecentemos	acrecent-áramos/ásemos
acrecentaríais	acrecentéis	acrecent-arais/aseis
acrecentarían	acrecienten	acrecent-aran/asen
Perfect	**Perfect**	**Pluperfect**
habría acrecentado	haya acrecentado	hub-iera/iese acrecentado

GERUND	PAST PARTICIPLE	IMPERATIVE
acrecentando	acrecentado	acrecienta, acrecentad acreciente (Vd), acrecienten (Vds)

Ha acrecentado su número de acciones. *He has increased his number of shares.*
El calor acrecienta a lo largo del día. *The heat increases throughout the day.*
Puedes acrecentar la temperatura del horno. *You can increase the oven temperature.*
Acrecentaré mi colección de plantas con esquejos. *I shall increase my plant collection with cuttings.*

Acrecentó su fortuna. *She increased her fortune.*
Su comportamiento ha acrecentado su influencia. *Her behaviour has increased her influence.*

un acrecentamiento *increase, growth*
acrecentante *increasing, incremental*
acrecentarse *to increase, grow*
acrecentador(a) *one that increases*
una acrecencia *increase, growth*

5 adestrar *to direct, train* tr.

INDICATIVE

Present	Imperfect	Perfect
adiestro	adestraba	he adestrado
adiestras	adestrabas	has adestrado
adiestra	adestraba	ha adestrado
adestramos	adestrábamos	hemos adestrado
adestráis	adestrabais	habéis adestrado
adiestran	adestraban	han adestrado
Future	**Pluperfect**	**Past Definite**
adestraré	había adestrado	adestré
adestrarás	habías adestrado	adestraste
adestrará	había adestrado	adestró
adestraremos	habíamos adestrado	adestramos
adestraréis	habíais adestrado	adestrasteis
adestrarán	habían adestrado	adestraron
Future Perfect	**Past Perfect**	
habré adestrado	hube adestrado	

CONDITIONAL	SUBJUNCTIVE	
Present	**Present**	**Imperfect**
adestraría	adiestre	adestr-ara/ase
adestrarías	adiestres	adestr-aras/ases
adestraría	adiestre	adestr-ara/ase
adestraríamos	adestremos	adestr-áramos/ásemos
adestraríais	adestréis	adestr-arais/aseis
adestrarían	adiestren	adestr-aran/asen
Perfect	**Perfect**	**Pluperfect**
habría adestrado	haya adestrado	hub-iera/iese adestrado

GERUND	PAST PARTICIPLE	IMPERATIVE
adestrando	adestrado	adiestra, adestrad adiestre (Vd), adiestren (Vds)

Adiestra perros. *She trains dogs.*
Te adiestraré cuando tengamos tiempo. *I shall coach you when we have more time.*
Adiestraban a los niños en el manejo de las armas. *They used to train children in the use of arms.*
No tiene paciencia para adestrar. *He is not patient enough to train.*

Soy diestro en ajedrez. *I am an expert at chess.*
Eres diestro en coches. *You are an expert on cars.*

un adiestramiento *training, drilling, practice*
adiestrador(a) *trainer, coach, teacher*
adiestrado *trained, trainee*
destreza *skill, dexterity, handiness*
adiestrable *trainable*
un diestro *matador, bullfighter, expert swordsman*
diestro/a *right, right hand, skilful, dexterous, handy*
la diestra *the right hand*

adquirir *to acquire* tr. 6

INDICATIVE

Present	Imperfect	Perfect
adquiero	adquiría	he adquirido
adquieres	adquirías	has adquirido
adquiere	adquiría	ha adquirido
adquirimos	adquiríamos	hemos adquirido
adquirís	adquiríais	habéis adquirido
adquieren	adquirían	han adquirido
Future	**Pluperfect**	**Past Definite**
adquiriré	había adquirido	adquirí
adquirirás	habías adquirido	adquiriste
adquirirá	había adquirido	adquirió
adquiriremos	habíamos adquirido	adquirimos
adquiriréis	habíais adquirido	adquiristeis
adquirirán	habían adquirido	adquirieron
Future Perfect	**Past Perfect**	
habré adquirido	hube adquirido	

CONDITIONAL	SUBJUNCTIVE	
Present	**Present**	**Imperfect**
adquiriría	adquiera	adquir-iera/iese
adquirirías	adquieras	adquir-ieras/ieses
adquiriría	adquiera	adquir-iera/iese
adquiriríamos	adquiramos	adquir-iéramos/iésemos
adquiriríais	adquiráis	adquir-ierais/ieseis
adquirirían	adquieran	adquir-ieran/iesen
Perfect	**Perfect**	**Pluperfect**
habría adquirido	haya adquirido	hub-iera/iese adquirido

GERUND	PAST PARTICIPLE	IMPERATIVE
adquiriendo	adquirido	adquiere, adquirid adquiera (Vd), adquieran (Vds)

Se adquiere aquí. *You can acquire it here.*
Lo adquirí en 1950. *I acquired it in 1950.*
Adquiriría uno si tuviera dinero. *I would get one if I had the money.*
¡Ojalá adquiramos uno! *I wish we could acquire one!*

bienes adquiridos *acquired wealth*
poder adquisitivo *buying power (of currency)*
adquiridor *acquirer, buyer*
adquirible *obtainable*
adquiriente *acquirer*
adquisición *acquisition*
adquisitivo *acquisitive (law); buying*

7 advertir *to warn, advise* tr.

INDICATIVE

Present	Imperfect	Perfect
advierto	advertía	he advertido
adviertes	advertías	has advertido
advierte	advertía	ha advertido
advertimos	advertíamos	hemos advertido
advertís	advertíais	habéis advertido
advierten	advertían	han advertido
Future	**Pluperfect**	**Past Definite**
advertiré	había advertido	advertí
advertirás	habías advertido	advertiste
advertirá	había advertido	advirtió
advertiremos	habíamos advertido	advertimos
advertiréis	habíais advertido	advertisteis
advertirán	habían advertido	advirtieron
Future Perfect	**Past Perfect**	
habré advertido	hube advertido	

CONDITIONAL	SUBJUNCTIVE	
Present	**Present**	**Imperfect**
advertiría	advierta	advirt-iera/iese
advertirías	adviertas	advirt-ieras/ieses
advertiría	advierta	advirt-iera/iese
advertiríamos	advirtamos	advirt-iéramos/iésemos
advertiríais	advirtáis	advirt-ierais/ieseis
advertirían	adviertan	advirt-ieran/iesen
Perfect	**Perfect**	**Pluperfect**
habría advertido	haya advertido	hub-iera/iese advertido

GERUND	PAST PARTICIPLE	IMPERATIVE
advirtiendo	advertido	advierte, advertid advierta (Vd), adviertan (Vds)

Te lo advierto, no lo hagas. *I warn you, don't do it.*
¿Has advertido que llevaba una caja? *Did you notice that he was carrying a box?*
Ya te lo había advertido. *I had warned you already.*
Pedro les advirtó ayer. *Pedro warned them yesterday.*

Te advierto que no vale la pena. *It's not worth it, I tell you.*
Me lo advirtieron en Madrid. *I was notified in Madrid.*
Te lo advierto por última vez. *I am warning you for the last time.*
Adviértele que se lleve el abrigo. *Remind him to take his coat.*

advertido/a *sharp, wide awake*
una advertencia *notice, warning*
un advertidor *detector*
advertidor local *audio warning device*
un advertimiento *warning notice*
advertidamente *knowingly, with forewarning*

alentar *to encourage, breathe* tr./intr. 8

INDICATIVE

Present	Imperfect	Perfect
aliento	alentaba	he alentado
alientas	alentabas	has alentado
alienta	alentaba	ha alentado
alentamos	alentábamos	hemos alentado
alentáis	alentabais	habéis alentado
alientan	alentaban	han alentado
Future	**Pluperfect**	**Past Definite**
alentaré	había alentado	alenté
alentarás	habías alentado	alentaste
alentará	había alentado	alentó
alentaremos	habíamos alentado	alentamos
alentaréis	habíais alentado	alentasteis
alentarán	habían alentado	alentaron
Future Perfect	**Past Perfect**	
habré alentado	hube alentado	

CONDITIONAL	SUBJUNCTIVE	
Present	**Present**	**Imperfect**
alentaría	aliente	alent-ara/ase
alentarías	alientes	alent-aras/ases
alentaría	aliente	alent-ara/ase
alentaríamos	alentemos	alent-áramos/ásemos
alentaríais	alentéis	alent-arais/aseis
alentarían	alienten	alent-aran/asen
Perfect	**Perfect**	**Pluperfect**
habría alentado	haya alentado	hub-iera/iese alentado

GERUND	PAST PARTICIPLE	IMPERATIVE
alentando	alentado	alienta, alentad aliente (Vd), alienten (Vds)

Juan siempre alienta a sus amigos. *Juan always encourages his friends.*
Me alentó a continuar. *She encouraged me to go on.*
Me alienta con su sonrisa. *She encourages me with her smile.*
Nos alentaron vuestros mensajes. *Your messages encouraged us.*

Todavía tiene aliento. *It is still alive.*
Tuvimos que alentar hondo. *We had to take a deep breath.*
Ni se mueve ni alienta. *He's not moving or breathing.*
En sus almas alientan patriotismo. *They are very patriotic.*

aliento *breath*
alentada *long breath*
alentador *encouraging, inspiring*
alentoso *brave, spirited*
alentado/a *tireless, comforting*
alentadamente *spiritedly, gallantly*

9 almorzar *to have lunch* tr./intr.

INDICATIVE

Present
almuerzo
almuerzas
almuerza
almorzamos
almorzáis
almuerzan

Imperfect
almorzaba
almorzabas
almorzaba
almorzábamos
almorzabais
almorzaban

Perfect
he almorzado
has almorzado
ha almorzado
hemos almorzado
habéis almorzado
han almorzado

Future
almorzaré
almorzarás
almorzará
almorzaremos
almorzaréis
almorzarán

Pluperfect
había almorzado
habías almorzado
había almorzado
habíamos almorzado
habíais almorzado
habían almorzado

Past Definite
almorcé
almorzaste
almorzó
almorzamos
almorzasteis
almorzaron

Future Perfect
habré almorzado

Past Perfect
hube almorzado

CONDITIONAL

Present
almorzaría
almorazarías
almorzaría
almorzaríamos
almorzaríais
almorzarían

Perfect
habría almorzado

SUBJUNCTIVE

Present
almuerce
almuerces
almuerce
almorcemos
almorcéis
almuercen

Imperfect
almorz-ara/ase
almorz-aras/ases
almorz-ara/ase
almorz-áramos/ásemos
almorz-arais/aseis
almorz-aran/asen

Perfect
haya almorzado

Pluperfect
hub-iera/iese almorzado

GERUND

almorzando

PAST PARTICIPLE

almorzado

IMPERATIVE

almuerza, almorzad
almuerce (Vd), almuercen (Vds)

En España almorzamos a las 11. *In Spain, we have brunch at 11.*
Almorzaremos tarde. *We'll have a late lunch.*
Almuerzo café con leche y un pastel. *I have white coffee and cake for elevenses.*
Vamos a tomar el almuerzo. *Let's have lunch/brunch/a late breakfast.*
El almuerzo duró 2 horas. *Lunch lasted for 2 hours.*

Vengo almorzado. *I have had lunch already.*

el almuerzo *lunch/brunch/elevenses/late breakfast*

amar *to love, be fond of* tr. 10

INDICATIVE

Present	Imperfect	Perfect
amo	amaba	he amado
amas	amabas	has amado
ama	amaba	ha amado
amamos	amábamos	hemos amado
amáis	amabais	habéis amado
aman	amaban	han amado
Future	**Pluperfect**	**Past Definite**
amaré	había amado	amé
amarás	habías amado	amaste
amará	había amado	amó
amaremos	habíamos amado	amamos
amaréis	habíais amado	amasteis
amarán	habían amado	amaron
Future Perfect	**Past Perfect**	
habré amado	hube amado	

CONDITIONAL / SUBJUNCTIVE

Present	Present	Imperfect
amaría	ame	am-ara/ase
amarías	ames	am-aras/ases
amaría	ame	am-ara/ase
amaríamos	amemos	am-áramos/ásemos
amaríais	améis	am-arais/aseis
amarían	amen	am-aran/asen
Perfect	**Perfect**	**Pluperfect**
habría amado	haya amado	hub-iera/iese amado

GERUND	PAST PARTICIPLE	IMPERATIVE
amando	amado	ama, amad ame (Vd), amen (Vds)

Amo a los niños. *I love children.*
Daphnis amaba a Chloe. *Daphnis loved Chloe.*
Es bello amar. *To love is beautiful.*
Los soldados aman a la patria. *Soldiers love their homeland.*

¡Con mil amores! *I'd love to!*
Nos sentamos al amor de la lumbre. *We sat by the fireplace.*
¡Por el amor de Dios! *For God's sake!*
Nos casamos por amor. *We married for love.*

amor *love*
amores *love affair*
amante *lover*
amoroso *loving, tender*
amor propio *pride, self-respect*
hacer el amor *to make love*
amoríos *love affairs, romance*
amorosamente *lovingly*

11 andar *to walk* tr./intr.

INDICATIVE

Present	Imperfect	Perfect
ando	andaba	he andado
andas	andabas	has andado
anda	andaba	ha andado
andamos	andábamos	hemos andado
andáis	andábais	habéis andado
andan	andaban	han andado
Future	**Pluperfect**	**Past Definite**
andaré	había andado	anduve
andarás	habías andado	anduviste
andará	había andado	anduvo
andaremos	habíamos andado	anduvimos
andaréis	habíais andado	anduvisteis
andarán	habían andado	anduvieron
Future Perfect	**Past Perfect**	
habré andado	hube andado	

CONDITIONAL	SUBJUNCTIVE	
Present	**Present**	**Imperfect**
andaría	ande	anduvi-era/ese
andarías	andes	anduvi-eres/eses
andaría	ande	anduvi-era/ese
andaríamos	andemos	anduvi-éramos/ésemos
andaríais	andéis	anduvi-erais/eseis
andarían	anden	anduvi-eran/esen
Perfect	**Perfect**	**Pluperfect**
habría andado	haya andado	hub-iera/iese andado

GERUND	PAST PARTICIPLE	IMPERATIVE
andando	andado	anda, andad ande (Vd), anden (Vds)

Vamos andando. *Let's walk.*
Anduvimos 3 km. *We walked 3 km.*
Subimos andando las escaleras. *We walked up the stairs.*
Andaré hasta la estación. *I shall walk to the station.*

Andaremos mal de tiempo. *We won't have enough time.*
¿Cómo andan los negocios? *How is business?*
Peter anda por las nubes. *Peter is absent-minded.*
No te andes por las ramas. *Don't beat about the bush.*

andante *walking, errant*
andar a gatas *to crawl*
andanza *event, occurrence*
andariego/a *wandering, wanderer*
andador(a) *wandering*
andado/a *trodden, frequented, common*
andadura *walking, pace*
andarín/andarina *walking, tireless walker*

apaciguar *to pacify, soothe* tr. 12

INDICATIVE

Present	Imperfect	Perfect
apaciguo	apaciguaba	he apaciguado
apaciguas	apaciguabas	has apaciguado
apacigua	apaciguaba	ha apaciguado
apaciguamos	apaciguábamos	hemos apaciguado
apaciguáis	apaciguabais	habéis apaciguado
apaciguan	apaciguaban	han apaciguado
Future	**Pluperfect**	**Past Definite**
apaciguaré	había apaciguado	apacigüé
apaciguarás	habías apaciguado	apaciguaste
apaciguará	había apaciguado	apaciguó
apaciguaremos	habíamos apaciguado	apaciguamos
apaciguaréis	habíais apaciguado	apaciguasteis
apaciguaran	habían apaciguado	apaciguaron
Future Perfect	**Past Perfect**	
habré apaciguado	hube apaciguado	

CONDITIONAL	SUBJUNCTIVE	
Present	**Present**	**Imperfect**
apaciguaría	apacigüe	apacigu-ara/ase
apaciguarías	apacigües	apacigu-aras/ases
apaciguaría	apacigüe	apacigu-ara/ase
apaciguaríamos	apacigüemos	apacigu-áramos/ásemos
apaciguaríais	apacigüéis	apacigu-arais/aseis
apaciguarían	apacigüen	apacigu-aran/asen
Perfect	**Perfect**	**Pluperfect**
habría apaciguado	haya apaciguado	hub-iera/iese apaciguado

GERUND	PAST PARTICIPLE	IMPERATIVE
apaciguando	apaciguado	apacigua, apaciguad apacigüe (Vd), apacigüen (Vds)

Se enfada muchísmo, pero se apacigua solo. *He gets very angry but he calms down after a while.*
Apacigua a los niños. *He calms the children down.*
Sabe apaciguar. *He knows how to calm people down.*
Apaciguó a los rebeldes. *He pacified the rebels.*

Se apacigua con música. *Music calms him down.*
Política de apaciguamiento. *Policy of appeasement.*

apaciguarse *to lull, calm down*
apacible *mild, placid*
apaciguado *pacified*
apaciguamiento *pacification, appeasement*
apaciguador(a) *soothing, calming*
apacibilidad *gentleness, calmness*

13 apostar *to bet, post* tr./intr.

INDICATIVE

Present	Imperfect	Perfect
apuesto	apostaba	he apostado
apuestas	apostabas	has apostado
apuesta	apostaba	ha apostado
apostamos	apostábamos	hemos apostado
apostáis	apostabais	habéis apostado
apuestan	apostaban	han apostado
Future	**Pluperfect**	**Past Definite**
apostaré	había apostado	aposté
apostarás	habías apostado	apostaste
apostará	había apostado	apostó
apostaremos	habíamos apostado	apostamos
apostaréis	habíais apostado	apostasteis
apostarán	habían apostado	apostaron
Future Perfect	**Past Perfect**	
habré apostado	hube apostado	

CONDITIONAL	SUBJUNCTIVE	
Present	**Present**	**Imperfect**
apostaría	apueste	apost-ara/ase
apostarías	apuestes	apost-aras/ases
apostaría	apueste	apost-ara/ase
apostaríamos	apostemos	apost-áramos/ásemos
apostaríais	apostéis	apost-arais/aseis
apostarían	apuesten	apost-aran/asen
Perfect	**Perfect**	**Pluperfect**
habría apostado	haya apostado	hub-iera/iese apostado

GERUND	PAST PARTICIPLE	IMPERATIVE
apostando	apostado	apuesta, apostad apueste (Vd), apuesten (Vds)

Les han apostado en Escocia. *They have been posted to Scotland.*
Apostaremos los caballos en el prado. *We'll station the horses on the field.*
Te apuesto un helado a que no viene. *I bet you an ice-cream he doesn't come.*

Se las apuesta con cualquiera a beber. *He drinks with anybody.*
¿Qué te apuestas? *What do you bet?*
¡Apuesto a que sí! *I bet it is!*

una apuesta *a bet*
apuesto/a *neat, elegant, handsome*
apostador(a) *professional bookmaker*
apostadamente *on purpose*
un apostadero *station post, naval station*
aposta *on purpose*

apretar *to grip, press together* tr./intr. 14

INDICATIVE

Present	Imperfect	Perfect
aprieto	apretaba	he apretado
aprietas	apretabas	has apretado
aprieta	apretaba	ha apretado
apretamos	apretábamos	hemos apretado
apretáis	apretabais	habéis apretado
aprietan	apretaban	han apretado
Future	**Pluperfect**	**Past Definite**
apretaré	había apretado	apreté
apretarás	habías apretado	apretaste
apretará	había apretado	apretó
apretaremos	habíamos apretado	apretamos
apretaréis	habíais apretado	apretasteis
apretarán	habían apretado	apretaron
Future Perfect	**Past Perfect**	
habré apretado	hube apretado	

CONDITIONAL / SUBJUNCTIVE

Present	Present	Imperfect
apretaría	apriete	apret-ara/ase
apretarías	aprietes	apret-aras/ases
apretaría	apriete	apret-ara/ase
apretaríamos	apretemos	apret-áramos/ásemos
apretaríais	apretéis	apret-arais/aseis
apretarían	aprieten	apret-aran/asen
Perfect	**Perfect**	**Pluperfect**
habría apretado	haya apretado	hub-iera/iese apretado

GERUND	PAST PARTICIPLE	IMPERATIVE
apretando	apretado	aprieta, apretad
		apriete (Vd), aprieten (Vds)

Peter me aprieta entre sus brazos. *Peter hugs me in his arms.*
¿Te aprietan los zapatos? *Are your shoes tight?*
Le apretó contra le pared. *He pinned him against the wall.*
Tuve que apretar la maleta. *I had to press hard to shut the case.*

Estamos apretados de dinero. *We are short of money.*
Tenemos que apretarnos el cinturón. *We have to economise.*
El calor aprieta. *The heat is unbearable.*
¡Aprieta a correr! *Start running!/Run faster/harder!*

apretadamente *tightly, densely*
apretadera *strap, rope, pressure*
apretado/a *tight, difficult*
apretador *wedge, tightening*
apretón *squeeze, grip*
aprieto *jam, trouble*

15 aprobar *to approve, pass* tr./intr.

INDICATIVE

Present	Imperfect	Perfect
apruebo	aprobaba	he aprobado
apruebas	aprobabas	has aprobado
aprueba	aprobaba	ha aprobado
aprobamos	aprobábamos	hemos aprobado
aprobáis	aprobabais	habéis aprobado
aprueban	aprobaban	han aprobado
Future	**Pluperfect**	**Past Definite**
aprobaré	había aprobado	aprobé
aprobarás	habías aprobado	aprobaste
aprobará	había aprobado	aprobó
aprobaremos	habíamos aprobado	aprobamos
aprobaréis	habíais aprobado	aprobasteis
aprobarán	habían aprobado	aprobaron
Future Perfect	**Past Perfect**	
habré aprobado	hube aprobado	

CONDITIONAL / SUBJUNCTIVE

Present (Conditional)	Present (Subjunctive)	Imperfect (Subjunctive)
aprobaría	apruebe	aprob-ara/ase
aprobarías	apruebes	aprob-aras/ases
aprobaría	apruebe	aprob-ara/ase
aprobaríamos	aprobemos	aprob-áramos/ásemos
aprobaríais	aprobéis	aprob-arais/aseis
aprobarían	aprueben	aprob-aran/asen
Perfect	**Perfect**	**Pluperfect**
habría aprobado	haya aprobado	hub-iera/iese aprobado

GERUND	PAST PARTICIPLE	IMPERATIVE
aprobando	aprobado	aprueba, aprobad apruebe (Vd), aprueben (Vds)

Se ha aprobado la propuesta. *The motion has been passed.*
Aprobé en español. *I passed in Spanish.*
Me ha aprobado el presupuesto. *He has passed my budget.*
Seguro que se aprobará mi proyecto. *I am sure my project will be approved.*

El ministro va a aprobar una resolución. *The minister is going to adopt a resolution.*
Quieren aprobar un contrato. *They want to ratify a contract.*
El juez aprobará la moción jurídica. *The judge will carry the motion.*
Ha aprobado la inspección. *He passed the inspection.*

aprobado *passed, approved*
aprobatoria *approving*
aprobación *approval, consent*
aprobación del Parlamento *parliamentary approval*
aprobar un documento *to certify a document*
aprobado oficialmente por las autoridades *officially approved by the authorities*

argüir *to argue, reason* tr./intr. 16

INDICATIVE

Present	Imperfect	Perfect
arguyo	argüía	ha argüido
arguyes	argüías	has argüido
arguye	argüía	ha argüido
argüimos	argüíamos	hemos argüido
argüís	argüíais	habéis argüido
arguyen	argüían	han argüido
Future	**Pluperfect**	**Past Definite**
argüiré	había argüido	argüí
argüirás	habías argüido	argüiste
argüirá	había argüido	arguyó
argüiremos	habíamos argüido	argüimos
argüiréis	habíais argüido	argüisteis
argüirán	habían argüido	arguyeron
Future Perfect	**Past Perfect**	
habré argüido	hube argüido	

CONDITIONAL	SUBJUNCTIVE	
Present	**Present**	**Imperfect**
argüiría	arguya	argu-yera/yese
argüirías	arguyas	argu-yeras/yeses
argüiría	arguya	argu-yera/yese
argüiríamos	arguyamos	argu-yéramos/yésemos
argüiríais	arguyáis	argu-yerais/yeseis
argüirían	arguyan	argu-yeran/yesen
Perfect	**Perfect**	**Pluperfect**
habría argüido	haya argüido	hub-iera/iese argüido

GERUND	PAST PARTICIPLE	IMPERATIVE
arguyendo	argüido	arguye, argüid arguya (Vd), arguyan (Vds)

No podemos argüir con él. *We can't reason with him.*
Arguyó que teníamos obligaciones con mi familia. *He argued that we had obligations to my family.*
Juan argüiría con cualquiera. *Juan would argue with anybody.*
Si arguyese bien el caso . . . *If only he argued the case well . . .*

argumento cornuto *long dilemma, on-going dilemma*
argumento decisivo *decisive argument*
argumentar la comedia *to outline the comedy*
argumento incontestable *an indisputable argument*

argumento *argument, plot, theme subject*
argumentación *argument, reasoning*
argumentista *script-writer, arguer*
argüitivo/a *argumentative*
argumentar *to argue, dispute*

17 arrendar *to lease, rent, hire* tr.

INDICATIVE

Present	**Imperfect**	**Perfect**
arriendo	arrendaba	he arrendado
arriendas	arrendabas	has arrendado
arrienda	arrendaba	ha arrendado
arrendamos	arrendábamos	hemos arrendado
arrendáis	arrendabais	habéis arrendado
arriendan	arrendaban	han arrendado
Future	**Pluperfect**	**Past Definite**
arrendaré	había arrendado	arrendé
arrendarás	habías arrendado	arrendaste
arrendará	había arrendado	arrendó
arrendaremos	habíamos arrendado	arrendamos
arrendaréis	habíais arrendado	arrendasteis
arrendarán	habían arrendado	arrendaron
Future Perfect	**Past Perfect**	
habré arrendado	hube arrendado	

CONDITIONAL	SUBJUNCTIVE	
Present	**Present**	**Imperfect**
arrendaría	arriende	arrend-ara/ase
arrendarías	arriendes	arrend-aras/ases
arrendaría	arriende	arrend-ara/ase
arrendaríamos	arrendemos	arrend-áramos/ásemos
arrendaríais	arrendéis	arrend-arais/aseis
arrendarían	arrienden	arrend-aran/asen
Perfect	**Perfect**	**Pluperfect**
habría arrendado	haya arrendado	hub-iera/iese arrendado

GERUND	PAST PARTICIPLE	IMPERATIVE
arrendando	arrendado	arrienda, arrendad arriende (Vd), arrienden (Vds)

Arrendaré una habitación. *I shall rent a room.*
Arrienda su casa y vive con su madre. *She rents out her house and lives with her mother.*
Han arrendado un hotel para pasar el verano. *They have rented a hotel for the summer.*
Yo que tú arrendaría el coche y usaría la moto. *If I were you, I would rent out the car and use the motorbike.*

No ha arrendado ganancia. *He has made no profits.*
Voy a arrendar la casa de nuevo. *I am going to re-lease the house.*
Pensamos tomar una casa en arrendamiento. *We are thinking about renting a house.*

arrendamiento *letting, leasing, hiring*
arrendajo *jay (bird)*
arrendatario/a *tenant, leaseholder*
arrendable *leaseable*
arrendador *landlord*
arrendamiento bruto *gross rent*
arrendamiento financiero *hire purchase*
arrendar de nuevo *re-lease*

asentar *to fix, set down* tr. 18

INDICATIVE

Present	Imperfect	Perfect
asiento	asentaba	he asentado
asientas	asentabas	has asentado
asienta	asentaba	ha asentado
asentamos	asentábamos	hemos asentado
asentáis	asentabais	habéis asentado
asientan	asentaban	han asentado
Future	**Pluperfect**	**Past Definite**
asentaré	había asentado	asenté
asentarás	habías asentado	asentaste
asentará	había asentado	asentó
asentaremos	habíamos asentado	asentamos
asentaréis	habíais asentado	asentasteis
asentarán	habían asentado	asentaron
Future Perfect	**Past Perfect**	
habré asentado	hube asentado	

CONDITIONAL	SUBJUNCTIVE	
Present	**Present**	**Imperfect**
asentaría	asiente	asent-ara/ase
asentarías	asientes	asent-aras/ases
asentaría	asiente	asent-ara/ase
asentaríamos	asentemos	asent-áramos/ásemos
asentaríais	asentéis	asent-arais/aseis
asentarían	asienten	asent-aran/asen
Perfect	**Perfect**	**Pluperfect**
habría asentado	haya asentado	hub-iera/iese asentado

GERUND	PAST PARTICIPLE	IMPERATIVE
asentando	asentado	asienta, asentad asiente (Vd), asienten (Vds)

Ricardo II se asentó en el trono. *Richard II sat on the throne.*
La lluvia ha asentado el polvo. *The rain has settled the dust.*
Debes asentar los cimientos del edificio. *You must lay the foundations of the building.*
Vamos a asentar el campamento al lado del río. *We are going to set up a camp by the river.*

Le asentó una bofetada. *He gave him a slap.*
Estoy asentando las costuras con la plancha. *I am pressing (ironing) the seams.*
Las mesas de tres patas asientan mejor que las de cuatro. *Tables with three legs are more stable than tables with four legs.*
Lo dejó bien asentado. *He stated it clearly.*

asiento *seat*
asentar el polvo *to settle the dust*
asentar en el libro *to enter into the books*
asentar ladrillos *to set bricks in cement*
asentar en el haber de . . . *to credit someone with . . .*
asentar al debe *to debit*

19 asentir *to assent, agree* intr.

INDICATIVE

Present	Imperfect	Perfect
asiento	asentía	he asentido
asientes	asentías	has asentido
ansiente	asentía	ha asentido
asentimos	asentíamos	hemos asentido
asentís	asentíais	habéis asentido
asienten	asentían	han asentido
Future	**Pluperfect**	**Past Definite**
asentiré	había asentido	asentí
asentirás	habías asentido	asentiste
asentirá	había asentido	asintió
asentiremos	habíamos asentido	asentimos
asentiréis	habíais asentido	asentisteis
asentirán	habían asentido	asintieron
Future Perfect	**Past Perfect**	
habré asentido	hube asentido	

CONDITIONAL	SUBJUNCTIVE	
Present	**Present**	**Imperfect**
asentiría	asienta	asint-iera/iese
asentirías	asientas	asint-ieras/ieses
asentiría	asienta	asint-iera/iese
asentiríamos	asintamos	asint-iéramos/iésemos
asentiríais	asintáis	asint-ierais/ieseis
asentirían	asientan	asint-ieran/iesen
Perfect	**Perfect**	**Pluperfect**
habría asentido	haya asentido	hub-iera/iese asentido

GERUND	PAST PARTICIPLE	IMPERATIVE
asintiendo	asentido	asiente, asentid asienta (Vd), asientan (Vds)

Todos asintieron a las palabras del presidente. *Everybody acquiesced to the words of the president.*
Asintió a todo. *He agreed to everything.*
Lo asentiremos mañana. *We shall agree to it tomorrow.*
No asintió a dejarse retratar. *She did not agree to have her picture taken.*

Asiente con la cabeza. *Nod your head.*
Asentí a la verdad de su razonamiento. *I recognized the truth of his reasoning.*
Asentimos por unanimidad. *We agreed unanimously.*
¡Asiente! *Agree on it!*

asentimiento *assent, consent*
asenso *consent*
consentimiento *consent*
asentista *contractor, supplier*

asir *to grasp, seize* tr./intr. 20

INDICATIVE

Present	Imperfect	Perfect
asgo	asía	he asido
ases	asías	has asido
ase	asía	ha asido
asimos	asíamos	hemos asido
asís	asíais	habéis asido
asen	asían	han asido
Future	**Pluperfect**	**Past Definite**
asiré	había asido	así
asirás	habías asido	asiste
asirá	había asido	asió
asiremos	habíamos asido	asimos
asiréis	habíais asido	asisteis
asirán	habían asido	asieron
Future Perfect	**Past Perfect**	
habré asido	hube asido	

CONDITIONAL	SUBJUNCTIVE	
Present	**Present**	**Imperfect**
asiría	asga	as-iera/iese
asirías	asgas	as-ieras/ieses
asiría	asga	as-iera/iese
asiríamos	asgamos	as-iéramos/iésemos
asiríais	asgáis	as-ierais/ieseis
asirían	asgan	as-ieran/iesen
Perfect	**Perfect**	**Pluperfect**
habría asido	haya asido	hub-iera/iese asido

GERUND	PAST PARTICIPLE	IMPERATIVE
asiendo	asido	ase, asid asga (Vd), asgan (Vds)

Hay que asir la jarra por el asa. *You must grasp the jug by the handle.*
Asiré el momento. *I shall seize the moment.*
Manuel sabe asir las oportunidades. *Manuel knows how to grasp opportunities.*
Los bebés no pueden asir bien. *Babies cannot grasp things properly.*

Ibamos asidos del brazo. *We went arm in arm.*
Se asieron después del accidente. *They grappled after the accident.*
Van a asirse de los pelos. *They are going to fly at each other's throat.*
Siempre tiene disculpas y se ase a las ramas. *She always comes out with plenty of reasons why she cannot do it.*

asir por el mango *to face a problem*
el asa *handle*
asidera *saddle-strap*
asidero *handle, handhold, pretext*

21 atender *to attend, pay attention* tr./intr.

INDICATIVE

Present	Imperfect	Perfect
atiendo	atendía	he atendido
atiendes	atendías	has atendido
atiende	atendía	ha atendido
atendemos	atendíamos	hemos atendido
atendéis	atendíais	habéis atendido
atienden	atendían	han atendido
Future	**Pluperfect**	**Past Definite**
atenderé	había atendido	atendí
atenderás	habías atendido	atendiste
atenderá	había atendido	atendió
atenderemos	habíamos atendido	atendimos
atenderéis	habíais atendido	atendisteis
atenderán	habían atendido	atendieron
Future Perfect	**Past Perfect**	
habré atendido	hube atendido	

CONDITIONAL	SUBJUNCTIVE	
Present	**Present**	**Imperfect**
atendería	atienda	atend-iera/iese
atenderías	atiendas	atend-ieras/ieses
atendería	atienda	atend-iera/iese
atenderíamos	atendamos	atend-iéramos/iésemos
atenderíais	atendáis	atend-ierais/ieseis
atenderían	atiendan	atend-ieran/iesen
Perfect	**Perfect**	**Pluperfect**
habría atendido	haya atendido	hub-iera/iese atendido

GERUND	PAST PARTICIPLE	IMPERATIVE
atendiendo	atendido	atiende, atended atienda (Vd), atiendan (Vds)

Tengo compromisos que atender. *I have got obligations to meet.*
Atendieron una orden. *They paid attention to the command.*
Atenderé una reunión el lunes. *I shall attend a meeting on Monday.*
Ya lo atiendo yo por tí. *I'll do it for you.*

Atenderemos el giro. *We shall honour the draft.*
El médico atendió un caso urgente. *The doctor had to see to an emergency.*
Sara llama la atención. *Everybody notices Sara.*
Marcial es atento con los niños. *Marcial is kind to children.*

la atención *attention, care*
¡Atención, cuidado con el perro! *Beware of the dog!*
en atención a esto . . . *regarding this . . .*
atento/a *attentive, observant, polite*
prestar atención *to pay attention*

atravesar *to cross, go through* tr. 22

INDICATIVE

Present	Imperfect	Perfect
atravieso	atrevesaba	he atravesado
atraviesas	atrevesabas	has atravesado
atraviesa	atrevesaba	ha atravesado
atravesamos	atrevesábamos	hemos atravesado
atravesáis	atravesabais	habéis atravesado
atraviesan	atravesaban	han atravesado
Future	**Pluperfect**	**Past Definite**
atravesaré	había atravesado	atravesé
atravesarás	habías atravesado	atravesaste
atravesará	había atravesado	atravesó
atravesaremos	habíamos atravesado	atravesamos
atravesaréis	habíais atravesado	atravesasteis
atravesarán	habían atravesado	atravesaron
Future Perfect	**Past Perfect**	
habré atravesado	hube atravesado	

CONDITIONAL	SUBJUNCTIVE	
Present	**Present**	**Imperfect**
atravesaría	atraviese	atraves-ara/ase
atravesarías	atravieses	atraves-aras/ases
atravesaría	atraviese	atraves-ara/ase
atravesaríamos	atravesemos	atraves-áramos/ásemos
atravesaríais	atraveséis	atraves-arais/aseis
atravesarían	atraviesen	atraves-aran/asen
Perfect	**Perfect**	**Pluperfect**
habría atravesado	haya atravesado	hub-iera/iese atravesado

GERUND	PAST PARTICIPLE	IMPERATIVE
atravesando	atravesado	atraviesa, atravesad atraviese (Vd), atraviesen (Vds)

Atravieso un momento feliz. *I am going through a happy time.*
La bala atravesó el metal. *The bullet passed through the metal.*
Atravesamos el río de noche. *We crossed the river at night.*
Atravesaremos la frontera el martes. *We shall cross the border on Tuesday.*

Le tengo atravesado. *I cannot stand him.*
Siempre atraviesa mis negocios. *He always meddles in my affairs.*
Me encanta atravesar en una conversación. *I love to butt in on a conversation.*
atravesar las defensas aéreas *to pierce the air defences*

atravesado/a *crossed, traverse*
atravesada *crossing, passage*
travesía *crossing*
atravesable *traversable*
atravesando las olas *broadside to the waves*

23 beber *to drink* tr./intr.

INDICATIVE

Present	Imperfect	Perfect
bebo	bebía	he bebido
bebes	bebías	has bebido
bebe	bebía	ha bebido
bebemos	bebíamos	hemos bebido
bebéis	bebíais	habéis bebido
beben	bebían	han bebido
Future	**Pluperfect**	**Past Definite**
beberé	había bebido	bebí
beberás	habías bebido	bebiste
beberá	había bebido	bebió
beberemos	habíamos bebido	bebimos
beberéis	habíais bebido	bebisteis
beberán	habían bebido	bebieron
Future Perfect	**Past Perfect**	
habré bebido	hube bebido	

CONDITIONAL	SUBJUNCTIVE	
Present	**Present**	**Imperfect**
bebería	beba	beb-iera/iese
beberías	bebas	beb-ieras/ieses
bebería	beba	beb-iera/iese
beberíamos	bebamos	beb-iéramos/iésemos
beberíais	bebáis	beb-ierais/ieseis
beberían	beban	beb-ieran/iesen
Perfect	**Perfect**	**Pluperfect**
habría bebido	haya bebido	hub-iera/iese bebido

GERUND	PAST PARTICIPLE	IMPERATIVE
bebiendo	bebido	bebe, bebed beba (Vd), beban (Vds)

Bebo café con leche por la mañana. *I drink white coffee in the mornings.*
Es abstemio, nunca bebe alcohol. *He is a teetotaler.*
Se bebió tres coñacs después de comer. *After lunch he had three brandies.*
Para celebrarlo beberemos champán. *We shall drink champagne to celebrate.*

Bebe como una cuba. *He drinks like a fish.*
Bebamos a la salud del rey. *Let's drink to the king's health.*
Se han dado a la bebida. *They have taken to drink.*
Está bebido. *He is tipsy (drunk).*

bebida *drink*
bebedor(a) *boozer, heavy drinker*
bebedizo *drinkable*
bebedero *water trough; spout (of drinking vessels)*
bebido *tipsy, drunk*

buscar *to look for* tr. 24

INDICATIVE

Present	Imperfect	Perfect
busco	buscaba	he buscado
buscas	buscabas	has buscado
busca	buscaba	ha buscado
buscamos	buscábamos	hemos buscado
buscáis	buscabais	habéis buscado
buscan	buscaban	han buscado

Future	Pluperfect	Past Definite
buscaré	había buscado	busqué
buscarás	habías buscado	buscaste
buscará	había buscado	buscó
buscaremos	habíamos buscado	buscamos
buscaréis	habíais buscado	buscasteis
buscarán	habían buscado	buscaron

Future Perfect	Past Perfect
habré buscado	hube buscado

CONDITIONAL	SUBJUNCTIVE	
Present	**Present**	**Imperfect**
buscaría	busque	busc-ara/ase
buscarías	busques	busc-aras/ases
buscaría	busque	busc-ara/ase
buscaríamos	busquemos	busc-áramos/ásemos
buscaríais	busquéis	busc-arais/aseis
buscarían	busquen	busc-aran/asen
Perfect	**Perfect**	**Pluperfect**
habría buscado	haya buscado	hub-iera/iese buscado

GERUND	PAST PARTICIPLE	IMPERATIVE
buscando	buscado	busca, buscad busque (Vd), busquen (Vds)

Busco un coche rojo. *I am looking for a red car.*
Le busqué por todas partes. *I looked for him everywhere.*
Nadie nos buscará aquí. *Nobody will look for us here.*
Está buscando un trabajo. *He is looking for a job.*

Tengo que buscar la referencia. *I've got to look up the reference.*
Miguel Angel ha tenido que buscarse la vida. *Miguel Angel has had to fend for himself.*
Se lo buscó ella misma. *She brought it on herself.*
¡Te la estás buscando! *You're asking for it!*

busca *search*
búsqueda *search*
buscador(a) *searcher*
buscón *petty thief, rogue*
buscona *whore*
buscavidas *meddler*
buscarruidos *troublemaker*

25 caber *to fit, have enough room* intr.

INDICATIVE

Present	**Imperfect**	**Perfect**
quepo	cabía	he cabido
cabes	cabías	has cabido
cabe	cabía	ha cabido
cabemos	cabíamos	hemos cabido
cabéis	cabíais	habéis cabido
caben	cabían	han cabido
Future	**Pluperfect**	**Past Definite**
cabré	había cabido	cupe
cabrás	habías cabido	cupiste
cabrá	había cabido	cupo
cabremos	habíamos cabido	cupimos
cabréis	habíais cabido	cupisteis
cabrán	habían cabido	cupieron
Future Perfect	**Past Perfect**	
habré cabido	hube cabido	

CONDITIONAL	SUBJUNCTIVE	
Present	**Present**	**Imperfect**
cabría	quepa	cup-iera/iese
cabrías	quepas	cup-ieras/ieses
cabría	quepa	cup-iera/iese
cabríamos	quepamos	cup-iéramos/iésemos
cabríais	quepáis	cup-ierais/ieseis
cabrían	quepan	cup-ieran/iesen
Perfect	**Perfect**	**Pluperfect**
habría cabido	haya cabido	hub-iera/iese cabido

GERUND	PAST PARTICIPLE	IMPERATIVE
cabiendo	cabido	cabe, cabed quepa (Vd), quepan (Vds)

No cabe por esa puerta. *It won't go through that door.*
¿Cabe el libro? *Is there room for the book?*
Caben más de tres en el ascensor. *There is room for more than three people in the lift.*
Caben tres litros en la botella. *The bottle holds three litres.*

Lo compro todo si cabe. *I'll buy everything if possible.*
Todo cabe en Carlos. *Carlos is capable of anything.*
¡No cabe más! *There's no more room./That's the lot!*
No cabía en sí de contenta. *She was overjoyed.*

cabida *space, room*
capacidad *capacity*
cabiendo *holding*
no cabe duda *there is no doubt*
no tiene cabida *it is not acceptable*

caer *to fall, drop* intr. 26

INDICATIVE

Present	**Imperfect**	**Perfect**
caigo	caía	he caído
caes	caías	has caído
cae	caía	ha caído
caemos	caíamos	hemos caído
caéis	caíais	habéis caído
caen	caían	han caído
Future	**Pluperfect**	**Past Definite**
caeré	había caído	caí
caerás	habías caído	caíste
caerá	había caído	cayó
caeremos	habíamos caído	caímos
caeréis	habíais caído	caísteis
caerán	habían caído	cayeron
Future Perfect	**Past Perfect**	
habré caído	hube caído	

CONDITIONAL	SUBJUNCTIVE	
Present	**Present**	**Imperfect**
caería	caiga	ca-yera/yese
caerías	caigas	ca-yeras/yeses
caería	caiga	ca-yera/yese
caeríamos	caigamos	ca-yéramos/yésemos
caeríais	caigáis	ca-yerais/yeseis
caerían	caigan	ca-yeran/yesen
Perfect	**Perfect**	**Pluperfect**
habría caído	haya caído	hub-iera/iese caído

GERUND	PAST PARTICIPLE	IMPERATIVE
cayendo	caído	cae, caed caiga (Vd), caigan (Vds)

Cayeron diez en la batalla. *There were ten casualties in the battle.*
Se ha caído del caballo. *She has fallen off the horse.*
Ha caído el gobierno. *The government has fallen.*

La noche está al caer. *Night is about to fall.*
Pam cayó en cama/enferma. *Pam fell ill.*
Pedro está al caer. *Pedro is about to arrive.*
Antonio no me cae bien. *I don't like Antonio.*
Carlos se cae de miedo. *Carlos is terrified.*
La fiesta cae en martes. *The party is on a Tuesday.*

caída *fall, tumble*
caedizo *weak, about to fall*
caído/a *fallen*
caedura *waste, loose, refuse*
caduco/a *expired, cancelled*

27 calentar *to warm, heat up* tr.

INDICATIVE

Present	Imperfect	Perfect
caliento	calentaba	he calentado
calientas	calentabas	has calentado
calienta	calentaba	ha calentado
calentamos	calentábamos	hemos calentado
calentáis	calentabais	habéis calentado
calientan	calentaban	han calentado
Future	**Pluperfect**	**Past Definite**
calentaré	había calentado	calenté
calentarás	habías calentado	calentaste
calentará	había calentado	calentó
calentaremos	habíamos calentado	calentamos
calentaréis	habíais calentado	calentasteis
calentarán	habían calentado	calentaron
Future Perfect	**Past Perfect**	
habré calentado	hube calentado	

CONDITIONAL	SUBJUNCTIVE	
Present	**Present**	**Imperfect**
calentaría	caliente	calent-ara/ase
calentarías	calientes	calent-aras/ases
calentaría	caliente	calent-ara/ase
calentaríamos	calentemos	calent-áramos/ásemos
calentaríais	calentéis	calent-arais/aseis
calentarían	calienten	calent-aran/asen
Perfect	**Perfect**	**Pluperfect**
habría calentado	haya calentado	hub-iera/iese calentado

GERUND	PAST PARTICIPLE	IMPERATIVE
calentando	calentado	calienta, calentad caliente (Vd), calienten (Vds)

Calienta la leche. *Warm up the milk.*
Nos calentamos al fuego. *We warmed up by the fire.*
El sol calentará la piedra. *The sun will warm up the stone.*
Me he calentado bastante. *I have warmed myself up enough.*

Lo calentó al rojo vivo. *He made it red hot.*
Pedro está caliente. *Pedro is angry.*
Les calentaron las orejas. *They told them off.*
Rodolfo está caliente. *Rodolfo is sexually aroused.*

calentador *heater*
calentador de inmersión *immersion heater*
calor *heat*
entrar en calor *to get warm*
hace calor *it is hot*
calentamiento *heating, warming*
ejercicios de calentamiento *warm-up exercises*
calentura *fever, high temperature*

caminar *to walk* tr./intr. 28

INDICATIVE

Present	Imperfect	Perfect
camino	caminaba	he caminado
caminas	caminabas	has caminado
camina	caminaba	ha caminado
caminamos	caminábamos	hemos caminado
camináis	caminabais	habéis caminado
caminan	caminaban	han caminado
Future	**Pluperfect**	**Past Definite**
caminaré	había caminado	caminé
caminarás	habías caminado	caminaste
caminará	había caminado	caminó
caminaremos	habíamos caminado	caminamos
caminaréis	habíais caminado	caminasteis
caminarán	habían caminado	caminaron
Future Perfect	**Past Perfect**	
habré caminado	hube caminado	

CONDITIONAL	SUBJUNCTIVE	
Present	**Present**	**Imperfect**
caminaría	camine	camin-ara/ase
caminarías	camines	camin-aras/ases
caminaría	camine	camin-ara/ase
caminaríamos	caminemos	camin-áramos/ásemos
caminaríais	caminéis	camin-arais/aseis
caminarían	caminen	camin-aran/asen
Perfect	**Perfect**	**Pluperfect**
habría caminado	haya caminado	hub-iera/iese caminado

GERUND	PAST PARTICIPLE	IMPERATIVE
caminando	caminado	camina, caminad
		camine (Vd), caminen (Vds)

Caminamos durante dos horas. *We walked for two hours.*
Caminé hasta la casa. *I walked to the house.*
Caminarán hasta el río. *They will walk to the river.*
¿Has caminado despacio? *Have you walked slowly?*

Don Francisco camina derecho. *Don Francisco behaves properly.*
Fredes camina con pena. *Fredes moves with difficulty.*
Me pilla de camino. *It is on my way.*
Sara va por buen camino. *Sara is on the right track.*

camino *road, way*
caminata *long walk, ramble*
caminante *walker*
caminero *road builder*
caminador(a) *fond of walking*
caminejo *rough road, dirt track*

29 cantar *to sing, chant* tr./intr.

INDICATIVE

Present	Imperfect	Perfect
canto	cantaba	he cantado
cantas	cantabas	has cantado
canta	cantaba	ha cantado
cantamos	cantábamos	hemos cantado
cantáis	cantabais	habéis cantado
cantan	cantaban	han cantado
Future	**Pluperfect**	**Past Definite**
cantaré	había cantado	canté
cantarás	habías cantado	cantaste
cantará	había cantado	cantó
cantaremos	habíamos cantado	cantamos
cantaréis	habíais cantado	cantasteis
cantarán	habían cantado	cantaron
Future Perfect	**Past Perfect**	
habré cantado	hube cantado	

CONDITIONAL	SUBJUNCTIVE	
Present	**Present**	**Imperfect**
cantaría	cante	cant-ara/ase
cantarías	cantes	cant-aras/ases
cantaría	cante	cant-ara/ase
cantaríamos	cantemos	cant-áramos/ásemos
cantaríais	cantéis	cant-arais/aseis
cantarían	canten	cant-aran/asen
Perfect	**Perfect**	**Pluperfect**
habría cantado	haya cantado	hub-iera/iese cantado

GERUND	PAST PARTICIPLE	IMPERATIVE
cantando	cantado	canta, cantad cante (Vd), canten (Vds)

Me gusta cantar. *I like singing.*
Marta canta en la ópera de Madrid. *Marta sings in the Madrid Opera.*
Plácido Domingo cantará en Mérida. *Placido Domingo will sing in Merida.*
Caruso cantó en el Amazonas. *Caruso sang in the Amazon.*

Sara y Elena cantan a dos voces. *Sara and Elena sing duets.*
Ana cantó de plano. *Ana made a full confession.*
Eso es otro cantar. *That is another thing./That's another story.*
Francisca cantará las claras. *Francisca will speak out frankly.*

canción *song*
cantar *song*
cantar de gesta *epic poem*
cántico *hymn, song*
cantante *singer*
cantante de ópera *opera singer*
cantarín, cantarina *tinkling, sing-song noise*

castigar *to punish, chastise* tr. 30

INDICATIVE

Present	Imperfect	Perfect
castigo	castigaba	he castigado
castigas	castigabas	has castigado
castiga	castigaba	ha castigado
castigamos	castigábamos	hemos castigado
castigáis	castigabais	habéis castigado
castigan	castigaban	han castigado
Future	**Pluperfect**	**Past Definite**
castigaré	había castigado	castigué
castigarás	habías castigado	castigaste
castigará	había castigado	castigó
castigaremos	habíamos castigado	castigamos
castigaréis	habíais castigado	castigasteis
castigarán	habían castigado	castigaron
Future Perfect	**Past Perfect**	
habré castigado	hube castigado	

CONDITIONAL	SUBJUNCTIVE	
Present	**Present**	**Imperfect**
castigaría	castigue	castig-ara/ase
castigarías	castigues	castig-aras/ases
castigaría	castigue	castig-ara/ase
castigaríamos	castiguemos	castig-áramos/ásemos
castigaríais	castiguéis	castig-arais/aseis
castigarían	castiguen	castig-aran/asen
Perfect	**Perfect**	**Pluperfect**
habría castigado	haya castigado	hub-iera/iese castigado

GERUND	PAST PARTICIPLE	IMPERATIVE
castigando	castigado	castiga, castigad castigue (Vd), castiguen (Vds)

No castigues al niño. *Don't punish the boy.*
Me castigaron por romper el vaso. *I was punished for breaking the glass.*
Si te portas mal te castigaré. *I shall punish you if you don't behave.*
Te vamos a castigar. *We are going to punish you.*

Pedro castiga mucho el caballo. *Pedro rides the horse hard.*
¡Eres mi castigo! *You are bad for me!*
¡Qué castigo, Señor! *What a hard time you give me!*
¡Esto es un castigo! *This is so very hard!*

castigo *punishment, penalty*
castigo corporal *corporal punishment*
castigador(a) *punisher, punishing*
castigación *punishment*
castigado/a *punished*

31 cazar *to hunt, chase* tr.

INDICATIVE

Present	Imperfect	Perfect
cazo	cazaba	he cazado
cazas	cazabas	has cazado
caza	cazaba	ha cazado
cazamos	cazábamos	hemos cazado
cazáis	cazabais	habéis cazado
cazan	cazaban	han cazado
Future	**Pluperfect**	**Past Definite**
cazaré	había cazado	cacé
cazarás	habías cazado	cazaste
cazará	había cazado	cazó
cazaremos	habíamos cazado	cazamos
cazaréis	habíais cazado	cazasteis
cazarán	habían cazado	cazaron
Future Perfect	**Past Perfect**	
habré cazado	hube cazado	

CONDITIONAL	SUBJUNCTIVE	
Present	**Present**	**Imperfect**
cazaría	cace	caz-ara/ase
cazarías	caces	caz-aras/ases
cazaría	cace	caz-ara/ase
cazaríamos	cacemos	caz-áramos/ásemos
cazaríais	cacéis	caz-arais/aseis
cazarían	cacen	caz-aran/asen
Perfect	**Perfect**	**Pluperfect**
habría cazado	haya cazado	hub-iera/iese cazado

GERUND	PAST PARTICIPLE	IMPERATIVE
cazando	cazado	caza, cazad cace (Vd), cacen (Vds)

Estaba cazando un león en Africa. *He was hunting a lion in Africa.*
Juanjo va de caza. *Juanjo goes hunting.*
Cazarán jabalíes en setiembre. *They will hunt wild boar in September.*
No me gusta cazar. *I don't like hunting.*

Por fín le cacé en la fiesta. *I finally ran him down at the party.*
Miguel las caza al vuelo. *Miguel is pretty sharp.*
Le cacé en el acto. *I caught him in the act.*
No le vas a cazar. *You will not catch him.*

caza *hunting*
caza mayor *big game*
cazador(a) *hunter*
cazador furtivo *poacher*
cazadora *leather jacket*
cazamoscas *flycatcher*
cazagenios *talent spotter*
cazadero *hunting ground*

cegar *to dazzle, blind* tr./intr. 32

INDICATIVE

Present	Imperfect	Perfect
ciego	cegaba	he cegado
ciegas	cegabas	has cegado
ciega	cegaba	ha cegado
cegamos	cegábamos	hemos cegado
cegáis	cegabais	habéis cegado
ciegan	cegaban	han cegado
Future	**Pluperfect**	**Past Definite**
cegaré	había cegado	cegué
cegarás	habías cegado	cegaste
cegará	había cegado	cegó
cegaremos	habíamos cegado	cegamos
cegaréis	habíais cegado	cegasteis
cegarán	habían cegado	cegaron
Future Perfect	**Past Perfect**	
habré cegado	hube cegado	

CONDITIONAL	SUBJUNCTIVE	
Present	**Present**	**Imperfect**
cegaría	ciegue	ceg-ara/ase
cegarías	ciegues	ceg-aras/ases
cegaría	ciegue	ceg-ara/ase
cegaríamos	cieguemos	ceg-áramos/ásemos
cegaríais	ceguéis	ceg-arais/aseis
cegarían	cieguen	ceg-aran/asen
Perfect	**Perfect**	**Pluperfect**
habría cegado	haya cegado	hub-iera/iese cegado

GERUND	PAST PARTICIPLE	IMPERATIVE
cegando	cegado	ciega, cegad ciege (Vd), ciegen (Vds)

El sol me ciega. *The sun is blinding me.*
La explosión me cegó. *The explosion blinded me.*
El árbol le ciega la vista. *The tree blocks his view.*
Ha cegado el agujero. *He has blocked up the hole.*

Se ha quedado ciega. *She has gone blind.*
Se cegaron de ira. *They were blinded with anger.*
Tiene ceguera nocturna. *He suffers from night blindness.*
La nieve me produce ceguera. *I suffer from snow blindness.*

cegato/a *short-sighted*
cegatón(a) *short-sighted (pejorative)*
ceguera *blindness*
ceguedad *blindness*
ciego/a *blind*
cegador(a) *blinding*
cegajoso/a *bleary-eyed*
cegarrita *squinting*

33 cerrar *to close, shut, lock* tr./intr.

INDICATIVE

Present	Imperfect	Perfect
cierro	cerraba	he cerrado
cierras	cerrabas	has cerrado
cierra	cerraba	ha cerrado
cerramos	cerrábamos	hemos cerrado
cerráis	cerrabais	habéis cerrado
cierran	cerraban	han cerrado
Future	**Pluperfect**	**Past Definite**
cerraré	había cerrado	cerré
cerrarás	habías cerrado	cerraste
cerrará	había cerrado	cerró
cerraremos	habíamos cerrado	cerramos
cerraréis	habíais cerrado	cerrasteis
cerrarán	habían cerrado	cerraron
Future Perfect	**Past Perfect**	
habré cerrado	hube cerrado	

CONDITIONAL	SUBJUNCTIVE	
Present	**Present**	**Imperfect**
cerraría	cierre	cerr-ara/ase
cerrarías	cierres	cerr-aras/ases
cerraría	cierre	cerr-ara/ase
cerraríamos	cerremos	cerr-áramos/ásemos
cerraríais	cerréis	cerr-arais/aseis
cerrarían	cierren	cerr-aran/asen
Perfect	**Perfect**	**Pluperfect**
habría cerrado	haya cerrado	hub-iera/iese cerrado

GERUND	PAST PARTICIPLE	IMPERATIVE
cerrando	cerrado	cierra, cerrad
		cierre (Vd), cierren (Vds)

Cierra la puerta. *Close the door.*
Han cerrado la frontera. *They have closed the border.*
Cerramos a las seis. *We close at six.*
La carretera está cerrada por la nieve. *The road is blocked by the snow.*

Cierro con llave. *I lock up.*
La fábrica ha cerrado. *The factory has closed down.*
La puerta cierra mal. *The door doesn't close properly.*
Se ha cerrado en hacerlo. *He persists stubbornly in doing it.*

cierre *closing*
cierre de radio y TV *close-down (radio and TV)*
cerradura *lock*
cerradura de seguridad *safety lock*
cerradura de combinación *combination lock*
cerrajero/a *locksmith*
cerrajería *locksmith's craft, trade, shop*

cocer *to boil, cook* tr./intr. 34

INDICATIVE

Present	Imperfect	Perfect
cuezo	cocía	he cocido
cueces	cocías	has cocido
cuece	cocía	ha cocido
cocemos	cocíamos	hemos cocido
cocéis	cocíais	habéis cocido
cuecen	cocían	han cocido
Future	**Pluperfect**	**Past Definite**
coceré	había cocido	cocí
cocerás	habías cocido	cociste
cocerá	había cocido	coció
coceremos	habíamos cocido	cocimos
coceréis	habíais cocido	cocisteis
cocerán	habían cocido	cocieron
Future Perfect	**Past Perfect**	
habré cocido	hube cocido	

CONDITIONAL	SUBJUNCTIVE	
Present	**Present**	**Imperfect**
cocería	cueza	coc-iera/iese
cocerías	cuezas	coc-ieras/ieses
cocería	cueza	coc-iera/iese
ceceríamos	cozamos	coc-iéramos/iésemos
coceríais	cozáis	coc-ierais/ieseis
cocerían	cuezan	coc-ieran/iesen
Perfect	**Perfect**	**Pluperfect**
habría cocido	haya cocido	hub-iera/iese cocido

GERUND	PAST PARTICIPLE	IMPERATIVE
cociendo	cocido	cuece, coced cueza (Vd), cuezan (Vds)

Tienes que cocer el agua. *You must boil the water.*
La leche está cociendo. *The milk is boiling.*
Coceré las patatas. *I shall boil the potatoes.*
Cocieron el pan al horno. *They baked the bread (in the oven).*

Me estoy cociendo viva. *I am extremely hot.*
¿Está bien cocido? *Is it well done?*
Lo cuezo a fuego lento. *I let it boil gently, I simmer it.*
Lo cueces a fuego vivo. *You boil it vigorously.*

cocer al horno *to bake*
cocido *stew*
cocido/a *boiled*
cocción *cooking, boiling time*
cocina *kitchen, cookery*
cocinero/a *cook*
cocido preliminar *prebake*
cocinilla *small kitchen, spirit stove*
un cocinillas *a meddler*

35 coger *to take, pick up, catch* tr./intr.

INDICATIVE

Present	Imperfect	Perfect
cojo	cogía	he cogido
coges	cogías	has cogido
coge	cogía	ha cogido
cogemos	cogíamos	hemos cogido
cogéis	cogíais	habéis cogido
cogen	cogían	han cogido
Future	**Pluperfect**	**Past Definite**
cogeré	había cogido	cogí
cogerás	habías cogido	cogiste
cogerá	había cogido	cogió
cogeremos	habíamos cogido	cogimos
cogeréis	habíais cogido	cogisteis
cogerán	habían cogido	cogieron
Future Perfect	**Past Perfect**	
habré cogido	hube cogido	

CONDITIONAL	SUBJUNCTIVE	
Present	**Present**	**Imperfect**
cogería	coja	cog-iera/iese
cogerías	cojas	cog-ieras/ieses
cogería	coja	cog-iera/iese
cogeríamos	cojamos	cog-iéramos/iésemos
cogeríais	cojáis	cog-ierais/ieseis
cogerían	cojan	cog-ieran/iesen
Perfect	**Perfect**	**Pluperfect**
habría cogido	haya cogido	hub-iera/iese cogido

GERUND	PAST PARTICIPLE	IMPERATIVE
cogiendo	cogido	coge, coged coja (Vd), cojan (Vds)

Coge la caja. *Pick up the box.*
Cogimos un taxi. *We took a taxi.*
Hemos cogido los billetes. *We have collected the tickets.*
Vamos a coger el tren. *We are going to take the train.*

He cogido cariño al gato. *I've taken a liking to the cat.*
Cogí celos a Juan. *I became jealous of Juan.*
Se ha cogido los dedos en la puerta. *He's caught his fingers in the door.*
Me has cogido desprevenido. *You have caught me at a disadvantage.*

cogestión *partnership in industry*
cogido *fold, pleat, tuck*
cogedura *gathering*
cogedizo/a *easy to pick*
cogedero *handle*
cogedero/a *ready for picking, ripe*
cogedor *dustpan*
cogienda *harvest*

colar *to filter, strain* tr./intr. 36

INDICATIVE

Present	Imperfect	Perfect
cuelo	colaba	he colado
cuelas	colabas	has colado
cuela	colaba	ha colado
colamos	colábamos	hemos colado
coláis	colabais	habéis colado
cuelan	colaban	han colado
Future	**Pluperfect**	**Past Definite**
colaré	había colado	colé
colarás	habías colado	colaste
colará	había colado	coló
colaremos	habíamos colado	colamos
colaréis	habíais colado	colasteis
colarán	habían colado	colaron
Future Perfect	**Past Perfect**	
habré colado	hube colado	

CONDITIONAL	SUBJUNCTIVE	
Present	**Present**	**Imperfect**
colaría	cuele	col-ara/ase
colarías	cueles	col-aras/ases
colaría	cuele	col-ara/ase
colaríamos	colemos	col-áramos/ásemos
colaríais	coléis	col-arais/aseis
colarían	cuelen	col-aran/asen
Perfect	**Perfect**	**Pluperfect**
habría colado	haya colado	hub-iera/iese colado

GERUND	PAST PARTICIPLE	IMPERATIVE
colando	colado	cuela, colad cuele (Vd), cuelen (Vds)

Voy a colar las verduras. *I am going to strain the vegetables.*
Cuela el café. *Filter the coffee.*
Colaremos los zumos. *We shall filter the juices.*
¿Has colado todo el café? *Have you filtered all the coffee?*

Coló su mentira. *They believed his lie.*
Trataba de colar un bilette falso. *He was trying to use a forged note.*
Me colé en el cine. *I managed to get into the cinema without paying.*
¡No cuela! *I don't believe you!*

colar con lejía *to bleach*
colador *strainer*
coladura *straining, mistake (fig.)*
colada *clothes to be washed*
hacer la colada *to do the washing*
cola *queue*
hacer cola *to queue, get into line*

37 colgar *to hang up* tr./intr.

INDICATIVE

Present	**Imperfect**	**Perfect**
cuelgo	colgaba	he colgado
cuelgas	colgabas	has colgado
cuelga	colgaba	ha colgado
colgamos	colgábamos	hemos colgado
colgáis	colgabais	habéis colgado
cuelgan	colgaban	han colgado
Future	**Pluperfect**	**Past Definite**
colgaré	había colgado	colgué
colgarás	habías colgado	colgaste
colgará	había colgado	colgó
colgaremos	habíamos colgado	colgamos
colgaréis	habíais colgado	colgasteis
colgarán	habían colgado	colgaron
Future Perfect	**Past Perfect**	
habré colgado	hube colgado	

CONDITIONAL	SUBJUNCTIVE	
Present	**Present**	**Imperfect**
colgaría	cuelgue	colg-ara/ase
colgarías	cuelgues	colg-aras/ases
colgaría	cuelgue	colg-ara/ase
colgaríamos	colguemos	colg-áramos/ásemos
colgaríais	colguéis	colg-arais/aseis
colgarían	cuelguen	colg-aran/asen
Perfect	**Perfect**	**Pluperfect**
habría colgado	haya colgado	hub-iera/iese colgado

GERUND	PAST PARTICIPLE	IMPERATIVE
colgando	colgado	cuelga, colgad cuelgue (Vd), cuelgen (Vds)

Cuelga la ropa en el jardín. *Hang out the clothes in the garden.*
Colgaremos el cuadro en la pared. *We'll hang the picture on the wall.*
¿Lo has colgado del clavo? *Have you hung it on the hook?*
Me colgó el teléfono. *He rang off./He hung up on me.*

Le colgaron la culpa a Juan. *They pinned the blame on Juan.*
¡Me quedé colgada! *I was left so disappointed!*
Hemos dejado colgado a Bob. *We let Bob down/failed him.*
¡Antes le veré colgado! *I'll see him hanged first!*

colgante *hanging*
puente colgante *suspension bridge*
colgadero *hanger, peg*
colgado/a *suspended, hanging down, uncertain*
colgador *hanger*
colgadura *drapery, tapestry*
colgajo *appendage, rag, tatters*
colgadizo/a *hanging, loose*

comenzar *to start, begin* tr./intr. 38

INDICATIVE

Present	Imperfect	Perfect
comienzo	comenzaba	he comenzado
comienzas	comenzabas	has comenzado
comienza	comenzaba	ha comenzado
comenzamos	comenzábamos	hemos comenzado
comenzáis	comenzabais	habéis comenzado
comienzan	comenzaban	han comenzado
Future	**Pluperfect**	**Past Definite**
comenzaré	había comenzado	comencé
comenzarás	habías comenzado	comenzaste
comenzará	había comenzado	comenzó
comenzaremos	habíamos comenzado	comenzamos
comenzaréis	habíais comenzado	comenzasteis
comenzarán	habían comenzado	comenzaron
Future Perfect	**Past Perfect**	
habré comenzado	hube comenzado	

CONDITIONAL	SUBJUNCTIVE	
Present	**Present**	**Imperfect**
comenzaría	comience	comenz-ara/ase
comenzarías	comiences	comenz-aras/ases
comenzaría	comience	comenz-ara/ase
comenzaríamos	comencemos	comenz-aramos/ásemos
comenzaríais	comencéis	comenz-arais/aseis
comenzarían	comiencen	comenz-aran/asen
Perfect	**Perfect**	**Pluperfect**
habría comenzado	haya comenzado	hub-iera/iese comenzado

GERUND	PAST PARTICIPLE	IMPERATIVE
comenzando	comenzado	comienza, comenzad comience (Vd), comiencen (Vds)

Siempre comienza el primero. *He always starts first.*
Comenzó a las cuatro. *He started at four.*
Comenzaremos con Juan. *We shall start with Juan.*
¡Quiero comenzar por el postre! *I want to start with the dessert!*

Comienza a regir en mayo. *It becomes operative in May.*
Comienza a ejercer sus funciones el lunes. *He takes up office on Monday.*
Cacho dio comienzo a la carrera. *Cacho started the race.*
El rey comenzará el acto. *The king will open the ceremony.*

comenzamiento *start, beginning*
comienzo *start, beginning*
al comienzo *at first, at the start*
en los comienzos de siglo *at the beginning of the century*
comenzante *beginning*
comenzadero *ready to start*
comienza y no acaba *it goes on for ever*

39 comer *to eat* tr./intr.

INDICATIVE

Present	Imperfect	Perfect
como	comía	he comido
comes	comías	has comido
come	comía	ha comido
comemos	comíamos	hemos comido
coméis	comíais	habéis comido
comen	comían	han comido
Future	**Pluperfect**	**Past Definite**
comeré	había comido	comí
comerás	habías comido	comiste
comerá	había comido	comió
comeremos	habíamos comido	comimos
comeréis	habíais comido	comisteis
comerán	habían comido	comieron
Future Perfect	**Past Perfect**	
habré comido	hube comido	

CONDITIONAL	SUBJUNCTIVE	
Present	**Present**	**Imperfect**
comería	coma	com-iera/iese
comerías	comas	com-ieras/ieses
comería	coma	com-iera/iese
comeríamos	comamos	com-iéramos/iésemos
comeríais	comáis	com-ierais/ieseis
comerían	coman	com-ieran/iesen
Perfect	**Perfect**	**Pluperfect**
habría comido	haya comido	hub-iera/iese comido

GERUND	PAST PARTICIPLE	IMPERATIVE
comiendo	comido	come, comed coma (Vd), coman (Vds)

En España se come a las dos. *In Spain lunch is at 2 p.m.*
Comimos en un hotel. *We had lunch in a hotel.*
Comeré un bocadillo con Juan. *I shall have a sandwich with Juan.*
Se habrá comido la tarta. *He must have eaten the cake.*

Da de comer al perro. *Feed the dog.*
Sin comerlo ni beberlo. *Without having anything to do with it.*
No comas a dos carrillos. *Don't gobble your food.*
Se lo come con los ojos. *His eyes are bigger than his belly.*

cama y comida *bed and board*
Somos de buen comer. *We are hearty eaters.*
Esos colores se comen. *These colours clash with each other.*
comida *food, meal*
comidilla *hobby, favourite pastime*
comedor *dining room*
comilón *big eater, glutton*

competir *to compete, contest* intr. 40

INDICATIVE

Present	Imperfect	Perfect
compito	competía	he competido
compites	competías	has competido
compite	competía	ha competido
competimos	competíamos	hemos competido
competís	competíais	habéis competido
compiten	competían	han competido
Future	**Pluperfect**	**Past Definite**
competiré	había competido	competí
competirás	habias competido	competiste
competirá	había competido	compitió
competiremos	habíamos competido	competimos
competiréis	habíais competido	competisteis
competirán	habían competido	compitieron
Future Perfect	**Past Perfect**	
habré competido	hube competido	

CONDITIONAL	SUBJUNCTIVE	
Present	**Present**	**Imperfect**
competiría	compita	compit-iera/iese
competirías	compitas	compit-ieras/ieses
competiría	compita	compit-iera/iese
competiríamos	compitamos	compit-iéramos/iésemos
competiríais	compitáis	compit-ierais/ieseis
competirían	compitan	compit-ieran/iesen
Perfect	**Perfect**	**Pluperfect**
habría competido	haya competido	hub-iera/iese competido

GERUND	PAST PARTICIPLE	IMPERATIVE
compitiendo	competido	compite, competid compita (Vd), compitan (Vds)

Los atletas compiten en Sevilla. *The athletes compete in Seville.*
Tom compite con Jerry. *Tom competes against Jerry.*
Compito con Carmen por el primer puesto. *I compete with Carmen for first position.*
Competirán en los Juegos Olímpicos. *They will compete in the Olympic Games.*

Están en competencia. *They are in competition.*
No es de mi competencia. *It is not my responsibility.*
Es otra de las cosas de su competencia. *It is another of his responsibilities.*
Sony compite en ventas. *Sony outsells its competitors.*

competición *competition*
competidor(a) *competitor, rival*
competidor *competing*
competitivo/a *competitive*
competencia *competition, rivalry, competitiveness*
competencia desleal *unfair competition*

41 comprar *to buy, purchase* tr.

INDICATIVE

Present	Imperfect	Perfect
compro	compraba	he comprado
compras	comprabas	has comprado
compra	compraba	ha comprado
compramos	comprábamos	hemos comprado
compráis	comprabais	habéis comprado
compran	compraban	han comprado
Future	**Pluperfect**	**Past Definite**
compraré	había comprado	compré
comprarás	habías comprado	compraste
comprará	había comprado	compró
compraremos	habíamos comprado	compramos
compraréis	habíais comprado	comprasteis
comprarán	habían comprado	compraron
Future Perfect	**Past Perfect**	
habré comprado	hube comprado	

CONDITIONAL	SUBJUNCTIVE	
Present	**Present**	**Imperfect**
compraría	compre	compr-ara/ase
comprarías	compres	compr-aras/ases
compraría	compre	compr-ara/ase
compraríamos	compremos	compr-áramos/ásemos
compraríais	compréis	compr-arais/aseis
comprarían	compren	compr-aran/asen
Perfect	**Perfect**	**Pluperfect**
habría comprado	haya comprado	hub-iera/iese comprado

GERUND	PAST PARTICIPLE	IMPERATIVE
comprando	comprado	compra, comprad compre (Vd), compren (Vds)

Me he comprado un coche. *I have bought a car.*
Compraremos pan mañana. *We shall buy bread tomorrow.*
Necesitamos comprar un piso. *We need to buy a flat.*
Compraron los regalos en Sevilla. *They bought the presents in Seville.*

Vamos de compras. *Let's go shopping.*
Francisca compra al contado. *Francisca pays cash.*
No compres al fiado. *Don't buy on credit.*
Lo han comprado a plazos. *They have bought it on hire purchase.*

compra *shopping, purchase, buying*
comprador(a) *buyer*
comprado/a *bought*
compraventa *buying and selling, dealing*
comprable *purchasable*
compradizo/a *purchasable*
comprante *buyer*

comprobar *to check, confirm* tr. 42

INDICATIVE

Present	**Imperfect**	**Perfect**
compruebo	comprobaba	he comprobado
compruebas	comprobabas	has comprobado
comprueba	comprobaba	ha comprobado
comprobamos	comprobábamos	hemos comprobado
comprobáis	comprobabais	habéis comprobado
comprueban	comprobaban	han comprobado
Future	**Pluperfect**	**Past Definite**
comprobaré	había comprobado	comprobé
comprobarás	habías comprobado	comprobaste
comprobará	había comprobado	comprobó
comprobaremos	habíamos comprobado	comprobamos
comprobaréis	habíais comprobado	comprobasteis
comprobarán	habían comprobado	comprobaron
Future Perfect	**Past Perfect**	
habré comprobado	hube comprobado	

CONDITIONAL	SUBJUNCTIVE	
Present	**Present**	**Imperfect**
comprobaría	compruebe	comprob-ara/ase
comprobarías	compruebes	comprob-aras/ases
comprobaría	compruebe	comprob-ara/ase
comprobaríamos	comprobemos	comprob-áramos/ásemos
comprobaríais	comprobéis	comprob-arais/aseis
comprobarían	comprueben	comprob-aran/asen
Perfect	**Perfect**	**Pluperfect**
habría comprobado	haya comprobado	hub-iera/iese comprobado

GERUND	PAST PARTICIPLE	IMPERATIVE
comprobando	comprobado	comprueba, comprobad compruebe (Vd), comprueben (Vds)

Esto lo comprueba. *This verifies it.*
He comprobado que es verdad. *I have verified it.*
Tenemos que comprobar las facturas. *We have to check the invoices.*
Lo comprobaré con rayos X. *I shall X-ray to check it.*

Comprobar los derechos literarios y musicales. *To clear the literary and musical rights*
Está comprobando la temperatura. *He is monitoring the temperature.*
Comprueban en obra. *They do spot checks.*

comprobable *provable, demonstrable*
comprobación *checking, proof*
comprobador *tester*
comprobante *voucher, receipt*
documento comprobante *supporting document*
comprobatorio/a *proving, confirming*

43 concebir *to conceive, imagine* tr./intr.

INDICATIVE

Present	**Imperfect**	**Perfect**
concibo	concebía	he concebido
concibes	concebías	has concebido
concibe	concebía	ha concebido
concebimos	concebíamos	hemos concebido
concebís	concebíais	habéis concebido
conciben	concebían	han concebido
Future	**Pluperfect**	**Past Definite**
concebiré	había concebido	concebí
concebirás	habías concebido	concebiste
concebirá	había concebido	concibió
concebiremos	habíamos concebido	concebimos
concebiréis	habíais concebido	concebisteis
concebirán	habían concebido	concibieron
Future Perfect	**Past Perfect**	
habré concebido	hube concebido	

CONDITIONAL	SUBJUNCTIVE	
Present	**Present**	**Imperfect**
concebiría	conciba	concib-iera/iese
concebirías	concibas	concib-ieras/ieses
concebiría	conciba	concib-iera/iese
concebiríamos	concibamos	concib-iéramos/iésemos
concebiríais	concibáis	concib-ierais/ieseis
concebirían	conciban	concib-ieran/iesen
Perfect	**Perfect**	**Pluperfect**
habría concebido	haya concebido	hub-iera/iese concebido

GERUND	PAST PARTICIPLE	IMPERATIVE
concibiendo	concebido	concibe, concebid conciba (Vd), conciban (Vds)

Ha concebido. *She is pregnant.*
Hemos concebido un plan. *We have made a plan.*
No concibo su plan. *I can't understand his plan.*
No lo puede concebir. *He can't imagine it.*

Concibo esperanzas. *I nourish hope.*
Concibió una antipatía por Simón. *He took a dislike to Simon.*
Me hizo concebir esperanzas. *It encouraged me.*
la Purísma Concepción *the Immaculate Conception*

concebible *conceivable, thinkable*
inconcebible *unthinkable*
concepción *conception, understanding*
anticonceptivos *contraceptives*
preconcebir *preconceive*
concepto *concept, idea, notion*
concebir un proyecto en líneas generales *to plan out a project*

concertar *to arrange, agree* tr./intr. 44

INDICATIVE

Present	Imperfect	Perfect
concierto	concertaba	he concertado
conciertas	concertabas	has concertado
concierta	concertaba	ha concertado
concertamos	concertábamos	hemos concertado
concertáis	concertabais	habéis concertado
conciertan	concertaban	han concertado
Future	**Pluperfect**	**Past Definite**
concertaré	había concertado	concerté
concertarás	habías concertado	concertaste
concertará	había concertado	concertó
concertaremos	habíamos concertado	concertamos
concertaréis	habíais concertado	concertasteis
concertarán	habían concertado	concertaron
Future Perfect	**Past Perfect**	
habré concertado	hube concertado	

CONDITIONAL	SUBJUNCTIVE	
Present	**Present**	**Imperfect**
concertaría	concierte	concert-ara/ase
concertarías	conciertes	concert-aras/ases
concertaría	concierte	concert-ara/ase
concertaríamos	concertemos	concert-áramos/ásemos
concertaríais	concertéis	concert-arais/aseis
concertarían	concierten	concert-aran/asen
Perfect	**Perfect**	**Pluperfect**
habría concertado	haya concertado	hub-iera/iese concertado

GERUND	PAST PARTICIPLE	IMPERATIVE
concertando	concertado	concierta, concertad concierte (Vd), concierten (Vds)

Hemos concertado el precio. *We have fixed the price.*
Quiero concertar la venta. *I want to coordinate the sale.*
Vamos a concertarlo. *Let's come to terms about it.*
No lo han concertado. *They have not agreed to do it.*

Lo concertamos para mañana. *We plan it for tomorrow.*
Tus noticias conciertan con las mías. *Your news coincides with mine.*
Están concertando un contrato. *They are drawing up a contract.*

concertado/a *orderly, concerted*
matrimonio concertado *arranged marriage*
concertista *player, performer*
concertante *concerning*
concierto *agreement; concert*
concertador(a) *arranging, arranger*
concertadamente *methodically*

45 conducir *to drive, conduct, lead* tr./intr.

INDICATIVE

Present	Imperfect	Perfect
conduzco	conducía	he conducido
conduces	conducías	has conducido
conduce	conducía	ha conducido
conducimos	conducíamos	hemos conducido
conducís	conducíais	habéis conducido
conducen	conducían	han conducido
Future	**Pluperfect**	**Past Definite**
conduciré	había conducido	conduje
conducirás	habías conducido	condujiste
conducirá	había conducido	condujo
conduciremos	habíamos conducido	condujimos
conduciréis	habíais conducido	condujisteis
conducirán	habían conducido	condujeron
Future Perfect	**Past Perfect**	
habré conducido	hube conducido	

CONDITIONAL	SUBJUNCTIVE	
Present	**Present**	**Imperfect**
conduciría	conduzca	conduj-era/ese
conducirías	conduzcas	conduj-eras/eses
conduciría	conduzca	conduj-era/ese
conduciríamos	conduzcamos	conduj-éramos/ésemos
conduciríais	conduzcáis	conduj-erais/eseis
conducirían	conduzcan	conduj-eran/esen
Perfect	**Perfect**	**Pluperfect**
habría conducido	haya conducido	hub-iera/iese conducido

GERUND	PAST PARTICIPLE	IMPERATIVE
conduciendo	conducido	conduce, conducid conduzca (Vd), conduzcan (Vds)

¿Sabes conducir? *Can you drive?*
Conduce muy deprisa. *She drives very fast.*
Nos condujeron por un túnel. *They led us along a tunnel.*
Estos cables conducen la electricidad. *These cables carry the electricity.*

No te conduce a nada. *It takes you nowhere.*
¿A qué conduce? *What's the point?*
La depresión le condujo a la bebida. *Depression drove him to drink.*

conducción *leading, driving*
conductor(a) *driver, conductor*
conducto *pipe, tube, conduit*
conductibilidad *conductivity*
conducencia *transportation*
conducente *conducive to, leading to*
conducta *conduct, behaviour, something transported*

confesar *to confess, admit* tr. 46

INDICATIVE

Present	**Imperfect**	**Perfect**
confieso	confesaba	he confesado
confiesas	confesabas	has confesado
confiesa	confesaba	ha confesado
confesamos	confesábamos	hemos confesado
confesáis	confesabais	habéis confesado
confiesan	confesaban	han confesado

Future	**Pluperfect**	**Past Definite**
confesaré	había confesado	confesé
confesarás	habías confesado	confesaste
confesará	había confesado	confesó
confesaremos	habíamos confesado	confesamos
confesaréis	habíais confesado	confesasteis
confesarán	habían confesado	confesaron

Future Perfect	**Past Perfect**
habré confesado	hube confesado

CONDITIONAL / SUBJUNCTIVE

Present (Conditional)	**Present** (Subjunctive)	**Imperfect** (Subjunctive)
confesaría	confiese	confes-ara/ase
confesarías	confieses	confes-aras/ases
confesaría	confiese	confes-ara/ase
confesaríamos	confesemos	confes-áramos/ásemos
confesaríais	confeséis	confes-arais/aseis
confesarían	confiesen	confes-aran/asen

Perfect	**Perfect**	**Pluperfect**
habría confesado	haya confesado	hub-iera/iese confesado

GERUND	PAST PARTICIPLE	IMPERATIVE
confesando	confesado	confiesa, confesad confiese (Vd), confiesen (Vds)

Me ha confesado su edad. *He has told me his age.*
Ha confesado el crimen. *He has admitted to the crime.*
Voy a confesar mis pecados. *I'm going to confess my sins.*
Confesó antes de ir a la cárcel. *He confessed before going to jail.*

confesar abiertamente *to confess openly*
confesar sin reservas *to admit without reservation*
confesión de culpabilidad *admission of guilt*
confesión judicial *deposition*

confesión *confession, admission*
confesional *confessional*
confesionario *confessional*
confesante *penitent*
confeso *confessed, converted*
confesor *confessor*

47 conocer *to know* tr./intr.

INDICATIVE

Present	Imperfect	Perfect
conozco	conocía	he conocido
conoces	conocías	has conocido
conoce	conocía	ha conocido
conocemos	conocíamos	hemos conocido
conocéis	conocíais	habéis conocido
conocen	conocían	han conocido
Future	**Pluperfect**	**Past Definite**
conoceré	había conocido	conocí
conocerás	habías conocido	conociste
conocerá	había conocido	conoció
conoceremos	habíamos conocido	conocimos
conoceréis	habíais conocido	conocisteis
conocerán	habían conocido	conocieron
Future Perfect	**Past Perfect**	
habré conocido	hube conocido	

CONDITIONAL	SUBJUNCTIVE	
Present	**Present**	**Imperfect**
conocería	conozca	conoc-iera/iese
conocerías	conozcas	conoc-ieras/ieses
conocería	conozca	conoc-iera/iese
conoceríamos	conozcamos	conoc-iéramos/iésemos
conoceríais	conozcáis	conoc-ierais/ieseis
conocerían	conozcan	conoc-ieran/iesen
Perfect	**Perfect**	**Pluperfect**
habría conocido	haya conocido	hub-iera/iese conocido

GERUND	PAST PARTICIPLE	IMPERATIVE
conociendo	conocido	conoce, conoced conozca (Vd), vonozcan (Vds)

Le conozco desde hace muchos años. *I've known him for years.*
Nos conocimos en Burgos. *We met in Burgos.*
¿Conoces Pamplona? *Have you every been to Pamplona?*
No conozco la Rioja. *I don't know la Rioja.*

Te daré a conocer en la fiesta. *I'll introduce you at the party.*
José Carreras es muy conocido. *José Carreras is very well known.*
¿De qué le conoces? *How come you know him?*
No me conoce de nada. *She doesn't know me.*

conocedor(a) *expert, knowledgeable*
conocido/a *well known, known*
conocimiento *knowledge*
conocencia *knowledge, confession*
conocible *knowable, recognisable*
conocidamente *clearly, distinctly*

conseguir *to obtain, achieve* tr. 48

INDICATIVE

Present	Imperfect	Perfect
consigo	conseguía	he conseguido
consigues	conseguías	has conseguido
consigue	conseguía	ha conseguido
conseguimos	conseguíamos	hemos conseguido
conseguís	conseguíais	habéis conseguido
consiguen	conseguían	han conseguido
Future	**Pluperfect**	**Past Definite**
conseguiré	había conseguido	conseguí
conseguirás	habías conseguido	conseguiste
conseguirá	había conseguido	consiguió
conseguiremos	habíamos conseguido	conseguimos
conseguiréis	habíais conseguido	conseguisteis
conseguirán	habían conseguido	consiguieron
Future Perfect	**Past Perfect**	
habré conseguido	hube conseguido	

CONDITIONAL	SUBJUNCTIVE	
Present	**Present**	**Imperfect**
conseguiría	consiga	consigu-iera/iese
conseguirías	consigas	consigu-ieras/ieses
conseguiría	consiga	consigu-iera/iese
conseguiríamos	consigamos	consigu-iéramos/iésemos
conseguiríais	consigáis	consigu-ierais/ieseis
conseguirían	consigan	consigu-ieran/iesen
Perfect	**Perfect**	**Pluperfect**
habría conseguido	haya conseguido	hub-iera/iese conseguido

GERUND	PAST PARTICIPLE	IMPERATIVE
consiguiendo	conseguido	consigue, conseguid consiga (Vd), consigan (Vds)

He conseguido hacerlo. *I have managed to do it.*
Consiguió un permiso especial. *He obtained a special permit.*
¿Ha conseguido vender el coche? *Has she managed to sell the car?*
Esperamos conseguirlo. *We hope to achieve It.*

He conseguido el apoyo de la OTAN. *I have enlisted the support of NATO.*
Tenemos que conseguir fondos. *We have to raise funds.*
Quiere conseguir un préstamo. *She wants to secure a loan.*
¡Si consiguiéramos una clientela! *If only we could build up a clientele!*

conseguido *achieved*
conseguimiento *achieved*
asequible *obtainable, available, feasible*
conseguible *obtainable*

49 consentir *to consent, allow* tr./intr.

INDICATIVE

Present	Imperfect	Perfect
consiento	consentía	he consentido
consientes	consentías	has consentido
consiente	consentía	ha consentido
consentimos	consentíamos	hemos consentido
consentís	consentíais	habéis consentido
consienten	consentían	han consentido
Future	**Pluperfect**	**Past Definite**
consentiré	había consentido	consentí
consentirás	habías consentido	consentiste
consentirá	había consentido	consintió
consentiremos	habíamos consentido	consentimos
consentiréis	habíais consentido	consentisteis
consentirán	habían consentido	consintieron
Future Perfect	**Past Perfect**	
habré consentido	hube consentido	

CONDITIONAL	SUBJUNCTIVE	
Present	**Present**	**Imperfect**
consentiría	consienta	consint-iera/iese
consentirías	consientas	consint-ieras/ieses
consentiría	consienta	consint-iera/iese
consentiríamos	consintamos	consint-iéramos/iésemos
consentiríais	consintáis	consint-ierais/ieseis
consentirían	consientan	consint-ieran/iesen
Perfect	**Perfect**	**Pluperfect**
habría consentido	haya consentido	hub-iera/iese consentido

GERUND	PAST PARTICIPLE	IMPERATIVE
consintiendo	consentido	consiente, consentid consienta (Vd), consientan (Vds)

No te consentirán hablar. *They won't let you speak.*
¡No se puede consentir eso! *We can't have that!*
No consiente más peso. *It won't take any more weight.*

Te consiento otro. *I'll allow you to have another one.*
Consiento en hacerlo. *I agree to do it.*
consentir la sentencia *to acquiesce in the judgement*

consentido/a *spoiled, pampered*
marido consentido *complaisant husband*
consentidor(a) *indulgent, weak, conniver*
consentimiento *consent*
consenso *consensus*
consentimiento implícito *constructive assent*
consentimiento expreso *express consent*

contar *to count, tell* tr./intr.

INDICATIVE

Present	Imperfect	Perfect
cuento	contaba	he contado
cuentas	contabas	has contado
cuenta	contaba	ha contado
contamos	contábamos	hemos contado
contáis	contabais	habéis contado
cuentan	contaban	han contado
Future	**Pluperfect**	**Past Definite**
contaré	había contado	conté
contarás	habías contado	contaste
contará	había contado	contó
contaremos	habíamos contado	contamos
contaréis	habíais contado	contasteis
contarán	habían contado	contaron
Future Perfect	**Past Perfect**	
habré contado	hube contado	

CONDITIONAL	SUBJUNCTIVE	
Present	**Present**	**Imperfect**
contaría	cuente	cont-ara/ase
contarías	cuentes	cont-aras/ases
contaría	cuente	cont-ara/ase
contaríamos	contemos	cont-áramos/ásemos
contaríais	contéis	cont-arais/aseis
contarían	cuenten	cont-aran/asen
Perfect	**Perfect**	**Pluperfect**
habría contado	haya contado	hub-iera/iese contado

GERUND	PAST PARTICIPLE	IMPERATIVE
contando	contado	cuenta, contad cuente (Vd), cuenten (Vds)

Cuenta del 1 al 10. *Count from 1 to 10.*
Me solía contar cuentos de hadas. *She used to tell me fairy tales.*
Te contaré lo que pasó. *I'll tell you what happened.*
Nos lo han contado ya. *We have already been told.*

Cuenta con que es más fuerte que tú. *Don't forget he's stronger than you are.*
¡Cuenta conmigo! *Trust me!*
Es muy largo de contar. *It's a long story.*
No contaba con Juan. *I was not expecting Juan.*

¿Qué cuentas? *How are things?*
¡Cuéntaselo a tu abuela! *Tell it to the marines!*
cuento *story, tale*
cuentista *gossip*
contador de cuentos *story teller*
cuenta *account, calculation, bill*
cuentagotas *dropper*
contante y sonante *ready cash*

51 convertir *to convert, change* tr.

INDICATIVE

Present	Imperfect	Perfect
convierto	convertía	he convertido
conviertes	convertías	has convertido
convierte	convertía	ha convertido
convertimos	convertíamos	hemos convertido
convertís	convertíais	habéis convertido
convierten	convertían	han convertido
Future	**Pluperfect**	**Past Definite**
convertiré	había convertido	convertí
convertirás	habías convertido	convertiste
convertirá	había convertido	convirtió
convertiremos	habíamos convertido	convertimos
convertiréis	habíais convertido	convertisteis
convertirán	habían convertido	convirtieron
Future Perfect	**Past Perfect**	
habré convertido	hube convertido	

CONDITIONAL / SUBJUNCTIVE

Present (Conditional)	Present (Subjunctive)	Imperfect (Subjunctive)
convertiría	convierta	convirt-iera/iese
convertirías	conviertas	convirt-ieras/ieses
convertiría	convierta	convirt-iera/iese
convertiríamos	convirtamos	convirt-iéramos/iésemos
convertiríais	convirtáis	convirt-ierais/ieseis
convertirían	conviertan	convirt-ieran/iesen
Perfect	**Perfect**	**Pluperfect**
habría convertido	haya convertido	hub-iera/iese convertido

GERUND	PAST PARTICIPLE	IMPERATIVE
convirtiendo	convertido	convierte, convertid convierta (Vd), conviertan (Vds)

Se ha convertido al catolicismo. *He has converted to Catholicism.*
Quiero convertir libras en pesetas. *I want to change pounds into pesetas.*
Se convirtió en una rana. *He turned into a frog.*
Convirtió decimales a binario. *He converted decimal to binary.*

Convertimos en divisas. *We change foreign currency.*
Lo van a convertir en dinero. *They are going to convert it into money.*
Coviértelo en efectivo. *Turn it into cash.*
Lo convertirán en numérico. *They will digitise it.*

conversor(a) *converter*
convertible *convertible*
convertidor(a) *converter*
conversión *conversion*
converso/a *converted, convert*
conversón/conversona *gossiping, talkative*
convertibilidad *convertibility*

corregir *to correct, put right* tr. 52

INDICATIVE

Present	Imperfect	Perfect
corrijo	corregía	he corregido
corriges	corregías	has corregido
corrige	corregía	ha corregido
corregimos	corregíamos	hemos corregido
corregís	corregíais	habéis corregido
corrigen	corregían	han corregido
Future	**Pluperfect**	**Past Definite**
corregiré	había corregido	corregí
corregirás	habías corregido	corregiste
corregirá	había corregido	corrigió
corregiremos	habíamos corregido	corregimos
corregiréis	habíais corregido	corregisteis
corregirán	habían corregido	corrigieron
Future Perfect	**Past Perfect**	
habré corregido	hube corregido	

CONDITIONAL	SUBJUNCTIVE	
Present	**Present**	**Imperfect**
corregiría	corrija	corrig-iera/iese
corregirías	corrijas	corrig-ieras/ieses
corregiría	corrija	corrig-iera/iese
corregiríamos	corrijamos	corrig-iéramos/iésemos
corregiríais	corrijáis	corrig-ierais/ieseis
corregirían	corrijan	corrig-ieran/iesen
Perfect	**Perfect**	**Pluperfect**
habría corregido	haya corregido	hub-iera/iese corregido

GERUND	PAST PARTICIPLE	IMPERATIVE
corrigiendo	corregido	corrige, corregid corrija (Vd), corrijan (Vds)

Tengo que corregir exámenes. *I have to mark exams.*
Voy a corregir un defecto. *I'm going to remove a defect.*
Me corrigió delante de todos. *He corrected me in front of everybody.*
Te lo he corregido. *I have put it right for you.*

Estuvo muy correcto conmigo. *He was very polite to me.*
corregir una prueba de imprenta *to read a proof*
Corrigen instrumentos. *They adjust instruments.*
Corrige con exceso. *She overcorrects.*

corrección *correction, adjustment*
correcto/a *right, correct, accurate*
corrector(a) *proofreader*
corregirse *to reform oneself*
correccional *reformatory*
corregible *rectifiable*

53 costar *to cost, be difficult* intr.

INDICATIVE

Present	Imperfect	Perfect
cuesto	costaba	he costado
cuestas	costabas	has costado
cuesta	costaba	ha costado
costamos	costábamos	hemos costado
costáis	costabais	habéis costado
cuestan	costaban	han costado
Future	**Pluperfect**	**Past Definite**
costaré	había costado	costé
costarás	habías costado	costaste
costará	había costado	costó
costaremos	habíamos costado	costamos
costaréis	habíais costado	costasteis
costarán	habían costado	costaron
Future Perfect	**Past Perfect**	
habré costado	hube costado	

CONDITIONAL	SUBJUNCTIVE	
Present	**Present**	**Imperfect**
costaría	cueste	cost-ara/ase
costarías	cuestes	cost-aras/ases
costaría	cueste	cost-ara/ase
costaríamos	costemos	cost-áramos/ásemos
costaríais	costéis	cost-arais/aseis
costarían	cuesten	cost-aran/asen
Perfect	**Perfect**	**Pluperfect**
habría costado	haya costado	hub-iera/iese costado

GERUND	PAST PARTICIPLE	IMPERATIVE
costando	costado	cuesta, costad cueste (Vd), cuesten (Vds)

¿Cuánto cuesta? *How much is it?*
Cuesta 1.000 pesetas. *It costs 1000 pesetas.*
No cuestan muy caras. *They are not very expensive.*
Nos costó encontrar la película. *It was hard to find the film.*

Me cuesta hablar español. *I find it difficult to speak Spanish.*
Nos costó creerlo. *We found it difficult to believe.*
Cuesta unos minutos hacerlo. *It takes a few minutes to do it.*
Cuesta un ojo de la cara. *It costs an arm and a leg.*

coste *cost, price*
costo *cost*
cuenta *bill*
costoso/a *expensive*
costo efectivo *effective cost*
costo de expedición *shipping charges*
costo, seguro y flete *cost, insurance and freight*

crecer *to grow, increase* intr. 54

INDICATIVE

Present	Imperfect	Perfect
crezco	crecía	he crecido
creces	crecías	has crecido
crece	crecía	ha crecido
crecemos	crecíamos	hemos crecido
crecéis	crecíais	habéis crecido
crecen	crecían	han crecido
Future	**Pluperfect**	**Past Definite**
creceré	había crecido	crecí
crecerás	habías crecido	creciste
crecerá	había crecido	creció
creceremos	habíamos crecido	crecimos
creceréis	habíais crecido	crecisteis
crecerán	habían crecido	crecieron
Future Perfect	**Past Perfect**	
habré crecido	hube crecido	

CONDITIONAL	SUBJUNCTIVE	
Present	**Present**	**Imperfect**
crecería	crezca	crec-iera/iese
crecerías	crezcas	crec-ieras/ieses
crecería	crezca	crec-iera/iese
creceríamos	crezcamos	crec-iéramos/iésemos
creceríais	crezcáis	crec-ierais/ieseis
crecerían	crezcan	crec-ieran/iesen
Perfect	**Perfect**	**Pluperfect**
habría crecido	haya crecido	hub-iera/iese crecido

GERUND	PAST PARTICIPLE	IMPERATIVE
creciendo	crecido	crece, creced crezca (Vd), crezcan (Vds)

Algunas plantas crecen rápidamente. *Some plants grow very quickly.*
Se deja crecer el pelo y la barba. *He lets his hair and beard grow.*
El niño ha crecido mucho. *The boy has grown a lot.*
El árbol no hace más que crecer. *The tree does not stop growing.*

El río crece todos los inviernos. *The river swells every winter.*
Crece un punto. *Increase a stitch.*
Enrique ve crecer la hierba. *Enrique is very sharp.*
Te lo devolveré con creces. *I shall repay you with interest.*

luna creciente *crescent moon*
crecimiento *growing, growth, increase, rise*
crecido/a *grown, numerous*
creces *increase, excess*
crecedero/a *growing*
crecida *swelling of a river*
crecidamente *amply, abundantly, in excess*

55 dar *to give* tr.

INDICATIVE

Present	Imperfect	Perfect
doy	daba	he dado
das	dabas	has dado
da	daba	ha dado
damos	dábamos	hemos dado
dais	dabais	habéis dado
dan	daban	han dado
Future	**Pluperfect**	**Past Definite**
daré	había dado	di
darás	habías dado	diste
dará	había dado	dio
daremos	habíamos dado	dimos
daréis	habíais dado	disteis
darán	habían dado	dieron
Future Perfect	**Past Perfect**	
habré dado	hube dado	

CONDITIONAL	SUBJUNCTIVE	
Present	**Present**	**Imperfect**
daría	dé	di-era/ese
darías	des	di-eras/eses
daría	dé	di-era/ese
daríamos	demos	di-éramos/ésemos
daríais	deis	di-erais/eseis
darían	den	di-eran/esen
Perfect	**Perfect**	**Pluperfect**
habría dado	haya dado	hub-iera/iese dado

GERUND	PAST PARTICIPLE	IMPERATIVE
dando	dado	da, dad dé (Vd), den (Vds)

Dame el libro por favor. *Give me the book, please.*
¿Le quieres dar el mensaje? *Can you give him the message?*
Me han dado un regalo? *I have been given a present.*
Le dimos el recado. *We gave him the message.*

¡Ahí me las den todas! *That won't bother me!*
Han dado las cuatro. *It's four o'clock.*
¡Y dale que dale! *Here we go again!*
Da lo mismo. *It doesn't matter.*
No se me da mal. *I'm not doing too badly.*

dador(a) *donor, giver, bearer*
dador de sangre *blood donor*
dares y tomares *give and take*
dación *giving, handing over*
dádiva *present, gift*
dar de comer *to feed*

deber *to owe, must, ought to* tr. 56

INDICATIVE

Present	**Imperfect**	**Perfect**
debo	debía	he debido
debes	debías	has debido
debe	debía	ha debido
debemos	debíamos	hemos debido
debéis	debíais	habéis debido
deben	debían	han debido
Future	**Pluperfect**	**Past Definite**
deberé	había debido	debí
deberás	habías debido	debiste
deberá	había debido	debió
deberemos	habíamos debido	debimos
deberéis	habíais debido	debisteis
deberán	habían debido	debieron
Future Perfect	**Past Perfect**	
habré debido	hube debido	

CONDITIONAL	SUBJUNCTIVE	
Present	**Present**	**Imperfect**
debería	deba	deb-iera/iese
deberías	debas	deb-ieras/ieses
debería	deba	deb-iera/iese
deberíamos	debamos	deb-iéramos/iésemos
deberíais	debáis	deb-ierais/ieseis
deberían	deban	deb-ieran/iesen
Perfect	**Perfect**	**Pluperfect**
habría debido	haya debido	hub-iera/iese debido

GERUND	PAST PARTICIPLE	IMPERATIVE
debiendo	debido	debe, debed deba (Vd), deban (Vds)

Me debes £5. *You owe me £5.*
Debo hacerlo. *I must do it.*
Debieran ir. *They ought to go.*
Debe ser así. *It must be like that.*

Has debido perderlo. *You must have lost it.*
Debe ser argentino. *He must be Argentinian.*
Debido al mal tiempo . . . *On account of the bad weather . . .*
¿A qué se debe esto? *What's that for?*
Cumplen con su deber. *They perform their duty.*

deber *duty*
deberes *homework*
debido/a *due*
debidamente *properly*
debe *debit*

57 decir *to say, tell* tr.

INDICATIVE

Present	Imperfect	Perfect
digo	decía	he dicho
dices	decías	has dicho
dice	decía	ha dicho
decimos	decíamos	hemos dicho
decís	decíais	habéis dicho
dicen	decían	han dicho

Future	Pluperfect	Past Definite
diré	había dicho	dije
dirás	habías dicho	dijiste
dirá	había dicho	dijo
diremos	habíamos dicho	dijimos
diréis	habíais dicho	dijisteis
dirán	habían dicho	dijeron

Future Perfect	Past Perfect
habré dicho	hube dicho

CONDITIONAL	SUBJUNCTIVE	
Present	**Present**	**Imperfect**
diría	diga	dij-iera/ese
dirías	digas	dij-ieras/eses
diría	diga	dij-iera/ese
diríamos	digamos	dij-iéramos/ésemos
diríais	digáis	dij-ierais/eseis
dirían	digan	dij-ieran/esen
Perfect	**Perfect**	**Pluperfect**
habría dicho	haya dicho	hub-iera/iese dicho

GERUND	PAST PARTICIPLE	IMPERATIVE
diciendo	dicho	di, decid diga (Vd), digan (Vds)

Dicen que hace calor. *They say it is hot.*
No dijo nada. *He said nothing.*
¿Cómo has dicho? *What did you say?*
Le dicen 'majo'. *They call him 'majo'.*

No lo digo por tí. *I don't mean you.*
Como quien dice . . . *So to speak . . .*
cómo quien no dice nada *casually*
digan lo que digan *whatever they may say*

un dicho *a saying*
dicho *said*
dicha *joy*
mejor dicho *rather*
dicho y hecho *no sooner said than done*
es un decir *it's just a saying*
decires *gossip*

defender *to defend* tr. 58

INDICATIVE

Present	Imperfect	Perfect
defiendo	defendía	he defendido
defiendes	defendías	has defendido
defiende	defendía	ha defendido
defendemos	defendíamos	hemos defendido
defendéis	defendíais	habéis defendido
defienden	defendían	han defendido

Future	Pluperfect	Past Definite
defenderé	había defendido	defendí
defenderás	habías defendido	defendiste
defenderá	había defendido	defendió
defenderemos	habíamos defendido	defendimos
defenderéis	habíais defendido	defendisteis
defenderán	habían defendido	defendieron

Future Perfect	Past Perfect
habré defendido	hube defendido

CONDITIONAL / SUBJUNCTIVE

Present (Conditional)	Present (Subjunctive)	Imperfect (Subjunctive)
defendería	defienda	defend-iera/iese
defenderías	defiendas	defend-ieras/ieses
defendería	defienda	defend-iera/iese
defenderíamos	defendamos	defend-iéramos/iésemos
defenderíais	defendáis	defend-ierais/ieseis
defenderían	defiendan	defend-ieran/iesen

Perfect	Perfect	Pluperfect
habría defendido	haya defendido	hub-iera/iese defendido

GERUND	PAST PARTICIPLE	IMPERATIVE
defendiendo	defendido	defiende, defended defienda (Vd), defiendan (Vds)

Se defienden de sus enemigos. *They defend themselves from their enemies.*
La gallina defiende a sus pollitos. *The hen defends her chicks.*
El muro nos defenderá del viento. *The wall will protect us from the wind.*
Sirve para defenderme contra el frío. *It's to protect me from the cold.*

Nos vamos defendiendo. *We are managing.*
Me defiendo en español. *I can get by in Spanish.*
Se defendieron bien. *They did well.*
¡Defiéndeme! *Help me!*

en defensa propia *in self defence*
defensa *defence*
defensa pasiva *civil defence*
defensa marítima *sea defence*
defensas costeras *coastal defences*
defensivo *defensive*
defensor *defender, protector*
estar a la defensiva *to be on the defensive*

59 deferir *to defer, delegate* tr./intr.

INDICATIVE

Present	Imperfect	Perfect
defiero	defería	he deferido
defieres	deferías	has deferido
defiere	defería	ha deferido
deferimos	deferíamos	hemos deferido
deferís	deferíais	habéis deferido
defieren	deferían	han deferido
Future	**Pluperfect**	**Past Definite**
deferiré	había deferido	deferí
deferirás	habías deferido	deferiste
deferirá	había deferido	defirió
deferiremos	habíamos deferido	deferimos
deferiréis	habíais deferido	deferisteis
deferirán	habían deferido	defirieron
Future Perfect	**Past Perfect**	
habré deferido	hube deferido	

CONDITIONAL	SUBJUNCTIVE	
Present	**Present**	**Imperfect**
deferiría	defiera	defir-iera/iese
deferirías	defieras	defir-ieras/ieses
deferiría	defiera	defir-iera/iese
deferiríamos	defiramos	defir-iéramos/iésemos
deferiríais	defiráis	defir-ierais/ieseis
deferirían	defieran	defir-ieran/iesen
Perfect	**Perfect**	**Pluperfect**
habría deferido	haya deferido	hub-iera/iese deferido

GERUND	PAST PARTICIPLE	IMPERATIVE
defiriendo	deferido	defiere, deferid defiera (Vd), defieran (Vds)

Quiero deferirle mi puesto. *I would like you to have my place.*
Te defiero mi responsabilidad. *I give you my responsibilities.*
No quiere deferir sus cargos. *He doesn't want to delegate his position.*
Estoy tan agradecida que les deferiré mis privilegios. *I am so grateful that I shall delegate my privileges to them.*

por deferencia *out of deference*
deferencia *deference*
deferente *deferential*
deferido/a *referred*
juramento deferido *oath*

delinquir *to break the law* intr. **60**

INDICATIVE

Present	**Imperfect**	**Perfect**
delinco	delinquía	he delinquido
delinques	delinquías	has delinquido
delinque	delinquía	ha delinquido
delinquimos	delinquíamos	hemos delinquido
delinquís	delinquíais	habéis delinquido
delinquen	delinquían	han delinquido
Future	**Pluperfect**	**Past Definite**
delinquiré	había delinquido	delinquí
delinquirás	habías delinquido	delinquiste
dclinquirá	había delinquido	delinquió
delinquiremos	habíamos delinquido	delinquimos
delinquiréis	habíais delinquido	delinquisteis
delinquirán	habían delinquido	delinquieron
Future Perfect	**Past Perfect**	
habré delinquido	hube delinquido	

CONDITIONAL	SUBJUNCTIVE	
Present	**Present**	**Imperfect**
delinquiría	delinca	delinqu-iera/iese
delinquirías	delincas	delinqu-ieras/ieses
delinquiría	delinca	delinqu-iera/iese
delinquiríamos	delincamos	delinqui-iéramos/ésemos
delinquiríais	delincáis	delinqui-ierais/eseis
delinquirían	delincan	delinqu-ieran/iesen
Perfect	**Perfect**	**Pluperfect**
habría delinquido	haya delinquido	hub-iera/iese delinquido

GERUND	PAST PARTICIPLE	IMPERATIVE
delinquiendo	delinquido	delinque, delinquid delinca (Vd), delincan (Vds)

No delinco por miedo. *I don't commit offences through fear of prosecution.*
Delinque por falta de dinero. *He is a delinquent because he hasn't got any money.*
Han delinquido en numerosas ocasiones. *They have committed numerous offences.*
No creo que delinca otra vez. *I don't think he will transgress again.*
Muchos drogadictos delinquen. *Many drug addicts are delinquent.*
En la guerra ambas partes delinquían. *In the war, both sides were delinquent.*

delito *crime, offence*
delito de incendio *arson*
delito común *common law crime*
delito consumado *consumated crime*
delito político *political crime*
delincuencia *delinquency*
delictivo/a *criminal*
delicto = delito *offence, crime*
delinquimiento *delinquency, guilt*
delincuente *delinquent*

61 demoler *to demolish, pull down* tr.

INDICATIVE

Present	Imperfect	Perfect
demuelo	demolía	he demolido
demueles	demolías	has demolido
demuele	demolía	ha demolido
demolemos	demolíamos	hemos demolido
demoléis	demolíais	habéis demolido
demuelen	demolían	han demolido
Future	**Pluperfect**	**Past Definite**
demoleré	había demolido	demolí
demolerás	habías demolido	demoliste
demolerá	había demolido	demolió
demoleremos	habíamos demolido	demolimos
demoleréis	habíais demolido	demolisteis
demolerán	habían demolido	demolieron
Future Perfect	**Past Perfect**	
habré demolido	hube demolido	

CONDITIONAL	SUBJUNCTIVE	
Present	**Present**	**Imperfect**
demolería	demuela	demol-iera/iese
demolerías	demuelas	demol-ieras/ieses
demolería	demuela	demol-iera/iese
demoleríamos	demolamos	demol-iéramos/iésemos
demoleríais	demoláis	demol-ierais/ieseis
demolerían	demuelan	demol-ieran/iesen
Perfect	**Perfect**	**Pluperfect**
habría demolido	haya demolido	hub-iera/iese demolido

GERUND	PAST PARTICIPLE	IMPERATIVE
demoliendo	demolido	demuele, demoled demuela (Vd), demuelan (Vds)

Voy a demoler el edificio. *I am going to have the building demolished.*
Está demoliendo la cocina. *He's demolishing the kitchen.*
Demolieron la catedral. *They demolished the cathedral.*
Los Godos demolieron el Imperio Romano. *The Goths demolished the Roman Empire.*

Quiere demoler los cimientos de la civilización. *He wants to demolish the very foundations of civilization.*
doctrinas demoledoras *destructive doctrines*
Su ambición es demoler la organización. *His ambition is to demolish the organization.*
demolición de edificios *house demolition*

demoledor(a) *wrecker*
argumento demoledor *powerful argument*
demolición *demolition*
ataque demoledor *shattering attack*
ovación demoledora *overwhelming ovation, thunderous applause*

demostrar *to prove, demonstrate* tr. 62

INDICATIVE

Present	Imperfect	Perfect
demuestro	demostraba	he demostrado
demuestras	demostrabas	has demostrado
demuestra	demostraba	ha demostrado
demostramos	demostrábamos	hemos demostrado
demostráis	demostrabais	habéis demostrado
demuestran	demostraban	han demostrado

Future	Pluperfect	Past Definite
demostraré	había demostrado	demostré
demonstrarás	habías demostrado	demostraste
demostrará	había demostrado	demostró
demostraremos	habíamos demostrado	demostramos
demostraréis	habíais demostrado	demostrasteis
demostrarán	habían demostrado	demostraron

Future Perfect	Past Perfect
habré demostrado	hube demostrado

CONDITIONAL / SUBJUNCTIVE

Conditional Present	Subjunctive Present	Subjunctive Imperfect
demostraría	demuestre	demostr-ara/ase
demostrarías	demuestres	demostr-aras/ases
demostraría	demuestre	demostr-ara/ase
demostraríamos	demostremos	demostr-áramos/ásemos
demostraríais	demostréis	demostr-arais/aseis
demostrarían	demuestren	demostr-aran/asen

Perfect	Perfect	Pluperfect
habría demostrado	haya demostrado	hub-iera/iese demostrado

GERUND	PAST PARTICIPLE	IMPERATIVE
demostrando	demostrado	demuestra, demostrad demuestre (Vd), demuestren (Vds)

Tengo una prueba para demostrarlo. *I've got something to prove it.*
Magallanes demostró que la tierra es redonda. *Magellan proved that the earth is round.*
Te demostraré el teorema. *I shall demonstrate the theorem.*
Nos demostró cómo funciona. *He showed us how it works.*
No puedes demostrarme nada. *You can't prove anything against me.*

demostración de cariño *show of affection*
demostración de fuerza *show of force*
demostración de cólera *display of anger*
demostración comercial *trade exhibition*
demostración indirecta *indirect proof*
demostrar que . . . *to show that . . .*
demostrativo *demonstrative*
demostrable *demonstrable, provable*
demostrabilidad *provability*

63 dentar *to indent* tr./intr.

INDICATIVE

Present	Imperfect	Perfect
diento	dentaba	he dentado
dientas	dentabas	has dentado
dienta	dentaba	ha dentado
dentamos	dentábamos	hemos dentado
dentáis	dentabais	habéis dentado
dientan	dentaban	han dentado
Future	**Pluperfect**	**Past Definite**
dentaré	había dentado	denté
dentarás	habías dentado	dentaste
dentará	había dentado	dentó
dentaremos	habíamos dentado	dentamos
dentaréis	habíais dentado	dentasteis
dentarán	habían dentado	dentaron
Future Perfect	**Past Perfect**	
habré dentado	hube dentado	

CONDITIONAL	SUBJUNCTIVE	
Present	**Present**	**Imperfect**
dentaría	diente	dent-ara/ase
dentarías	dientes	dent-aras/ases
dentaría	diente	dent-ara/ase
dentaríamos	dentemos	dent-áramos/ásemos
dentaríais	dentéis	dent-arais/aseis
dentarían	dienten	dent-aran/asen
Perfect	**Perfect**	**Pluperfect**
habría dentado	haya dentado	hub-iera/iese dentado

GERUND	PAST PARTICIPLE	IMPERATIVE
dentando	dentado	dienta, dentad diente (Vd), dienten (Vds)

Este carpintero dienta a mano. *This carpenter saws by hand.*
Dienta con la sierra. *He cuts it with the teeth of the saw.*
Quiero dentar la hoja de papel. *I want to make a jagged edge on the paper.*
¿Lo habéis dentado? *Have you indented it?*

un sello sin dentar *imperforate stamp*
¿Ha dentado el bebé? *Has the baby cut any teeth?*
Tiene mala dentadura. *He has got bad teeth.*

dentado/a *toothed, jagged edge, indented*
dentación *dentation*
dental *dental*
dentadura *dentures, teeth*
dentadura postiza *false teeth*
dentellado/a *serrated, dented*
dientes *teeth*

derretir *to melt, thaw* tr. 64

INDICATIVE

Present	Imperfect	Perfect
derrito	derretía	he derretido
derrites	derretías	has derretido
derrite	derretía	ha derretido
derretimos	derretíamos	hemos derretido
derretís	derretíais	habéis derretido
derriten	derretían	han derretido

Future	Pluperfect	Past Definite
derretiré	había derretido	derretí
derretirás	habías derretido	derretiste
derretirá	había derretido	derritió
derretiremos	habíamos derretido	derretimos
derretiréis	habíais derretido	derretisteis
derretirán	habían derretido	derritieron

Future Perfect	Past Perfect
habré derretido	hube derretido

CONDITIONAL / SUBJUNCTIVE

Present (Conditional)	Present (Subjunctive)	Imperfect (Subjunctive)
derretiría	derrita	derrit-iera/iese
derretirías	derritas	derrit-ieras/ieses
derretiría	derrita	derrit-iera/iese
derretiríamos	derritamos	derrit-iéramos/iésemos
derretiríais	derritáis	derrit-ierais/ieseis
derretirían	derritan	derrit-ieran/iesen

Perfect	Perfect	Pluperfect
habría derretido	haya derretido	hub-iera/iese derretido

GERUND	PAST PARTICIPLE	IMPERATIVE
derritiendo	derretido	derrite, derretid derrita (Vd), derritan (Vds)

Derrite la mantequilla primero. *First melt the butter.*
Se me ha derretido el helado. *My ice-cream has melted.*
El sol derretirá la nieve. *The sun will thaw the snow.*
El calor derrite. *The heat melts things.*

Don Juan derrite a las señoras. *Don Juan makes the ladies fall in love with him.*
Se derrite por Pedro. *She is crazy about Pedro.*
Miguel me derrite con sus bromas. *Miguel exasperates me with his jokes.*
Acabo de derretir mi billete de 10.000 pts. *I've just changed my 10,000 peseta note.*

derretido *melted, thawed*
derretimiento *melting, thawing; (fig.) squandering*
derretirse *to liquefy*
derretido al vapor *reduced to steam*

65 desalentar *make breathless* tr.

INDICATIVE

Present	**Imperfect**	**Perfect**
desaliento	desalentaba	he desalentado
desalientas	desalentabas	has desalentado
desalienta	desalentaba	ha desalentado
desalentamos	desalentábamos	hemos desalentado
desalentáis	desalentabais	habéis desalentado
desalientan	desalantaban	han desalentado
Future	**Pluperfect**	**Past Definite**
desalentaré	había desalentado	desaltenté
desalentarás	habías desalentado	desalentaste
desalentará	había desalentado	desalentó
desalentaremos	habíamos desalentado	desalentamos
desalentaréis	habíais desalentado	desalentasteis
desalentarán	habían desalentado	desalentaron
Future Perfect	**Past Perfect**	
habré desalentado	hube desalentado	

CONDITIONAL	SUBJUNCTIVE	
Present	**Present**	**Imperfect**
desalentaría	desaliente	desalent-ara/ase
desalentarías	desalientes	desalent-aras/ases
desalentaría	desaliente	desalent-ara/ase
desalentaríamos	desalentemos	desalent-aramos/ásemos
desalentaríais	desalentéis	desalent-arais/aseis
desalentarían	desalienten	desalent-aran/asen
Perfect	**Perfect**	**Pluperfect**
habría desalentado	haya desalentado	hub-iera/iese desalentado

GERUND	PAST PARTICIPLE	IMPERATIVE
desalentando	desalentado	desalienta, desalentad desaliente (Vd), desalienten (Vds)

El correr me desalienta. *Running makes me breathless.*
La muerte de su mujer le desalentó mucho. *His wife's death affected him badly.*
Están desalentados porque han perdido el partido. *They are discouraged because they have lost the match.*
Se desalientan subiendo las escaleras. *Going upstairs makes them breathless.*

No desalientes a Pedro. *Don't discourage Pedro.*
Traigo noticias desalentadoras. *I have brought disheartening news.*

desalentarse *to lose heart, get discouraged*
desaliento *discouragement, depression*
desalentado/a *discouraged*
desalentador(a) *discouraging*
desalentadamente *dispiritedly, faintly*

descender *to descend, go down* tr./intr. 66

INDICATIVE

Present	Imperfect	Perfect
desciendo	descendía	he descendido
desciendes	descendías	has descendido
desciende	descendía	ha descendido
descendemos	descendíamos	hemos descendido
descendéis	descendíais	habéis descendido
descienden	descendían	han descendido
Future	**Pluperfect**	**Past Definite**
descenderé	había descendido	descendí
descenderás	habías descendido	descendiste
descenderá	había descendido	descendió
descenderemos	habíamos descendido	descendimos
descenderéis	habíais descendido	descendisteis
descenderán	habían descendido	descendieron
Future Perfect	**Past Perfect**	
habré descendido	hube descendido	

CONDITIONAL	SUBJUNCTIVE	
Present	**Present**	**Imperfect**
descendería	descienda	descend-iera/iese
descenderías	desciendas	descend-ieras/ieses
descendería	descienda	descend-iera/iese
descenderíamos	descendamos	descend-iéramas/iésemos
descenderíais	descendáis	descend-ierais/ieseis
descenderían	desciendan	descend-ieran/iesen
Perfect	**Perfect**	**Pluperfect**
habría descendido	haya descendido	hub-iera/iese descendido

GERUND	PAST PARTICIPLE	IMPERATIVE
descendiendo	descendido	desciende, descended descienda (Vd), desciendan (Vds)

Desciende las escaleras. *She goes down the stairs.*
Ha descendido el nivel del agua. *The level of water has gone down.*
Anoche descendió la temperatura. *The temperature dropped last night.*
¿Le descenderá la temperatura? *Will his temperature come down?*

La tribu desciende del Tibet. *The tribe comes from Tibet.*
El Cid no desciende de linaje de reyes. *El Cid does not come from a line of kings.*
'Verbo' desciende de 'verbum'. *'Verbo' derives from 'verbum'.*
Las cifras han experimentado un brusco descenso. *The figures show a sharp fall.*

descenso *descent, going down, drop, fall*
descendiente *descendant*
descendimiento *lowering, descent*
descendente *descending*
descendencia *origin, offspring, descendants*

67 descolgar *to take down, unhook* tr.

INDICATIVE

Present	Imperfect	Perfect
descuelgo	descolgaba	he descolgado
descuelgas	descolgabas	has descolgado
descuelga	descolgaba	ha descolgado
descolgamos	descolgábamos	hemos descolgado
descolgáis	descolgabais	habéis descolgado
descuelgan	descolgaban	han descolgado
Future	**Pluperfect**	**Past Definite**
descolgaré	había descolgado	descolgué
descolgarás	habías descolgado	descolgaste
descolgará	había descolgado	descolgó
descolgaremos	habíamos descolgado	descolgamos
descolgaréis	habíais descolgado	descolgasteis
descolgarán	habían descolgado	descolgaron
Future Perfect	**Past Perfect**	
habré descolgado	hube descolgado	

CONDITIONAL	SUBJUNCTIVE	
Present	**Present**	**Imperfect**
descolgaría	descuelgue	descolg-ara/ase
descolgarías	descuelgues	descolg-aras/ases
descolgaría	descuelgue	descolg-ara/ase
descolgaríamos	descolguemos	descolg-áramos/ásemos
descolgaríais	descolguéis	descolg-arais/aseis
descolgarían	descuelguen	descolg-aran/asen
Perfect	**Perfect**	**Pluperfect**
habría descolgado	haya descolgado	hub-iera/iese descolgado

GERUND	PAST PARTICIPLE	IMPERATIVE
descolgando	descolgado	descuelga, descolgad descuelgue (Vd), descuelguen (Vds)

Descuelga el cuadro. *Take down the picture.*
Voy a descolgar las cortinas. *I am going to take the curtains down.*
Nos descolgamos cuesta abajo. *We went down hill slowly.*

Descuelga el teléfono. *Pick up the phone.*
Se descolgará por la pared. *He will climb down the wall.*
Se han descolgado las nubes. *Suddenly there are a few clouds.*
Siempre se descuelga con una estupidez. *He always comes out with a silly remark.*
El teléfono está descolgado. *The phone is off the hook.*
Nos descolgaremos pidiéndole el dinero. *We'll ask him for the money when he least expects it.*

descolgamiento de pintura *lifting of the paint*
descolgarse con . . . *to come out with*
descolgado/a *unhooked*

desconcertar *to upset, disconcert* tr. 68

INDICATIVE

Present	Imperfect	Perfect
desconcierto	desconcertaba	he desconcertado
desconciertas	desconcertabas	has desconcertado
desconcierta	desconcertaba	ha desconcertado
desconcertamos	desconcertábamos	hemos desconcertado
desconcertáis	desconcertabais	habéis desconcertado
desconciertan	desconcertaban	han desconcertado
Future	**Pluperfect**	**Past Definite**
desconcertaré	había desconcertado	desconcerté
desconcertarás	habías desconcertado	desconcertaste
desconcertará	había desconcertado	desconcertó
desconcertaremos	habíamos desconcertado	desconcertamos
desconcertaréis	habíais desconcertado	desconcertasteis
desconcertarán	habían desconcertado	desconcertaron
Future Perfect	**Past Perfect**	
habré desconcertado	hube desconcertado	

CONDITIONAL / SUBJUNCTIVE

Present (Conditional)	Present (Subjunctive)	Imperfect (Subjunctive)
desconcertaría	desconcierte	desconcert-ara/ase
desconcertarías	desconciertes	desconcert-aras/ases
desconcertaría	desconcierte	desconcert-ara/ase
desconcertaríamos	desconcertemos	desconcert-áramos/ásemos
desconcertaríais	desconcertéis	desconcert-arais/aseis
desconcertarían	desconcierten	desconcert-aran/asen
Perfect	**Perfect**	**Pluperfect**
habría desconcertado	haya desconcertado	hub-iera/iese desconcertado

GERUND	PAST PARTICIPLE	IMPERATIVE
desconcertando	desconcertado	desconcierta, desconcertad desconcierte (Vd), desconcierten (Vds)

Este niño me desconcierta. *This boy upsets me.*
Le desconcertó verme con Miguel. *It disconcerted him to see me with Miguel.*
Se me ha desconcertado el estómago. *I've got an upset stomach.*
Estoy tan desconcertado que no se qué pensar. *I am so taken aback that I don't know what to think.*

Hay desconcierto en el partido. *There is confusion in the party.*
Desconcierta hasta el más sosegado. *It would upset anybody.*
Su visita contribuye al desconcierto. *His visit increases the chaos.*

desconcertado *disconcerted*
desconcertador *disconcerting*
desconcertante *embarrassing, puzzling*
desconcierto *disorder, trouble, chaos*

69 descontar *to discount, take away* tr.

INDICATIVE

Present	Imperfect	Perfect
descuento	descontaba	he descontado
descuentas	descontabas	has descontado
descuenta	descontaba	ha descontado
descontamos	descontábamos	hemos descontado
descontáis	descontabais	habéis descontado
descuentan	descontaban	han descontado

Future	Pluperfect	Past Definite
descontaré	había descontado	desconté
descontarás	habías descontado	descontaste
descontará	había descontado	descontó
descontaremos	habíamos descontado	descontamos
descontaréis	habíais descontado	descontasteis
descontarán	habían descontado	descontaron

Future Perfect	Past Perfect
habré descontado	hube descontado

CONDITIONAL	SUBJUNCTIVE	
Present	**Present**	**Imperfect**
descontaría	descuente	descont-ara/ase
descontarías	descuentes	descont-aras/ases
descontaría	descuente	descont-ara/ase
descontaríamos	descontemos	descont-áramos/ásemos
descontaríais	descontéis	descont-arais/aseis
descontarían	descuenten	descont-aran/asen
Perfect	**Perfect**	**Pluperfect**
habría descontado	haya descontado	hub-iera/iese descontado

GERUND	PAST PARTICIPLE	IMPERATIVE
descontando	descontado	descuenta, descontad descuente (Vd), descuenten (Vds)

Me ha descontado el 10%. *I've got a 10% discount.*
Te descontaré el precio de la botella. *I will not charge you for the price of the bottle.*
Si descuentas diez me quedan veinte. *If you take away ten I am left with twenty.*
Han descontado los intereses. *They have discounted the interest.*

Da por descontado que . . . *Assume that . . .*
Lo podemos dar por descontado. *We can take that for granted.*
Hay mucho descontento. *There is a lot of unrest.*
Estoy descontenta del resultado. *I am dissatisfied with the result.*

por descontado *obviously, of course*
(con) descuento *(at a) discount*
¡Descuéntalo! *Forget it!*

despedir *to dismiss, say goodbye* tr. 70

INDICATIVE

Present	Imperfect	Perfect
despido	despedía	he despedido
despides	despedías	has despedido
despide	despedía	ha despedido
despedimos	despedíamos	hemos despedido
despedís	despedíais	habéis despedido
despiden	despedían	han despedido
Future	**Pluperfect**	**Past Definite**
despediré	había despedido	despedí
despedirás	habías despedido	despediste
despedirá	había despedido	despidió
despediremos	habíamos despedido	despedimos
despediréis	habíais despedido	despedisteis
despedirán	habían despedido	despidieron
Future Perfect	**Past Perfect**	
habré despedido	hube despedido	

CONDITIONAL	SUBJUNCTIVE	
Present	**Present**	**Imperfect**
despediría	despida	despid-iera/iese
despedirías	despidas	despid-ieras/ieses
despediría	despida	despid-iera/iese
despediríamos	despidamos	despid-iéramos/iésemos
despediríais	despidáis	despid-ierais/ieseis
despedirían	despidan	despid-ieran/iesen
Perfect	**Perfect**	**Pluperfect**
habría despedido	haya despedido	hub-iera/iese despedido

GERUND	PAST PARTICIPLE	IMPERATIVE
despidiendo	despedido	despide, despedid despida (Vd), despidan (Vds)

Voy a despedirme de Juan. *I'm going to say goodbye to Juan.*
Fuimos a la estación a despedirles. *We went to the station to see them off.*
Me despediré luego. *I shall say goodbye later.*
Se despidieron. *They said goodbye to each other.*

Van a despedir a los obreros. *The workers are going to get the sack.*
Ya puedes despedirte de ello. *You'd better forget about it.*
Le han despedido. *He has been fired.*
Hamlet despide el espíritu. *Hamlet gives up the ghost.*
Les despidieron en el acto. *They were fired on the spot.*
Me pienso despedir yo misma. *I'm going to quit.*

¡Estás despedido! *You're fired!*
despido *sack, dismissal, sacking*
despedida *farewell*
cena de despedida *farewell dinner*
regalo de despedida *parting gift*
despedida de aguas *drainage*

71 despertar *to awake, wake up* tr.

INDICATIVE

Present	**Imperfect**	**Perfect**
despierto	despertaba	he despertado
despiertas	despertabas	has despertado
despierta	despertaba	ha despertado
despertamos	despertábamos	hemos despertado
despertáis	despertabais	habéis despertado
despiertan	despertaban	han despertado
Future	**Pluperfect**	**Past Definite**
despertaré	había despertado	desperté
despertarás	habías despertado	despertaste
despertará	había despertado	despertó
despertaremos	habíamos despertado	despertamos
despertaréis	habíais despertado	despertasteis
despertarán	habían despertado	despertaron
Future Perfect	**Past Perfect**	
habré despertado	hube despertado	

CONDITIONAL	SUBJUNCTIVE	
Present	**Present**	**Imperfect**
despertaría	despierte	despert-ara/ase
despertarías	despiertes	despert-aras/ases
despertaría	despierte	despert-ara/ase
despertaríamos	despertemos	despert-áramos/ásemos
despertaríais	despertéis	despert-arais/aseis
despertarían	despierten	despert-aran/asen
Perfect	**Perfect**	**Pluperfect**
habría despertado	haya despertado	hub-iera/iese despertado

GERUND	PAST PARTICIPLE	IMPERATIVE
despertando	despertado	despierta, despertad despierte (Vd), despierten (Vds)

Me despierto a las 7. *I wake up at 7 a.m.*
Te despertaré a las 6. *I'll wake you up at 6.*
Nos despertó la tormenta. *The storm woke us up.*
¿Les despertamos? *Shall we wake them up?*

El despertar de la primavera. *The awakening of spring.*
Ya se despertará a la realidad. *She'll wake up to reality.*
Sueña despierta. *She daydreams.*
Por fin despertó de su error. *At last he realised his mistake.*
Elena despierta simpatías. *Everybody loves Elena.*

despertador *alarm clock*
despertador de viaje *travelling alarm clock*
despertador(a) *awakening, arousing*
despertamiento *awakening, revival, rebirth*
despierto/a *awake, wide awake, sharp, alert*

desplegar *to unfold, spread* tr. 72

INDICATIVE

Present	Imperfect	Perfect
despliego	desplegaba	he desplegado
despliegas	desplegabas	has desplegado
despliega	desplegaba	ha desplegado
desplegamos	desplegábamos	hemos desplegado
desplegáis	desplegabais	habéis desplegado
despliegan	desplegaban	han desplegado
Future	**Pluperfect**	**Past Definite**
desplegaré	había desplegado	desplegué
desplegarás	habías desplegado	desplegaste
desplegará	había desplegado	desplegó
desplegaremos	habíamos desplegado	desplegamos
desplegaréis	habíais desplegado	desplegasteis
desplegarán	habían desplegado	desplegaron
Future Perfect	**Past Perfect**	
habré desplegado	hube desplegado	

CONDITIONAL	SUBJUNCTIVE	
Present	**Present**	**Imperfect**
desplegaría	despliegue	despleg-ara/ase
desplegarías	despliegues	despleg-aras/ases
desplegaría	despliegue	despleg-ara/ase
desplegaríamos	despleguemos	despleg-áramos/ásemos
desplegaríais	despleguéis	despleg-arais/aseis
desplegarían	desplieguen	despleg-aran/asen
Perfect	**Perfect**	**Pluperfect**
habría desplegado	haya desplegado	hub-iera/iese desplegado

GERUND	PAST PARTICIPLE	IMPERATIVE
desplegando	desplegado	despliega, desplegad despliegue (Vd), desplieguen (Vds)

Despliego un pañuelo. *I unfold a scarf.*
Paqui desplegó el periódico. *Paqui unfolded the newspaper.*
Desplegarán la bandera. *They will unfurl the flag.*
Vamos a desplegar las velas del barco. *We are going to unfurl the sails of the boat.*

sin desplegar los labios *without uttering a word*
Desplegó mucha astucia. *He was cunning.*
Desplegaremos las alas. *We shall spread our wings.*
desplegar en abanico *to fan out*

despliegue *display, deployment, exhibition, show*
desplegado *displayed, splay*
desplegadura *unfolding, spreading*
desplegadamente *openly*
a velas desplegadas *with the sails set*
con banderas desplegadas *with the flags unfurled*

73 desterrar *to exile, banish* tr.

INDICATIVE

Present	Imperfect	Perfect
destierro	desterraba	he desterrado
destierras	desterrabas	has desterrado
destierra	desterraba	ha desterrado
desterramos	desterrábamos	hemos desterrado
desterráis	desterrabais	habéis desterrado
destierran	desterraban	han desterrado

Future	Pluperfect	Past Definite
desterraré	había desterrado	desterré
desterrarás	habías desterrado	desterraste
desterrará	había desterrado	desterró
desterraremos	habíamos desterrado	desterramos
desterraréis	habíais desterrado	desterrasteis
desterrarán	habían desterrado	desterraron

Future Perfect	Past Perfect	
habré desterrado	hube desterrado	

CONDITIONAL	SUBJUNCTIVE	
Present	**Present**	**Imperfect**
desterraría	destierre	desterr-ara/ase
desterrarías	destierres	desterr-aras/ases
desterraría	destierre	desterr-ara/ase
desterraríamos	desterremos	desterr-áramos/ásemos
desterraríais	desterréis	desterr-arais/aseis
desterrarían	destierren	desterr-aran/asen
Perfect	**Perfect**	**Pluperfect**
habría desterrado	haya desterrado	hub-iera/iese desterrado

GERUND	PAST PARTICIPLE	IMPERATIVE
desterrando	desterrado	destierra, desterrand destierre (Vd), destierren (Vds)

Hay que desterrar esas ideas. *Those ideas have to be banished.*
El gobierno ha desterrado el uso de las armas de fuego. *The government has banished the use of firearms.*
El rey desterró al Cid. *The king exiled el Cid.*
Deberíamos desterrar las armas nucleares. *We ought to banish nuclear arms.*

Desterramos toda sospecha. *We banish all suspicions from our minds.*
Vive en el destierro. *She lives in exile.*
Lo pintó en el destierro. *He painted that in exile.*

tierra *soil, earth*
desterrar *to remove soil from (mines)*
desterrado/a *exile, outlaw, outcast*
destierro *exile, banishment*

destruir *to destroy, ruin* tr. 74

INDICATIVE

Present	Imperfect	Perfect
destruyo	destruía	he destruido
destruyes	destruías	has destruido
destruye	destruía	ha destruido
destruimos	destruíamos	hemos destruido
destruís	destruíais	habéis destruido
destruyen	destruían	han destruido

Future	Pluperfect	Past Definite
destruiré	había destruido	destruí
destruirás	habías destruido	destruiste
destruirá	había destruido	destruyó
destruiremos	habíamos destruido	destruimos
destruiréis	habíais destruido	destruisteis
destruirán	habían destruido	destruyeron

Future Perfect	Past Perfect
habré destruido	hube destruido

CONDITIONAL / SUBJUNCTIVE

Conditional Present	Subjunctive Present	Subjunctive Imperfect
destruiría	destruya	destru-yera/yese
destruirías	destruyas	destru-yeras/yeses
destruiría	destruya	destru-yera/yese
destruiríamos	destruyamos	destru-yéramos/yésemos
destruiríais	destruyáis	destru-yerais/yeseis
destruirían	destruyan	destru-yeran/yesen

Perfect	Perfect	Pluperfect
habría destruido	haya destruido	hub-iera/iese destruido

GERUND	PAST PARTICIPLE	IMPERATIVE
destruyendo	destruido	destruye, destruid destruya (Vd), destruyan (Vds)

No destruyas ese trabajo. *Do not destroy that work.*
La bomba destruyó la estación. *The bomb destroyed the station.*
He destruido la información. *I have destroyed the information.*
Los romanos destruyeron Numancia. *The Romans destroyed Numancia.*

Lo van a destruir con explosivos. *They are going to blow it up.*
Ha sido destruido por un incendio. *It has been gutted by fire.*
Lo destruiré soplando. *I shall blow it out.*
La ciudad ha sido destruida por la acción enemiga. *The town has been destroyed by the enemy action.*

destruirse *to cancel (math)*
destruíble *destroyable, destructible*
destructor(a) *destroyer, destructive*
destrucción *wreck, destruction*
destruyente *destructive*
destructible *destructible*
destructivamente *destructively*
destructibilidad *destructibility*

75 devolver *to return, give back* tr.

INDICATIVE

Present	Imperfect	Perfect
devuelvo	devolvía	he devuelto
devuelves	devolvías	has devuelto
devuelve	devolvía	ha devuelto
devolvemos	devolvíamos	hemos devuelto
devolvéis	devolvíais	habéis devuelto
devuelven	devolvían	han devuelto
Future	**Pluperfect**	**Past Definite**
devolveré	había devuelto	devolví
devolverás	habías devuelto	devolviste
devolverá	había devuelto	devolvió
devolveremos	habíamos devuelto	devolvimos
devolveréis	habíais devuelto	devolvisteis
devolverán	habían devuelto	devolvieron
Future Perfect	**Past Perfect**	
habré devuelto	hube devuelto	

CONDITIONAL	SUBJUNCTIVE	
Present	**Present**	**Imperfect**
devolvería	devuelva	devolv-iera/iese
devolverías	devuelvas	devolv-ieras/ieses
devolvería	devuelva	devolv-iera/iese
devolveríamos	devolvamos	devolv-iéramos/iésemos
devoleríais	devolváis	devolv-ierais/ieseis
devolverían	devuelvan	devolv-ieran/iesen
Perfect	**Perfect**	**Pluperfect**
habría devuelto	haya devuelto	hub-iera/iese devuelto

GERUND	PAST PARTICIPLE	IMPERATIVE
devolviendo	devuelto	devuelve, devolved devuelva (Vd), devuelvan (Vds)

Te devolveré tu libro mañana. *I'll return your book tomorrow.*
Le devolvió su regalo. *He returned his present.*
Me devolvieron el dinero. *I got my money back.*
El espejo devuelve la imagen. *The mirror reflects the image.*
Han devuelto el castillo a su antiguo explendor. *They have restored the castle to its former glory.*

devolver mal por bien *to return bad for good*
devolver dinero *to refund money*
devolver una visita *to return a visit*
devolver la pelota *to pass the buck*

devolución *return, refund*
devolución de impuestos *tax refunds*
devolutivo/a *returnable*
devolver *to vomit, be sick (med)*
devolución de las inversiones *return on investments*

diferir *to postpone, differ* tr./intr. 76

INDICATIVE

Present	Imperfect	Perfect
difiero	difería	he diferido
difieres	diferías	has diferido
difiere	difería	ha diferido
diferimos	diferíamos	hemos diferido
diferís	deferíais	habéis diferido
difieren	diferían	han diferido
Future	**Pluperfect**	**Past Definite**
diferiré	había diferido	diferí
diferirás	habías diferido	diferiste
diferirá	había diferido	difirió
diferiremos	habíamos diferido	diferimos
diferiréis	habíais diferido	diferisteis
diferirán	habían diferido	difirieron
Future Perfect	**Past Perfect**	
habré diferido	hube diferido	

CONDITIONAL	SUBJUNCTIVE	
Present	**Present**	**Imperfect**
diferiría	difiera	difir-iera/iese
diferirías	difieras	difir-ieras/ieses
diferiría	difiera	difir-iera/iese
diferiríamos	difiramos	difir-iéramos/iésemos
diferiríais	difiráis	difir-ierais/ieseis
diferirían	difieran	difir-ieran/iesen
Perfect	**Perfect**	**Pluperfect**
habría diferido	haya diferido	hub-iera/iese diferido

GERUND	PAST PARTICIPLE	IMPERATIVE
difiriendo	diferido	difiere, diferid difiera (Vd), difieran (Vds)

Han diferido la boda hasta el otoño. *The wedding has been postponed until the autumn.*
Esta obra difiere de las anteriores. *This work is different from the previous ones.*
Vamos a diferir la reunión por unos días. *Let's defer the meeting for a few days.*
Nos conviene diferir la venta. *We should postpone the sale.*

Hay que hacer una diferencia entre . . . *We have to make a distinction between . . .*
diferir en *to be different in*
diferir de *to be different from*
a diferencia de . . . *unlike . . .*

diferente *different*
por diferentes razones *for various reasons*
diferencia *difference*
diferenciar *to differentiate*
diferenciarse *to differ*
diferentemente *differently*
diferible *deferrable*

77 digerir *to digest, absorb* tr.

INDICATIVE

Present	Imperfect	Perfect
digiero	digería	he digerido
digieres	digerías	has digerido
digiere	digería	ha digerido
digerimos	digeríamos	hemos digerido
digerís	digeríais	habéis digerido
digieren	digerían	han digerido
Future	**Pluperfect**	**Past Definite**
digeriré	había digerido	digerí
digerirás	habías digerido	digeriste
digerirá	había digerido	digirió
digeriremos	habíamos digerido	digerimos
digeriréis	habíais digerido	digeristeis
digerirán	habían digerido	digirieron
Future Perfect	**Past Perfect**	
habré digerido	hube digerido	

CONDITIONAL	SUBJUNCTIVE	
Present	**Present**	**Imperfect**
digeriría	digiera	digir-iera/iese
digerirías	digieras	digir-ieras/ieses
digeriría	digiera	digir-iera/iese
digeriríamos	digiramos	digir-iéramos/iésemos
digeriríais	digiráis	digir-ierais/ieseis
digerirían	digieran	digir-ieran/iesen
Perfect	**Perfect**	**Pluperfect**
habría digerido	haya digerido	hub-iera/iese digerido

GERUND	PAST PARTICIPLE	IMPERATIVE
digiriendo	digerido	digiere, digerid digiera (Vd), digieran (Vds)

Tiene una úlcera y no puede digerir bien. *He has an ulcer and cannot digest well.*
No pude digerir la cena. *I couldn't digest the supper.*
Ya lo he digerido. *I have already assimilated it.*
Me cuesta digerir su argumento. *I find his argument hard to digest.*

Necesito leerlo tres veces para digerirlo. *I need to read it three times in order to assimilate it.*
Lo digeriremos mañana. *We shall absorb it tomorrow.*
No puedo digerir a Dalí. *I cannot stand Dalí.*
No lo podré digerir nunca. *I shall never be able to digest it.*

digerible *digestible*
digestible *digestible*
digestión *digestion*
digesto *digest*
indigesto *indigestible*
digestivo/a *digestive*
digestibilidad *digestibility*
digestor *digester*

disolver *to dissolve, melt* tr. 78

INDICATIVE

Present	Imperfect	Perfect
disuelvo	disolvía	he disuelto
disuelves	disolvías	has disuelto
disuelve	disolvía	ha disuelto
disolvemos	disolvíamos	hemos disuelto
disolvéis	disolvíais	habéis disuelto
disuelven	disolvían	han disuelto
Future	**Pluperfect**	**Past Definite**
disolveré	había disuelto	disolví
disolverás	habías disuelto	disolviste
disolverá	había disuelto	disolvió
disolveremos	habíamos disuelto	disolvimos
disolveréis	habíais disuelto	disolvisteis
disolverán	habían disuelto	disolvieron
Future Perfect	**Past Perfect**	
habré disuelto	hube disuelto	

CONDITIONAL	SUBJUNCTIVE	
Present	**Present**	**Imperfect**
disolvería	disuelva	disolv-iera/iese
disolverías	disuelvas	disolv-ieras/ieses
disolvería	disuelva	disolv-iera/iese
disolveríamos	disolvamos	disolv-iéramos/iésemos
disolveríais	disolváis	disolv-ierais/ieseis
disolverían	disuelvan	disolv-ieran/iesen
Perfect	**Perfect**	**Pluperfect**
habría disuelto	haya disuelto	hub-iera/iese disuelto

GERUND	PAST PARTICIPLE	IMPERATIVE
disolviendo	disuelto	disuelve, disolved disuelva (Vd), disuelvan (Vds)

Quería disolver la reunión. *He wanted to break up the meeting.*
El parlamento se disuelve en agosto. *Parliament breaks up in August.*
Se disuelve en agua. *It dissolves in water.*
Se ha disuelto el matrimonio. *The marriage has been dissolved.*
Tejero quería disolver las Cortes. *Tejero wanted to dissolve las Cortes.*
La policía disolvió la manifestación. *The police broke up the demonstration.*

disolvente impuro *contaminated agent*
disolvente oxygenado *oxygenated solvent*
disolvente de grasas *fat-dissolving agent*

disolvente *solvent, dissolvent*
disolvedor *dissolver*
disolución *solution*
disoluble *dissoluble*
disoluto *dissolute, dissipated*

79 distinguir *to distinguish* tr.

INDICATIVE

Present	Imperfect	Perfect
distingo	distinguía	he distinguido
distingues	distinguías	has distinguido
distingue	distinguía	ha distinguido
distinguimos	distinguíamos	hemos distinguido
distinguís	distinguíais	habéis distinguido
distinguen	distinguían	han distinguido

Future	Pluperfect	Past Definite
distinguiré	había distinguido	distinguí
distinguirás	habías distinguido	distinguiste
distinguirá	había distinguido	distinguió
distinguiremos	habíamos distinguido	distinguimos
distinguiréis	habíais distinguido	distinguisteis
distinguirán	habían distinguido	distinguieron

Future Perfect	Past Perfect
habré distinguido	hube distinguido

CONDITIONAL / SUBJUNCTIVE

Present (Conditional)	Present (Subjunctive)	Imperfect (Subjunctive)
distinguiría	distinga	distingu-iera/iese
distinguirías	distingas	distingu-ieras/ieses
distinguiría	distinga	distingu-iera/iese
distinguiríamos	distingamos	distingu-iéramos/iésemos
distinguiríais	distingáis	distingu-ierais/ieseis
distinguirían	distingan	distingu-ieran/iesen

Perfect (Conditional)	Perfect (Subjunctive)	Pluperfect (Subjunctive)
habría distinguido	haya distinguido	hub-iera/iese distinguido

GERUND	PAST PARTICIPLE	IMPERATIVE
distinguiendo	distinguido	distingue, distinguid distinga (Vd), distingan (Vds)

No distingo mi jersey. *I can't tell which is my jumper.*
Lo sabría distinguir entre 1.000. *I could distinguish it from a 1000.*
¿Distingues los dos aspectos? *Can you distinguish between the two aspects?*
No les puedo distinguir. *I can't tell them apart.*

Mike es muy distinguido. *Mike is very distinguished.*
Leonor sabe distinguir. *Leonor is a discriminating person.*
Rodrigo les distingue con su amistad. *Rodrigo honours them with his friendship.*
Sé distinguir. *I know the difference. I can tell.*

distinción *distinction, difference*
distinguible *distinguishible*
distinguido/a *well-known, refined, distinguished*
distintivo/a *distinctive*
distinto/a *distinct, clear; different; several*

divertir *to amuse, distract* tr. 80

INDICATIVE

Present	Imperfect	Perfect
divierto	divertía	he divertido
diviertes	divertías	has divertido
divierte	divertía	ha divertido
divertimos	divertíamos	hemos divertido
divertís	divertíais	habéis divertido
divierten	divertían	han divertido
Future	**Pluperfect**	**Past Definite**
divertiré	había divertido	divertí
divertirás	habías divertido	divertiste
divertirá	había divertido	divirtió
divertiremos	habíamos divertido	divertimos
divertiréis	habíais divertido	divertisteis
divertirán	habían divertido	divirtieron
Future Perfect	**Past Perfect**	
habré divertido	hube divertido	

CONDITIONAL	SUBJUNCTIVE	
Present	**Present**	**Imperfect**
divertiría	divierta	divirt-iera/iese
divertirías	diviertas	divirt-ieras/ieses
divertiría	divierta	divirt-iera/iese
divertiríamos	divirtamos	divirt-iéramos/iésemos
divertiríais	divirtáis	divirt-ierais/ieseis
divertirían	diviertan	divirt-ieran/iesen
Perfect	**Perfect**	**Pluperfect**
habría divertido	haya divertido	hub-iera/iese divertido

GERUND	PAST PARTICIPLE	IMPERATIVE
divirtiendo	divertido	divierte, divertid divierta (Vd), diviertan (Vds)

El payaso divierte a los niños. *The clown amuses the children.*
Le divierte hacer eso. *That amuses him.*
Nos divertimos mucho. *We had a good time.*
¡Divierte el tráfico! *Divert the traffic!*

El médico va a divertir ahora. *The doctor is going to draw away the body fluid now.*
No te escucha, está divertido. *He is distracted (he is not listening).*
Están totalmente divertidos. *They are drunk.*
Intenta divertir a Juan. *Try to catch Juan's attention.*

diversiforme *diversiform*
diversión *diversion, entertainment, amusement*
diversivo/a *diversive*
divertido/a *amusing, entertaining, merry*
divertimiento *diversion, amusement, distraction*

81 doler *to ache, hurt* intr.

INDICATIVE

Present	Imperfect	Perfect
duelo	dolía	he dolido
dueles	dolías	has dolido
duele	dolía	ha dolido
dolemos	dolíamos	hemos dolido
doléis	dolíais	habéis dolido
duelen	dolían	han dolido

Future	Pluperfect	Past Definite
doleré	había dolido	dolí
dolerás	habías dolido	doliste
dolerá	había dolido	dolió
doleremos	habíamos dolido	dolimos
doleréis	habíais dolido	dolisteis
dolerán	habían dolido	dolieron

Future Perfect	Past Perfect
habré dolido	hube dolido

CONDITIONAL	SUBJUNCTIVE	
Present	**Present**	**Imperfect**
dolería	duela	dol-iera/iese
dolerías	duelas	dol-ieras/ieses
dolería	duela	dol-iera/iese
doleríamos	dolamos	dol-iéramos/iésemos
doleríais	doláis	dol-ierais/ieseis
dolerían	duelan	dol-ieran/iesen
Perfect	**Perfect**	**Pluperfect**
habría dolido	haya dolido	hub-iera/iese dolido

GERUND	PAST PARTICIPLE	IMPERATIVE
doliendo	dolido	duele, doled duela (Vd), duelan (Vds)

¿Te duele mucho? *Does it hurt much?*
Me duelen los brazos. *My arms ache.*
Le duele la cabeza. *He has got a headache.*
No nos ha dolido nada. *It did not hurt us a bit.*

¡Ahí le duele! *You have put your finger on it!*
Aún le duele le pérdida. *He is still mourning the loss.*
No me duele el dinero. *I don't mind about the money.*
¡Duélete de mí! *Pity me!*

dolencia *ailment, complaint*
doliente *suffering, sad*
dolo *fraud*
dolor *pain, ache*
dolor de cabeza *headache*
dolorido/a *sore, tender*
dolor crónico *chronic pain*
dolerse *to grieve, regret*

dormir *to sleep* tr./intr.

INDICATIVE

Present
duermo
duermes
duerme
dormimos
dormís
duermen

Imperfect
dormía
dormías
dormía
dormíamos
dormíais
dormían

Perfect
he dormido
has dormido
ha dormido
hemos dormido
habéis dormido
han dormido

Future
dormiré
dormirás
dormirá
dormiremos
dormiréis
dormirán

Pluperfect
había dormido
habías dormido
había dormido
habíamos dormido
habíais dormido
habían dormido

Past Definite
dormí
dormiste
durmió
dormimos
dormisteis
durmieron

Future Perfect
habré dormido

Past Perfect
hube dormido

CONDITIONAL

Present
dormiría
dormirías
dormiría
dormiríamos
dormiríais
dormirían

Perfect
habría dormido

SUBJUNCTIVE

Present
duerma
duermas
duerma
durmamos
durmáis
duerman

Imperfect
durm-iera/iese
durm-ieras/ieses
durm-iera/iese
durm-iéramos/iésemos
durm-ierais/ieseis
durm-ieran/iesen

Perfect
haya dormido

Pluperfect
hub-iera/iese dormido

GERUND

durmiendo

PAST PARTICIPLE

dormido

IMPERATIVE

duerme, dormid
duerma (Vd), duerman (Vds)

Me gusta dormir. *I love sleeping.*
Pedro duerme ocho horas al día. *Pedro sleeps eight hours a day.*
La reina Leonor durmió aquí. *Queen Eleonor slept here.*
Dormiremos en un hotel. *We'll sleep in a hotel.*

Tiene que dormirla. *He has to sleep it off.*
Creo que va a dormir la mona esta mañana. *I think she is going to sleep off her hangover this morning.*
Estaba dormido como un lirón/tronco. *He was fast asleep.*
He dormido como un santo/bendito. *I have slept peacefully.*
Durmieron a pierna suelta. *They slept soundly.*

dormida *sleep*
dormidero = sestil *sleeping place* (for animals)
dormidera *opium poppy*
dormilón/dormilona *sleepyhead*
dormitorio *bedroom*

83 echar *to throw, pour* tr./intr.

INDICATIVE

Present	Imperfect	Perfect
echo	echaba	he echado
echas	echabas	has echado
echa	echaba	ha echado
echamos	echábamos	hemos echado
echáis	echabais	habéis echado
echan	echaban	han echado
Future	**Pluperfect**	**Past Definite**
echaré	había echado	eché
echarás	habías echado	echaste
echará	había echado	echó
echaremos	habíamos echado	echamos
echaréis	habíais echado	echasteis
echarán	habían echado	echaron
Future Perfect	**Past Perfect**	
habré echado	hube echado	

CONDITIONAL	SUBJUNCTIVE	
Present	**Present**	**Imperfect**
echaría	eche	ech-ara/ase
echarías	eches	ech-aras/ases
echaría	eche	ech-ara/ase
echaríamos	echemos	ech-áramos/ásemos
echaríais	echéis	ech-arais/aseis
echarían	echen	ech-aran/asen
Perfect	**Perfect**	**Pluperfect**
habría echado	haya echado	hub-iera/iese echado

GERUND	PAST PARTICIPLE	IMPERATIVE
echando	echado	echa, echad eche (Vd), echen (Vds)

Echa azúcar al café. *Put some sugar in the coffee.*
¿Te echo un poco de agua? *Shall I pour some water for you?*
Cuando protesté me echaron. *When I protested they threw me out.*
¡Que le echen fuera! *Chuck him out!*

Echó el cuerpo atrás. *He leaned his body backwards.*
El bebé ha echado un diente. *The baby has cut a tooth.*
He echado raíces aquí. *I have put down roots here.*
Voy a echar la choza abajo. *I'm going to knock down the hut.*
La lluvia echó a perder la fruta. *The rain spoiled the fruit.*

echar de comer a los animales *to feed the animals*
echar a suertes *to draw lots*
echar a correr *to start running*
echarse *to lie down*
echadora de cartas *fortune teller*
echada *throw, cast, boast*
echar a perder *to waste*

elegir *to select, choose* tr. 84

INDICATIVE

Present	Imperfect	Perfect
elijo	elegía	he elegido
eliges	elegías	has elegido
elige	elegía	ha elegido
elegimos	elegíamos	hemos elegido
elegís	elegíais	habéis elegido
eligen	elegían	han elegido
Future	**Pluperfect**	**Past Definite**
elegiré	había elegido	elegí
elegirás	habías elegido	elegiste
elegirá	había elegido	eligió
elegiremos	habíamos elegido	elegimos
elegiréis	habíais elegido	elegisteis
elegirán	habían elegido	eligieron
Future Perfect	**Past Perfect**	
habré elegido	hube elegido	

CONDITIONAL	SUBJUNCTIVE	
Present	**Present**	**Imperfect**
elegiría	elija	elig-iera/iese
elegirías	elijas	elig-ieras/ieses
elegiría	elija	elig-iera/iese
elegiríamos	elijamos	elig-iéramos/iésemos
elegiríais	elijáis	elig-ierais/ieseis
elegirían	elijan	elig-ieran/iesen
Perfect	**Perfect**	**Pluperfect**
habría elegido	haya elegido	hub-iera/iese elegido

GERUND	PAST PARTICIPLE	IMPERATIVE
eligiendo	elegido	elige, elegid elija (Vd), elijan (Vds)

Te toca elegir. *It's your turn to choose.*
¿Has elegido ya? *Have you chosen already?*
Siempre elijo chocolate. *I always choose chocolate.*
Le eligieron entre los dos. *He was selected by both of them.*

¡Elige el que quieras! *The choice is yours!*
Se elige por sorteo. *It is chosen by lottery.*
Me eligieron por votación. *I was voted in.*
Han elegido el camino más difícil. *They have made the worst choice.*

elegible *eligible, selectable*
elegido *chosen, selected*
elección *choice, selection, option*
elecciones generales *general elections*
elecciones parciales *by-elections*
elector(a) *voter, elector*
potencia electoral *voting power*
elegibilidad *elegibility*

85 empezar *to begin, start* tr./intr.

INDICATIVE

Present	Imperfect	Perfect
empiezo	empezaba	he empezado
empiezas	empezabas	has empezado
empieza	empezaba	ha empezado
empezamos	empezábamos	hemos empezado
empezáis	empezabais	habéis empezado
empiezan	empezaban	han empezado
Future	**Pluperfect**	**Past Definite**
empezaré	había empezado	empecé
empezarás	habías empezado	empezaste
empezará	había empezado	empezó
empezaremos	habíamos empezado	empezamos
empezaréis	habíais empezado	empezasteis
empezarán	habían empezado	empezaron
Future Perfect	**Past Perfect**	
habré empezado	hube empezado	

CONDITIONAL	SUBJUNCTIVE	
Present	**Present**	**Imperfect**
empezaría	empiece	empez-ara/ase
empezarías	empieces	empez-aras/ases
empezaría	empiece	empez-ara/ase
empezaríamos	empecemos	empez-áramos/ásemos
empezaríais	empecéis	empez-arais/aseis
empezarían	empiecen	empez-aran/asen
Perfect	**Perfect**	**Pluperfect**
habría empezado	haya empezado	hub-iera/iese empezado

GERUND	PAST PARTICIPLE	IMPERATIVE
empezando	empezado	empieza, empezad empiece (Vd), empiecen (Vds)

El curso empieza en octubre. *The course starts in October.*
¡No empieces el trabajo! *Don't start the work!*
Ayer empezó a hacer calor. *Yesterday it started to get hot.*
Empecé diciendo que . . . *I started by saying that . . .*

Bueno, para empezar . . . *Well, to start with . . .*
Empezará a regir mañana. *It will come into force tomorrow.*
Voy a empezar a disparar. *I am going to open fire.*
Empiezan la excavación el lunes. *They break ground on Monday.*
empezar la casa por el tejado *to put the cart before the horse*

empiece *starting, beginning*
empezado *underway*
para empezar *first of all, to start with*
empiezo *beginning, start*
empezar por *to begin by*

encender *to light* tr. 86

INDICATIVE

Present	Imperfect	Perfect
enciendo	encendía	he encendido
enciendes	encendías	has encendido
enciende	encendía	ha encendido
encendemos	encendíamos	hemos encendido
encendéis	encendíais	habéis encendido
encienden	encendían	han encendido

Future	Pluperfect	Past Definite
encenderé	había encendido	encendí
encenderás	habías encendido	encendiste
encenderá	había encendido	encendió
encenderemos	habíamos encendido	encendimos
encenderéis	habíais encendido	encendisteis
encenderán	habían encendido	encendieron

Future Perfect	Past Perfect
habré encendido	hube encendido

CONDITIONAL / SUBJUNCTIVE

Conditional Present	Subjunctive Present	Subjunctive Imperfect
encendería	encienda	encend-iera/iese
encenderías	enciendas	encend-ieras/ieses
encendería	encienda	encend-iera/iese
encenderíamos	encendamos	encend-iéramos/iésemos
encenderíais	encendáis	encend-ierais/ieseis
encenderían	enciendan	encend-ieran/iesen

Perfect	Perfect	Pluperfect
habría encendido	haya encendido	hub-iera/iese encendido

GERUND	PAST PARTICIPLE	IMPERATIVE
encendiendo	encendido	enciende, encended encienda (Vd), enciendan (Vds)

¡Enciende una cerilla! *Light a match!*
Encendió la luz. *She turned on the light.*
¿Has encendido el horno? *Have you switched on the oven?*
Ya habían encendido la radio. *They had already switched on the radio.*

encender un fósforo *to strike a match*
Se encendió con la noticia. *He got very excited with the news.*
Es tímida y se enciende enseguida. *She is shy and blushes easily.*
Está encendido. *It is alight./It is on.*

encendedor *lighter*
encendido a mano *hand firing*
encenderse *to catch fire*
encendida *beating*
encendidamente *passionately, ardently*
encendedor de llama *flame igniter*
encendedor de mecha *fuse igniter*
encender fuego *to light a fire*

87 encerrar *to shut in, lock up* tr.

INDICATIVE

Present	Imperfect	Perfect
encierro	encerraba	he encerrado
encierras	encerrabas	has encerrado
encierra	encerraba	ha encerrado
encerramos	encerrábamos	hemos encerrado
encerráis	encerrabais	habéis encerrado
encierran	encerraban	han encerrado

Future	Pluperfect	Past Definite
encerraré	había encerrado	encerré
encerrarás	habías encerrado	encerraste
encerrará	había encerrado	encerró
encerraremos	habíamos encerrado	encerramos
encerraréis	habíais encerrado	encerrasteis
encerrarán	habían encerrado	encerraron

Future Perfect	Past Perfect
habré encerrado	hube encerrado

CONDITIONAL / SUBJUNCTIVE

Present (Conditional)	Present (Subjunctive)	Imperfect (Subjunctive)
encerraría	encierre	encerr-ara/ase
encerrarías	encierres	encerr-aras/ases
encerraría	encierre	encerr-ara/ase
encerraríamos	encerremos	encerr-áramos/ásemos
encerraríais	encerréis	encerr-arais/aseis
encerrarían	encierren	encerr-aran/asen

Perfect	Perfect	Pluperfect
habría encerrado	haya encerrado	hub-iera/iese encerrado

GERUND	PAST PARTICIPLE	IMPERATIVE
encerrando	encerrado	encierra, encerrad encierre (Vd), encierren (Vds)

El libro encierra toda la historia. *The book contains the whole story.*
Se encerró en el baño. *She shut herself in the bathroom.*
¿Has encerrado las gallinas? *Have you locked the hens in?*
Encerraremos los documentos en una caja fuerte. *We'll lock the documents in a safe.*

Me encerraré en el silencio. *I shall maintain a total silence.*
Les encerraron en un calabozo. *They were locked in jail.*
Camille fue encerrada en un manicomio. *Camille was put in a madhouse.*
Hay que encerrarlo entre comas o paréntesis. *It needs two commas or to be in brackets.*

encerradero *fold, pen*
encierro *closing, confinement, shutting in, locking*
encierre *penning*
encerrado/a *contained*
'encerrado entre cristales' *'glass enclosed'*
encerramiento *enclosure*

encomendar *to entrust* tr./intr. 88

INDICATIVE

Present	Imperfect	Perfect
encomiendo	encomendaba	he encomendado
encomiendas	encomendabas	has encomendado
encomienda	encomendaba	ha encomendado
encomendamos	encomendábamos	hemos encomendado
encomendáis	encomendabais	habéis encomendado
encomiendan	encomendaban	han encomendado
Future	**Pluperfect**	**Past Definite**
encomendaré	había encomendado	encomendé
encomendarás	habías encomendado	encomendaste
encomendará	había encomendado	encomendó
encomendaremos	habíamos encomendado	encomendamos
encomendaréis	habíais encomendado	encomendasteis
encomendarán	habían encomendado	encomendaron
Future Perfect	**Past Perfect**	
habré encomendado	hube encomendado	

CONDITIONAL	SUBJUNCTIVE	
Present	**Present**	**Imperfect**
encomendaría	encomiende	encomend-ara/ase
encomendarías	encomiendes	encomend-aras/ases
encomendaría	encomiende	encomend-ara/ase
encomendaríamos	encomendemos	encomend-áramos/ásemos
encomendaríais	encomendéis	encomend-arais/aseis
encomendarían	encomienden	encomend-aran/asen
Perfect	**Perfect**	**Pluperfect**
habría encomendado	haya encomendado	hub-iera/iese encomendado

GERUND	PAST PARTICIPLE	IMPERATIVE
encomendando	encomendado	encomienda, encomendad encomiende (Vd), encomienden (Vds)

Jim, te encomiendo mi casa. *Jim, I entrust you with my house.*
Encomendó el niño a su madre. *She entrusted the child to her mother.*
Se ha encomendado un traje nuevo. *He has ordered a new suit.*

Me encomiendo a Dios. *I put my trust in God.*
Lo encomendó contra reembolso. *He sent a parcel cash on delivery.*
Encomiéndame a tu mujer. *Send my regards to your wife.*

encomienda *concession, holding, commission, patronage*
encomiendas *regards, respects*
encomendado/a *entrusted*
encomiar *to commend*
encomendable *commendable*
encomendamiento *charge, task*

89 encontrar *to find, meet* tr./intr.

INDICATIVE

Present	Imperfect	Perfect
encuentro	encontraba	he encontrado
encuentras	encontrabas	has encontrado
encuentra	encontraba	ha encontrado
encontramos	encontrábamos	hemos encontrado
encontráis	encontrabais	habéis encontrado
encuentran	encontraban	han encontrado
Future	**Pluperfect**	**Past Definite**
encontraré	había encontrado	encontré
encontrarás	habías encontrado	encontraste
encontrará	había encontrado	encontró
encontraremos	habíamos encontrado	encontramos
encontraréis	habíais encontrado	encontrasteis
encontrarán	habían encontrado	encontraron
Future Perfect	**Past Perfect**	
habré encontrado	hube encontrado	

CONDITIONAL	SUBJUNCTIVE	
Present	**Present**	**Imperfect**
encontraría	encuentre	encontr-ara/ase
encontrarías	encuentres	encontr-aras/ases
encontraría	encuentre	encontr-ara/ase
encontraríamos	encontremos	encontr-áramos/ásemos
encontraríais	encontréis	encontr-arais/aseis
encontrarían	encuentren	encontr-aran/asen
Perfect	**Perfect**	**Pluperfect**
habría encontrado	haya encontrado	hub-iera/iese encontrado

GERUND	PAST PARTICIPLE	IMPERATIVE
encontrando	encontrado	encuentra, encontrad encuentre (Vd), encuentren (Vds)

¿Qué tal lo encuentras? *How do you find it?*
Lo encuentro bastante fácil. *I find it rather easy.*
No lo encontramos. *We can't find it.*
Me voy a encontrar con Sara en la biblioteca. *I'm going to meet Sara in the library.*

¿Qué tal te encuentras? *How are you?*
No sé lo que le encuentran. *I don't know what they see in him.*
Me encontré con un obstáculo. *I ran into an obstacle.*
Se encuentra enferma. *She is ill.*
¡Te la vas a encontrar! *You are going to get it!*

hacerse el encontradizo *to bump into someone*
encontrado/a *found*
encontrón *crash, collision*
encuentro *encounter*
encuentro fortuito *meeting by chance*
encontronazo *crash, collision*

enmendar *to correct, amend* tr. 90

INDICATIVE

Present	Imperfect	Perfect
enmiendo	enmendaba	he enmendado
enmiendas	enmendabas	has enmendado
enmienda	enmendaba	ha enmendado
enmendamos	enmendábamos	hemos enmendado
enmendáis	enmendabais	habéis enmendado
enmiendan	enmendaban	han enmendado
Future	**Pluperfect**	**Past Definite**
enmendaré	había enmendado	enmendé
enmendarás	habías enmendado	enmendaste
enmendará	había enmendado	enmendó
enmendaremos	habíamos enmendado	enmendamos
enmendaréis	habíais enmendado	enmendasteis
enmendarán	habían enmendado	enmendaron
Future Perfect	**Past Perfect**	
habré enmendado	hube enmendado	

CONDITIONAL	SUBJUNCTIVE	
Present	**Present**	**Imperfect**
enmendaría	enmiende	enmend-ara/ase
enmendarías	enmiendes	enmend-aras/ases
enmendaría	enmiende	enmend-ara/ase
enmendaríamos	enmendemos	enmend-áramos/ásemos
enmendaríais	enmendéis	enmend-arais/aseis
enmendarían	enmienden	enmend-aran/asen
Perfect	**Perfect**	**Pluperfect**
habría enmendado	haya enmendado	hub-iera/iese enmendado

GERUND	PAST PARTICIPLE	IMPERATIVE
enmendando	enmendado	enmienda, enmendad enmiende (Vd), enmienden (Vds)

Y no se puede enmendar. *It cannot be revised.*
Enmendaré el documento. *I shall amend the document.*
No hemos enmendado los errores. *We haven't corrected the errors.*
Te enmendaremos por ello. *We shall compensate you for it.*

enmendar buques *to shift boats*
El avión tuvo que enmendar el rumbo. *The plane had to change course.*
No tiene enmienda. *He is incorrigible.*
propósito de enmienda *a firm resolution to mend one's ways*

enmendarse *to reform*
enmendación *emendation, correction*
enmienda *emendation, reform, indemnity, correction*
la Quinta Enmienda *the Fifth Amendment*
enmienda constitucional *amendment to the constitution*
enmienda de poca importancia *minor amendment*
enmienda sobre el trabajo de menores *child labour amendment*

91 entender *to understand* tr./intr.

INDICATIVE

Present	Imperfect	Perfect
entiendo	entendía	he entendido
entiendes	entendías	has entendido
entiende	entendía	ha entendido
entendemos	entendíamos	hemos entendido
entendéis	entendíais	habéis entendido
entienden	entendían	han entendido
Future	**Pluperfect**	**Past Definite**
entenderé	había entendido	entendí
entenderás	habías entendido	entendiste
entenderá	había entendido	entendió
entenderemos	habíamos entendido	entendimos
entenderéis	habíais entendido	entendisteis
entenderán	habían entendido	entendieron
Future Perfect	**Past Perfect**	
habré entendido	hube entendido	

CONDITIONAL	SUBJUNCTIVE	
Present	**Present**	**Imperfect**
entendería	entienda	entend-iera/iese
entenderías	entiendas	entend-ieras/ieses
entendería	entienda	entend-iera/iese
entenderíamos	entendamos	entend-iéramos/iésemos
entenderíais	entendáis	entend-ierais/ieseis
entenderían	entiendan	entend-ieran/iesen
Perfect	**Perfect**	**Pluperfect**
habría entendido	haya entendido	hub-iera/iese entendido

GERUND	PAST PARTICIPLE	IMPERATIVE
entendiendo	entendido	entiende, entended entienda (Vd), entiendan (Vds)

No, no lo entiendo. *No, I do not understand it.*
Te lo pienso hacer entender. *I'll make you understand.*
Nos hicimos entender. *We made ourselves understood.*

No entiendo ni una palabra. *It's all Greek to me.*
a mi entender . . . *in my opinion*
¿Qué entiendes por eso? *What do you mean by that?*
¡Yo me entiendo! *I know what I am doing!*

entendederas *brain (col.)*
entendedor(a) *understanding*
entendido/a *understand, expert*
entendimiento *understanding, comprehension, intelligence*

entenderse *to be understood* r. 92

INDICATIVE

Present	Imperfect	Perfect
me entiendo	me entendía	me he entendido
te entiendes	te entendías	te has entendido
se entiende	se entendía	se ha entendido
nos entendemos	nos entendíamos	nos hemos entendido
os entendéis	os entendíais	os habéis entendido
se entienden	se entendían	se han entendido

Future	Pluperfect	Past Definite
me entenderé	me había entendido	me entendí
te entenderás	te habías entendido	te entendiste
se entenderá	se había entendido	se entendió
nos entenderemos	nos habíamos entendido	nos entendimos
os entenderéis	os habíais entendido	os entendisteis
se entenderán	se habían entendido	se entendieron

Future Perfect	Past Perfect
me habré entendido	me hube entendido

CONDITIONAL / SUBJUNCTIVE

Present (Conditional)	Present (Subjunctive)	Imperfect (Subjunctive)
me entendería	me entienda	me entend-iera/iese
te entenderías	te entiendas	te entend-ieras/ieses
se entendería	se entienda	se entend-iera/iese
nos entenderíamos	nos entendamos	nos entend-iéramos/iésemos
os entenderíais	os entendáis	os entend-ierais/ieseis
se entenderían	se entiendan	se entend-ieran/iesen

Perfect	Perfect	Pluperfect
me habría entendido	me haya entendido	me hub-iera/iese entendido

GERUND	PAST PARTICIPLE	IMPERATIVE
entendiéndose	entendido	entiende, entended entienda (Vd), entiendan (Vds)

¿Qué se entiende por eso? *What is meant by that?*
Se entiende que no es bueno. *It is known to be no good.*
Me he entendido con mi jefe. *I have come to an arrangement with my boss.*
¿Te entiendes con él? *Do you get on with him?*
Se entiende. *It is understood.*
Yo me entiendo. *I know what I am doing.*
Paula y Marcial se entienden bien. *Paula and Marcial get on well together.*
Ana se entiende con Luis. *Ana is having an affair with Luis.*
Creo que él se entiende. *I think he knows what he's on about.*
No me entiendo con el ordenador. *I don't know how the computer works.*
¿Te entiendes con ese lío de cables? *Would you know what to do with all those cables?*
Para el precio, entiéndete con el gerente. *Discuss the price with the manager.*

93 enterrar *to bury, forget* tr.

INDICATIVE

Present	Imperfect	Perfect
entierro	enterraba	he enterrado
entierras	enterrabas	has enterrado
entierra	enterraba	ha enterrado
enterramos	enterrábamos	hemos enterrado
enterráis	enterrabais	habéis enterrado
entierran	enterraban	han enterrado
Future	**Pluperfect**	**Past Definite**
enterraré	había enterrado	enterré
enterrarás	habías enterrado	enterraste
enterrará	había enterrado	enterró
enterraremos	habíamos enterrado	enterramos
enterraréis	habíais enterrado	enterrasteis
enterrarán	habían enterrado	enterraron
Future Perfect	**Past Perfect**	
habré enterrado	hube enterrado	

CONDITIONAL	SUBJUNCTIVE	
Present	**Present**	**Imperfect**
enterraría	entierre	enterr-ara/ase
enterrarías	entierres	enterr-aras/ases
enterraría	entierre	enterr-ara/ase
enterraríamos	enterremos	enterr-áramos/ásemos
enterraríais	enterréis	enterr-arais/aseis
enterrarían	entierren	enterr-aran/asen
Perfect	**Perfect**	**Pluperfect**
habría enterrado	haya enterrado	hub-iera/iese enterrado

GERUND	PAST PARTICIPLE	IMPERATIVE
enterrando	enterrado	entierra, enterrad entierre (Vd), entierren (Vds)

Queremos que la entierren en su pueblo. *We want her to be buried in her village.*
La enterron el sábado. *She was buried on Saturday.*
Le van a enterrar dentro de tres días. *He is going to be buried in three days.*
¿Han enterrado ya a las víctimas? *Have the victims been buried already?*

enterrar en el olvido *to forget*
Lo enterraré para siempre. *I shall never mention it or think about it again.*
El abuelo nos enterrará a todos. *Grandfather will survive us all.*
Se enterró en vida. *He retired to a quiet place.*

enterradero *burial ground*
enterrado/a *buried*
enterrada *ingrowing nail*
enterrador *grave digger*
enterramiento *burial, interment*
entierro *burial, funeral*
tesoro enterrado *treasure trove*
enterrado por la lava *buried in lava*

enviar *to send* tr. 94

INDICATIVE

Present	Imperfect	Perfect
envío	enviaba	he enviado
envías	enviabas	has enviado
envía	enviaba	ha enviado
enviamos	enviábamos	hemos enviado
enviáis	enviabais	habéis enviado
envían	enviaban	han enviado
Future	**Pluperfect**	**Past Definite**
enviaré	había enviado	envié
enviarás	habías enviado	enviaste
enviará	había enviado	envió
enviaremos	habíamos enviado	enviamos
enviaréis	habíais enviado	enviasteis
enviarán	habían enviado	enviaron
Future Perfect	**Past Perfect**	
habré enviado	hube enviado	

CONDITIONAL	SUBJUNCTIVE	
Present	**Present**	**Imperfect**
enviaría	envíe	envi-ara/ase
enviarías	envíes	envi-aras/ases
enviaría	envíe	envi-ara/ase
anviaríamos	enviemos	envi-áramos/ásemos
enviaríais	enviéis	envi-arais/aseis
enviarían	envíen	envi-aran/asen
Perfect	**Perfect**	**Pluperfect**
habría enviado	haya enviado	hub-iera/iese enviado

GERUND	PAST PARTICIPLE	IMPERATIVE
enviando	enviado	envía, enviad envíe (Vd), envíen (Vds)

Te enviaré un recado. *I'll send you a message.*
Hemos enviado un regalo a mi madre. *We have sent my mother a present.*
Me lo envía Juan. *Juan is sending it for me.*
Angy me envío a recoger su paquete. *Angy sent me to collect her parcel.*

Terry es un enviado especial. *Terry is a special envoy.*
Lo envió contra reembolso. *He sent it cash on delivery.*
Voy a enviar un parte. *I'm going to file a dispatch.*
Enviaron a Carlos de paseo. *They sent Carlos packing.*

envío *dispatch*
gastos de envío *transport charges, postage and packing*
envión *push*
enviado/a *envoy*
enviada *sending, shipment, consignment*
enviadizo/a *sent, ready to be sent*

95 envolver *to wrap up* tr.

INDICATIVE

Present	Imperfect	Perfect
envuelvo	envolvía	he envuelto
envuelves	envolvías	has envuelto
envuelve	envolvía	ha envuelto
envolvemos	envolvíamos	hemos envuelto
envolvéis	evolvíais	habéis envuelto
envuelven	envolvían	han envuelto
Future	**Pluperfect**	**Past Definite**
envolveré	había envuelto	envolví
envolverás	habías envuelto	envolviste
envolverá	había envuelto	envolvió
envolveremos	habíamos envuelto	envolvimos
envolveréis	habíais envuelto	envolvisteis
envolverán	habían envuelto	envolvieron
Future Perfect	**Past Perfect**	
habré envuelto	hube envuelto	

CONDITIONAL	SUBJUNCTIVE	
Present	**Present**	**Imperfect**
envolvería	envuelva	envolv-iera/iese
envolverías	envuelvas	envolv-ieras/ieses
envolvería	envuelva	envolv-iera/iese
envolveríamos	envolvamos	envolv-iéramos/iésemos
envolveríais	envolváis	envolv-ierais/ieseis
envolverían	envuelvan	envolv-ieran/iesen
Perfect	**Perfect**	**Pluperfect**
habría envuelto	haya envuelto	hub-iera/iese envuelto

GERUND	PAST PARTICIPLE	IMPERATIVE
envolviendo	envuelto	envuelve, envolved envuelva (Vd), envuelvan (Vds)

¿Te lo envuelvo? *Shall I wrap it up for you?*
Lo envolvió en un periódico. *She wrapped it up in a newspaper.*
La niebla envuelve la ciudad. *The fog covers the town.*
Envolvieron a Miguel. *Miguel was involved in it.*

Lo voy a envolver con cinta. *I am going to tape it up.*
Estaba envuelta en una capa. *She was wrapped in a cloak.*
El misterio envuelve la situación. *Mystery surrounds the situation.*
Peter me envuelve en cariño. *Peter surrounds me with love.*

envoltura *cover, wrapper, wrapping, case*
envoltura externa *outer wrapping*
envoltura comestible *edible casing*
envolvedero *cover, wrapper, wrapping*
envolvente *surrounding*
envolvimiento *wrapping, involvement*
envoltorio *package, wrapping*
envoltijo *bundle*

erguir *to stand up straight, raise* tr. 96

INDICATIVE

Present	Imperfect	Perfect
irgo/yergo	erguía	he erguido
irgues/yergues	erguías	has erguido
irgue/yergue	erguía	ha erguido
erguimos	erguíamos	hemos erguido
erguís	erguíais	habéis erguido
yerguen	erguían	han erguido
Future	**Pluperfect**	**Past Definite**
erguiré	había erguido	erguí
erguirás	habías erguido	erguiste
erguirá	había erguido	irguió
erguiremos	habíamos erguido	erguimos
erguiréis	habíais erguido	erguisteis
erguirán	habían erguido	irguieron
Future Perfect	**Past Perfect**	
habré erguido	hube erguido	

CONDITIONAL	SUBJUNCTIVE	
Present	**Present**	**Imperfect**
erguiría	yerga/irga	irgu-iera/iese
erguirías	yergas/irgas	irgu-ieras/ieses
erguiría	yerga/irga	irgu-iera/iese
erguiríamos	irgamos	irgu-iéramos/iésemos
erguiríais	irgáis	irgu-ierais/ieseis
erguirían	irgan	irgu-ieran/iesen
Perfect	**Perfect**	**Pluperfect**
habría erguido	haya erguido	hub-iera/iese erguido

GERUND	PAST PARTICIPLE	IMPERATIVE
irguiendo	erguido	yergue/irgue, erguid yerga/irga (Vd), yergan/irgan (Vds)

Le gusta erguirse para parecer más alto. *He likes to stand up straight to appear taller.*
¡Irgue/yergue la cabeza! *Raise your head.*
El caballo irguió las orejas. *The horse pricked up his ears.*
Se irguieron de repente. *They stood up suddenly.*

Martín siempre está dispuesto a erguir las orejas. *Martin is always ready to prick up his ears.*
¡Vamos a erguir la cabeza! *Let's hold our heads high!*
Doña Lupe lleva la cabeza bien erguida. *Doña Lupe is proud.*

erguido/a *erect, straight, proud*
erección *erection, raising*
erecto/a *standing, straight*
erector del lanzador *launcher, erector*
erguimiento *erection, straightening up*
estar muy erguido *to puff up with pride*

97 errar *to err, miss* tr./intr.

INDICATIVE

Present	Imperfect	Perfect
yerro	erraba	he errado
yerras	errabas	has errado
yerra	erraba	ha errado
erramos	errábamos	hemos errado
erráis	errabais	habéis errado
yerran	erraban	han errado
Future	**Pluperfect**	**Past Definite**
erraré	había errado	erré
errarás	habías errado	erraste
errará	había errado	erró
erraremos	habíamos errado	erramos
erraréis	habíais errado	errasteis
errarán	habían errado	erraron
Future Perfect	**Past Perfect**	
habré errado	hube errado	

CONDITIONAL	SUBJUNCTIVE	
Present	**Present**	**Imperfect**
erraría	yerre	err-ara/ase
errarías	yerres	err-aras/ases
erraría	yerre	err-ara/ase
erraríamos	erremos	err-áramos/ásemos
erraríais	erréis	err-arais/aseis
errarían	yerren	err-aran/asen
Perfect	**Perfect**	**Pluperfect**
habría errado	haya errado	hub-iera/iese errado

GERUND	PAST PARTICIPLE	IMPERATIVE
errando	errado	yerra, errad yerre (Vd), yerren (Vds)

Perdóname si he errado. *Please forgive me if I was at fault.*
Erramos por el parque. *We wandered in the park.*
He errado en mi elección. *I have made a mistake in my choice.*
Errar es humano. *To err is human.*

Caperucita Roja erró el camino. *Little Red Riding Hood lost her way.*
Enrique erró el golpe. *Enrique missed the target.*
El que mucho habla mucho yerra. *The more you talk, the more mistakes you make.*

error *error*
errante *wandering, travelling, erratic*
estrella errante *wandering star*
error de escritura *graphic error*
error de entrega *misdelivery*
error de imprenta *misprint*
errático/a *erratic*
erróneo *faulty, wrong*

escribir *to write, enrol, enlist* tr. 98

INDICATIVE

Present	Imperfect	Perfect
escribo	escribía	he escrito
escribes	escribías	has escrito
escribe	escribía	ha escrito
escribimos	escribíamos	hemos escrito
escribís	escribíais	habéis escrito
escriben	escribían	han escrito
Future	**Pluperfect**	**Past Definite**
escribiré	había escrito	escribí
escribirás	habías escrito	escribiste
escribirá	había escrito	escribió
escribiremos	habíamos escrito	escribimos
escribiréis	habíais escrito	escribisteis
escribirán	habían escrito	escribieron
Future Perfect	**Past Perfect**	
habré escrito	hube escrito	

CONDITIONAL	SUBJUNCTIVE	
Present	**Present**	**Imperfect**
escribiría	escriba	escrib-iera/iese
escribirías	escribas	escrib-ieras/ieses
escribiría	escriba	escrib-iera/iese
escribiríamos	escribamos	escrib-iéramos/iésemos
escribiríais	escribáis	escrib-ierais/ieseis
escribirían	escriban	escrib-ieran/iesen
Perfect	**Perfect**	**Pluperfect**
habría escrito	haya escrito	hub-iera/iese escrito

GERUND	PAST PARTICIPLE	IMPERATIVE
escribiendo	escrito	escribe, escribid escriba (Vd), escriban (Vds)

Leonor escribe artículos para El País. *Leonor writes for El País.*
Paqui lo escribirá todo a máquina. *Paqui will type everything.*
Elvira escribe muy bien. *Elvira writes beautifully.*
Grego escribía muchas cartas. *Grego used to write a lot of letters.*

'Burro' se escribe con b. *'Burro' is spelt with a b.*
¿Cómo se escribe? *How do you spell it?*
Voy a ponerlo por escrito. *I'm going to put it in writing.*
Fredes no sabía escribir. *Fredes didn't know how to write.*

escribir a máquina *to type*
escribir a mano *to write longhand*
escriba *scribe*
escribanía *writing desk, clerkship*
escribano *clerk*
escribiente *copylst*
escritor(a) *writer*
escritura *writing*
escritorio *desk*

99 estar *to be* (location) intr. (aux.)

INDICATIVE

Present	Imperfect	Perfect
estoy	estaba	he estado
estás	estabas	has estado
está	estaba	ha estado
estamos	estábamos	hemos estado
estáis	estabais	habéis estado
están	estaban	han estado
Future	**Pluperfect**	**Past Definite**
estaré	había estado	estuve
estrarás	habías estado	estuviste
estará	había estado	estuvo
estaremos	habíamos estado	estuvimos
estaréis	habíais estado	estuvisteis
estarán	habían estado	estuvieron
Future Perfect	**Past Perfect**	
habré estado	hube estado	

CONDITIONAL	SUBJUNCTIVE	
Present	**Present**	**Imperfect**
estaría	esté	estuv-iera/iese
estarías	estés	estuv-ieras/ieses
estaría	esté	estuv-iera/iese
estaríamos	estemos	estuv-iéramos/iésemos
estaríais	estéis	estuv-ierais/ieseis
estarían	estén	estuv-ieran/iesen
Perfect	**Perfect**	**Pluperfect**
habría estado	haya estado	hub-iera/iese estado

GERUND	PAST PARTICIPLE	IMPERATIVE
estando	estado	está, estad esté (Vd), estén (Vds)

Estamos en Burgos. *We are in Burgos.*
Estaré en el Escorial mañana. *I shall be in el Escorial tomorrow.*
El Prado está en Madrid. *The Prado is in Madrid.*
Estuve en Berlín en 1982. *I was in Berlin in 1982.*

Estoy enamorada de Peter. *I'm in love with Peter.*
¿Cómo estás? *How are you?*
Está más viejo. *He looks older.*
Enseguida estará. *It will be ready soon.*
¡Ya estamos! *There we go again!*

¡Estáte quieto! *Keep still!*
¿Estamos? *Agreed?*
estancia *dwelling*
Estoy de vacaciones *I am on holiday*
Estoy contenta. *I'm happy.*
Está enfermo. *He's ill.*
Está cansada. *She is tired.*
Está dormida. *She is alseep.*

evacuar *to evacuate* tr.

INDICATIVE

Present	Imperfect	Perfect
evacuo	evacuaba	he evacuado
evacuas	evacuabas	has evacuado
evacua	evacuaba	ha evacuado
evacuamos	evacuábamos	hemos evacuado
evacuáis	evacuabais	habéis evacuado
evacuan	evacuaban	han evacuado
Future	**Pluperfect**	**Past Definite**
evacuaré	había evacuado	evacué
evacuarás	habías evacuado	evacuaste
evacuará	había evacuado	evacuó
evecuaremos	habíamos evacuado	evacuamos
evacuaréis	habíais evacuado	evacuasteis
evacuarán	habían evacuado	evacuaron
Future Perfect	**Past Perfect**	
habré evacuado	hube evacuado	

CONDITIONAL	SUBJUNCTIVE	
Present	**Present**	**Imperfect**
evacuaría	evacue	evacu-ara/ase
evacuarías	evacues	evacu-aras/ases
evacuaría	evacue	evacu-ara/ase
evacuaríamos	evacuemos	evacu-áramos/ásemos
evacuaríais	evacuéis	evacu-arais/aseis
evacuarían	evacuen	evacu-aran/asen
Perfect	**Perfect**	**Pluperfect**
habría evacuado	haya evacuado	hub-iera/iese evacuado

GERUND	PAST PARTICIPLE	IMPERATIVE
evacuando	evacuado	evacua, evacuad evacue (Vd), evacuen (Vds)

Hay que evacuar el edificio. *We must evacuate the building.*
Se ha evacuado la ciudad por culpa de la guerra. *The town has been evacuated because of the war.*
Evacuaré el recipiente mañana. *I shall empty the container tomorrow.*

Está evacuando cenizas. *He is raking out ashes.*
Peter va a evacuar la máquina. *Peter is going to drain the engine.*
Están evacuando a los heridos. *They are taking the wounded out.*

evacuación *evacuation*
evacuado/a *evacuee*
evacuatorio *public lavatory*
evacuante *diureteic, evacuant*
evacuador *evacuator; wasteway, escape, spillway*
evacuativo/a *evacuative, purge, purgative*

101 fregar *to wash up, scrub* tr.

INDICATIVE

Present	Imperfect	Perfect
friego	fregaba	he fregado
friegas	fregabas	has fregado
friega	fregaba	ha fregado
fregamos	fregábamos	hemos fregado
fregáis	fregabais	habéis fregado
friegan	fregaban	han fregado
Future	**Pluperfect**	**Past Definite**
fregaré	había fregado	fregué
fregarás	habías fregado	fregaste
fregará	había fregado	fregó
fregaremos	habíamos fregado	fregamos
fregaréis	habíais fregado	fregasteis
fregarán	habían fregado	fregaron
Future Perfect	**Past Perfect**	
habré fregado	hube fregado	

CONDITIONAL	SUBJUNCTIVE	
Present	**Present**	**Imperfect**
fregaría	friegue	freg-ara/ase
fregarías	friegues	freg-aras/ases
fregaría	friegue	freg-ara/ase
fregaríamos	freguemos	freg-áramos/ásemos
fregaríais	freguéis	freg-arais/aseis
fregarían	frieguen	freg-aran/asen
Perfect	**Perfect**	**Pluperfect**
habría fregado	haya fregado	hub-iera/iese fregado

GERUND	PAST PARTICIPLE	IMPERATIVE
fregando	fregado	friega, fregad friegue (Vd), frieguen (Vds)

¿Has fregado los platos? *Have you done the washing-up?*
Me toca fregar mañana. *Tomorrow is my turn to do the washing-up.*
Tienes que fregar el suelo. *You are to mop the floor.*
Están fregando las paredes. *They are scrubbing the walls.*

¡No me friegues! *Stop bothering me!*
Está fregando a los niños. *He is pestering the children.*
Había fregación en la sala. *There was some friction in the room.*

fregada *nuisance, misfortune*
fregadero/a *sink, scullery; nuisance, annoyance*
fregador(a) *sink, mop, rubber*
fregasuelos *mop, cleaner*
fregona *mop, cleaner*
fregón *cleaner; silly, stupid, tiresome*
friegaplatos *dishwasher*
fregado *scrubbing*
fregadura *scouring*

freír *to fry* tr. 102

INDICATIVE

Present	Imperfect	Perfect
frío	freía	he frito
fríes	freías	has frito
fríe	freía	ha frito
freímos	freíamos	hemos frito
freís	freíais	habéis frito
fríen	freían	han frito
Future	**Pluperfect**	**Past Definite**
freiré	había frito	freí
freirás	habías frito	freíste
freirá	había frito	frío
freiremos	habíamos frito	freímos
freiréis	habíais frito	freísteis
freirán	habían frito	frieron
Future Perfect	**Past Perfect**	
habré frito	hube frito	

CONDITIONAL	SUBJUNCTIVE	
Present	**Present**	**Imperfect**
freiría	fría	fr-iera/iese
freirías	frías	fr-ieras/ieses
freiría	fría	fr-iera/iese
freiríamos	friamos	fr-iéramos/iésemos
freiríais	friáis	fr-ierais/ieseis
freirían	frían	fr-ieran/iesen
Perfect	**Perfect**	**Pluperfect**
habría frito	haya frito	hub-iera/iese frito

GERUND	PAST PARTICIPLE	IMPERATIVE
friendo	freído/frito	fríe, freíd fría (Vd), frían (Vds)

Voy a freír las patatas. *I am going to fry the potatoes.*
¿Has frito la carne? *Have you fried the meat?*
No lo has frito bastante. *You have not fried it enough.*
Freiremos el pescado. *We'll fry the fish.*
Quiero que frías el pan. *I would like you to fry the bread.*

Al freír será el reír. *The proof of the pudding is in the eating.*
¡Vete a freír espárragos! *Go to hell!*
Me frío de calor. *I am extremely hot.*
Se la he frito a Carlos. *I have deceived Carlos.*
¡Me tienes frito! *I am fed up with you.*

freidera *frying pan, fryer*
fritada *frying dish*
freiduría de pescado *fried fish shop*
frito/a *fried*
fritillas *fritters*
freidor(a) *one who fries*

103 gobernar *to govern, rule* tr./intr.

INDICATIVE

Present	Imperfect	Perfect
gobierno	gobernaba	he gobernado
gobiernas	gobernabas	has gobernado
gobierna	gobernaba	ha gobernado
gobernamos	gobernábamos	hemos gobernado
gobernáis	gobernabais	habéis gobernado
gobiernan	gobernaban	han gobernado
Future	**Pluperfect**	**Past Definite**
gobernaré	había gobernado	goberné
gobernarás	habías gobernado	gobernaste
gobernará	había gobernado	gobernó
gobernaremos	habíamos gobernado	gobernamos
gobernaréis	habíais gobernado	gobernasteis
gobernarán	habían gobernado	gobernaron
Future Perfect	**Past Perfect**	
habré gobernado	hube gobernado	

CONDITIONAL	SUBJUNCTIVE	
Present	**Present**	**Imperfect**
gobernaría	gobierne	gobern-ara/ase
gobernarías	gobiernes	gobern-aras/ases
gobernaría	gobierne	gobern-ara/ase
gobernaríamos	gobernemos	gobern-áramos/ásemos
gobernaríais	gobernéis	gobern-arais/aseis
gobernarían	gobiernen	gobern-aran/asen
Perfect	**Perfect**	**Pluperfect**
habría gobernado	haya gobernado	hub-iera/iese gobernado

GERUND	PAST PARTICIPLE	IMPERATIVE
gobernando	gobernado	gobierna, gobernad gobierne (Vd), gobiernen (Vds)

La madre gobierna esta familia. *It is the mother who rules this family.*
Franco gobernó desde 1939. *Franco ruled from 1939.*
El rey no gobierna. *The king does not govern.*
Le gobierna su mujer *His wife rules him.*

No sabe gobernar. *She doesn't know how to behave.*
gobernar mal *to misgovern*
gobierno doméstico *housekeeping*
Ministerio de la Gobernación *Home Office*
Ministro de la Gobernación *Home Secretary*

gobernanta *governess*
gobernante *ruler, governor*
gobierno *government*
gobierno de coalición *coalition cabinet*
gobierno de empresas *management*
gobernador *ruler*
gobernación *governing*
gobernable *governable*

haber *to have* tr. (aux.) **104**

INDICATIVE

Present	**Imperfect**	**Perfect**
he	había	he habido
has	habías	has habido
ha	había	ha habido
hemos	habíamos	hemos habido
habéis	habíais	habéis habido
han	habían	han habido
Future	**Pluperfect**	**Past Definite**
habré	había habido	hube
habrás	habías habido	hubiste
habrá	había habido	hubo
habremos	habíamos habido	hubimos
habréis	habíais habido	hubisteis
habrán	habían habido	hubieron
Future Perfect	**Past Perfect**	
habré habido	hube habido	

CONDITIONAL	SUBJUNCTIVE	
Present	**Present**	**Imperfect**
habría	haya	hub-iera/iese
habrías	hayas	hub-ieras/ieses
habría	haya	hub-iera/iese
habríamos	hayamos	hub-iéramos/iésemos
habríais	hayáis	hub-ierais/ieseis
habrían	hayan	hub-ieran/iesen
Perfect	**Perfect**	**Pluperfect**
habría habido	haya habido	hub-iera/iese habido

GERUND	PAST PARTICIPLE	IMPERATIVE
habiendo	habido	hé, habed haya (Vd), hayan (Vds)

Hay dos libros en la mesa. *There are two books on the table.*
Hay un libro en la silla. *There is a book on the chair.*
Francisca lee cuantos libros puede haber. *Francisca reads all the books she can lay her hands on.*
Se comería todos los pasteles habidos y por haber. *She would eat all the cakes that she could lay her hands on.*
en el partido habido ayer *yesterday's match*
La baja de temperatura habida ayer. *The fall in temperature recorded yesterday.*

Hay café. *There is some coffee.*
Hay libros. *There are some books.*
Tomaré lo que haya. *I'll have whatever is going.*
Hay que hacerlo. *It has to be done.*
tres años ha *three years ago.*

105 hablar *to speak, talk* tr./intr.

INDICATIVE

Present	Imperfect	Perfect
hablo	hablaba	he hablado
hablas	hablabas	has hablado
habla	hablaba	ha hablado
hablamos	hablábamos	hemos hablado
habláis	hablabais	habéis hablado
hablan	hablaban	han hablado
Future	**Pluperfect**	**Past Definite**
hablaré	había hablado	hablé
hablarás	habías hablado	hablaste
hablará	había hablado	habló
hablaremos	habíamos hablado	hablamos
hablaréis	habíais hablado	hablasteis
hablarán	habían hablado	hablaron
Future Perfect	**Past Perfect**	
habré hablado	hube hablado	

CONDITIONAL	SUBJUNCTIVE	
Present	**Present**	**Imperfect**
hablaría	hable	habl-ara/ase
hablarías	hables	habl-aras/ases
hablaría	hable	habl-ara/ase
hablaríamos	hablemos	habl-áramos/ásemos
hablaríais	habléis	habl-arais/aseis
hablarían	hablen	habl-aran/asen
Perfect	**Perfect**	**Pluperfect**
habría hablado	haya hablado	hub-iera/iese hablado

GERUND	PAST PARTICIPLE	IMPERATIVE
hablando	hablado	habla, hablad hable (Vd), hablen (Vds)

¿Hablan español? *Do you speak Spanish?*
¡Lo hablas todo! *You always tell everything!*
¿Hablaste con Juan? *Did you talk to Juan?*
Hablaremos con franquenza. *We will talk frankly.*

Eso es hablar por hablar. *That's just wasted breath.*
Susanita habla por los codos. *Susanita talks nineteen to the dozen.*
Hablan a tontas y a locas. *They talk without reason.*
No se te ocurra hablar por hablar. *Don't talk for the sake of talking.*

habla *speech*
hablador(a) *talkative, chatterbox, gossipy*
habladas *boasting, bragging*
habladurías *gossip, nasty talk*
hablante *talking, speaker*
hablista *good speaker*
hablilla *rumour, story*
hablantín = hablanchín *talkative*

hacer *to do, make* tr./intr.

INDICATIVE

Present	Imperfect	Perfect
hago	hacía	he hecho
haces	hacías	has hecho
hace	hacía	ha hecho
hacemos	hacíamos	hemos hecho
hacéis	hacíais	habéis hecho
hacen	hacían	han hecho
Future	**Pluperfect**	**Past Definite**
haré	había hecho	hice
harás	habías hecho	hiciste
hará	había hecho	hizo
haremos	habíamos hecho	hicimos
haréis	habíais hecho	hicisteis
harán	habían hecho	hicieron
Future Perfect	**Past Perfect**	
habré hecho	hube hecho	

CONDITIONAL	SUBJUNCTIVE	
Present	**Present**	**Imperfect**
haría	haga	hic-iera/iese
harías	hagas	hic-ieras/ieses
haría	haga	hic-iera/iese
haríamos	hagamos	hic-iéramos/iésemos
haríais	hagáis	hic-ierais/ieseis
harían	hagan	hic-ieran/iesen
Perfect	**Perfect**	**Pluperfect**
habría hecho	haya hecho	hub-iera/iese hecho

GERUND	PAST PARTICIPLE	IMPERATIVE
haciendo	hecho	haz, haced haga (Vd), hagan (Vds)

Estoy haciendo café. *I'm making some coffee.*
¿Has hecho la cama? *Have you made the bed?*
No sabe qué hacer. *She doesn't know what to do.*
¿Qué haces ahí? *What are you doing there?*

El árbol hace sombra. *The tree casts a shadow.*
Hacen lo que quieren. *They do as they please.*
¡La has hecho buena! *A fine mess you've made!*
Elena hizo el borrador. *Elena draughted it.*

hacendoso/a *industrious, hard working*
hecho *fact*
hecho/a *agreed, finished, done made*
hacedero/a *practicable, feasible*
hacedero/a *that can/will be done*
hechura *making, creation*
malhechor(a) *criminal*
hacedor(a) *maker*

107 helar *to freeze, chill* tr./intr.

INDICATIVE

Present	Imperfect	Perfect
hielo	helaba	he helado
hielas	helabas	has helado
hiela	helaba	ha helado
helamos	helábamos	hemos helado
heláis	helabais	habéis helado
hielan	helaban	han helado

Future	Pluperfect	Past Definite
helaré	había helado	helé
helarás	habías helado	helaste
helará	había helado	heló
helaremos	habíamos helado	helamos
helaréis	habíais helado	helasteis
helarán	habían helado	helaron

Future Perfect	Past Perfect
habré helado	hube helado

CONDITIONAL / SUBJUNCTIVE

CONDITIONAL Present	SUBJUNCTIVE Present	Imperfect
helaría	hiele	hel-ara/ase
helarías	hieles	hel-aras/ases
helaría	hiele	hel-ara/ase
helaríamos	helemos	hel-áramos/ásemos
helaríais	heléis	hel-arais/aseis
helarían	hielen	hel-aran/asen

Perfect	Perfect	Pluperfect
habría helado	haya helado	hub-iera/iese helado

GERUND	PAST PARTICIPLE	IMPERATIVE
helando	helado	hiela, helad hiele (Vd), hielen (Vds)

Va a helar. *It's going to freeze.*
¿Helará mañana? *Is there going to be a frost tomorrow?*
Voy a helar la fruta. *I'm going to freeze the fruit.*
¿Se helarán las plantas? *Will the plants freeze?*

Estoy helada. *I'm frozen.*
Se ha helado el agua. *The water has frozen.*
Me fui porque me estaba helando. *I left because I was frozen.*
Ha caído una helada. *There is a frost.*

helada *frost*
helada tardía *late frost*
helada temprana *early frost*
helado *ice-cream*
hielo *ice*
heladura *chilling*
heladería *ice-cream shop*
helero *glacier*

herir *to wound, hurt, harm* tr. 108

INDICATIVE

Present	Imperfect	Perfect
hiero	hería	he herido
hieres	herías	has herido
hiere	hería	ha herido
herimos	heríamos	hemos herido
herís	heríais	habéis herido
hieren	herían	han herido

Future	Pluperfect	Past Definite
heriré	había herido	herí
herirás	habías herido	heriste
herirá	había herido	hirió
heriremos	habíamos herido	herimos
heriréis	habíais herido	heristeis
herirán	habían herido	hirieron

Future Perfect	Past Perfect
habré herido	hube herido

CONDITIONAL / SUBJUNCTIVE

Present (Conditional)	Present (Subjunctive)	Imperfect (Subjunctive)
heriría	hiera	hir-iera/iese
herirías	hieras	hir-ieras/ieses
heriría	hiera	hir-iera/iese
heriríamos	hiramos	hir-iéramos/iésemos
heriríais	hiráis	hir-ierais/ieseis
herirían	hieran	hir-ieran/iesen

Perfect (Conditional)	Perfect (Subjunctive)	Pluperfect (Subjunctive)
habría herido	haya herido	hub-iera/iese herido

GERUND	PAST PARTICIPLE	IMPERATIVE
hiriendo	herido	hiere, herid hiera (Vd), hieran (Vds)

Ha sido herido en el brazo. *He has been wounded in the arm.*
Se ha herido la pierna. *She has hurt her leg.*
El cristal le hirió en la cabeza. *The glass injured him in the head.*
El accidente hirió su confianza. *The accident dented his confidence.*

Esos ruidos me hieren los oídos. *Those noises hurt my ears.*
Ese color me hiere la vista. *That colour hurts my eyes.*
Hizo un comentario hiriente. *She made a cutting remark.*
Se tuvo que lamer las heridas. *She had to lick her wounds.*

herida *wound*
herida de mal aspecto *angry wound*
herida de bala *gunshot injury*
herido/a *wounded*
hiriente *wounding, cutting*
comentario hiriente *cutting remark*

109 hervir *to boil* intr.

INDICATIVE

Present	Imperfect	Perfect
hiervo	hervía	he hervido
hierves	hervías	has hervido
hierve	hervía	ha hervido
hervimos	hervíamos	hemos hervido
hervís	hervíais	habéis hervido
hierven	hervían	han hervido
Future	**Pluperfect**	**Past Definite**
herviré	había hervido	herví
hervirás	habías hervido	herviste
hervirá	había hervido	hirvió
herviremos	habíamos hervido	hervimos
herviréis	habíais hervido	hervisteis
hervirán	habían hervido	hirvieron
Future Perfect	**Past Perfect**	
habré hervido	hube hervido	

CONDITIONAL	SUBJUNCTIVE	
Present	**Present**	**Imperfect**
herviría	hierva	hirv-iera/iese
hervirías	hiervas	hirv-ieras/ieses
herviría	hierva	hirv-iera/iese
herviríamos	hirvamos	hirv-iéramos/iésemos
herviríais	hirváis	hirv-ierais/ieseis
hervirían	hiervan	hirv-ieran/iesen
Perfect	**Perfect**	**Pluperfect**
habría hervido	haya hervido	hub-iera/iese hervido

GERUND	PAST PARTICIPLE	IMPERATIVE
hirviendo	hervido	hierve, hervid hierva (Vd), hiervan (Vds)

Hierve el agua. *Boil the water.*
Herviré las verduras antes de cenar. *I'll boil the vegetables before supper.*
Lo herviremos a fuego lento. *We'll simmer it.*
La tienda hervía de gente. *The shop was very crowded.*

Me hierve la sangre. *I get very worked up.*
Empieza a hervir. *It's coming to the boil.*
La alfombra hervía de pulgas. *The carpet was swarming with fleas.*
dar un hervor *to boil for a short time*
Hervir y dejar reposar. *Boil and allow to settle.*
alzar/levantar el hervor *to come to the boil*

hervor *boiling*
hervir a borbotones *to boil fast*
hervidor *kettle, boiler*
hervidero *boiling, bubbling*
hervido/a *boiled, stew*
hervederas *heartburn, indigestion*

huir *to run away, escape* tr./intr. 110

INDICATIVE

Present	Imperfect	Perfect
huyo	huía	he huido
huyes	huías	has huido
huye	huía	ha huido
huimos	huíamos	hemos huido
huís	huíais	habéis huido
huyen	huían	han huido
Future	**Pluperfect**	**Past Definite**
huiré	había huido	huí
huirás	habías huido	huiste
huirá	había huido	huyó
huiremos	habíamos huido	huimos
huiréis	habíais huido	huisteis
huirán	habían huido	huyeron
Future Perfect	**Past Perfect**	
habré huido	hube huido	

CONDITIONAL	SUBJUNCTIVE	
Present	**Present**	**Imperfect**
huiría	huya	hu-yera/yese
huirías	huyas	hu-yeras/yeses
huiría	huya	hu-yera/yese
huiríamos	huyamos	hu-yéramos/yésemos
huiríais	huyáis	hu-yerais/yeseis
huirían	huyan	hu-yeran/yesen
Perfect	**Perfect**	**Pluperfect**
habría huido	haya huido	hub-iera/iese huido

GERUND	PAST PARTICIPLE	IMPERATIVE
huyendo	huido	huye, huid huya (Vd), huyan (Vds)

Siempre huye del peligro. *He always runs away from danger.*
Huyen de la guerra. *They are running away from the war.*
El prisionero huyó de la cárcel. *The prisoner escaped from jail.*
El pájaro huirá del nido. *The bird will flee the nest.*

la huída de capitales *flight of capital*
huir a la desbandada *to escape in a mad rush*
Rehuiré de la tentación. *I shall flee from temptation.*
¡A huir que azotan! *Let's get out of here!*

¡Huye! *Run!*
huida *flight, escape*
huidizo *shy, elusive, receding*
rehuir *avoid*
huido/a *fugitive*
huidero *fleeting, short lived, transitory*
huidor *fleeing*

111 impedir *to impede, hinder, prevent* tr.

INDICATIVE

Present
impido
impides
impide
impedimos
impedís
impiden

Imperfect
impedía
impedías
impedía
impedíamos
impedíais
impedían

Perfect
he impedido
has impedido
ha impedido
hemos impedido
habéis impedido
han impedido

Future
impediré
impedirás
impedirá
impediremos
impediréis
impedirán

Pluperfect
había impedido
habías impedido
había impedido
habíamos impedido
habíais impedido
habían impedido

Past Definite
impedí
impediste
impidió
impedimos
impedisteis
impidieron

Future Perfect
habré impedido

Past Perfect
hube impedido

CONDITIONAL

Present
impediría
impedirías
impediría
impediríamos
impediríais
impedirían

Perfect
habría impedido

SUBJUNCTIVE

Present
impida
impidas
impida
impidamos
impidáis
impidan

Imperfect
impid-iera/iese
impid-ieras/ieses
impid-iera/iese
impid-iéramos/iésemos
impid-ierais/ieseis
impid-ieran/iesen

Perfect
haya impedido

Pluperfect
hub-iera/iese impedido

GERUND

impidiendo

PAST PARTICIPLE

impedido

IMPERATIVE

impide, impedid
impida (Vd), impidan (Vds)

Sus obligaciones le impiden venir. *His obligations prevent him from coming.*
Quiso impedirme hablar. *He tried to stop me from talking.*
Tratamos de impedir el accidente. *We tried to prevent the accident.*
Me veo impedida para ir. *I'm prevented from going.*
Me impidió hacerlo. *He stopped me from doing it.*

Hay que impedir el tráfico. *We have to block the traffic.*
No lo pude impedir. *I could not prevent it.*

impedido/a *crippled, disabled*
impeditivo *preventitive*
impedimento *impediment, obstacle*
impedimentos *handicaps, impairments, impediments*
impedimento común *common bar, general ban*
impedimenta *impedimenta*

invertir *to invert, turn upside down* tr. 112

INDICATIVE

Present	Imperfect	Perfect
invierto	invertía	he invertido
inviertes	invertías	has invertido
invierte	invertía	ha invertido
invertimos	invertíamos	hemos invertido
invertís	invertíais	habéis invertido
invierten	invertían	han invertido
Future	**Pluperfect**	**Past Definite**
invertiré	había invertido	invertí
invertirás	habías invertido	invertiste
invertirá	había invertido	invirtió
invertiremos	habíamos invertido	invertimos
invertiréis	habíais invertido	invertisteis
invertirán	habían invertido	invirtieron
Future Perfect	**Past Perfect**	
habré invertido	hube invertido	

CONDITIONAL	SUBJUNCTIVE	
Present	**Present**	**Imperfect**
invertiría	invierta	invirt-iera/iese
invertirías	inviertas	invirt-ieras/ieses
invertiría	invierta	invirt-iera/iese
invertiríamos	invirtamos	invirt-iéramos/iésemos
invertiríais	invirtáis	invirt-ierais/ieseis
invertirían	inviertan	invirt-ieran/iesen
Perfect	**Perfect**	**Pluperfect**
habría invertido	haya invertido	hub-iera/iese invertido

GERUND	PAST PARTICIPLE	IMPERATIVE
invirtiendo	invertido	invierte, invertid invierta (Vd), inviertan (Vds)

He invertido los papeles. *I've turned the papers upside down.*
Invirtieron dos días en el viaje. *They spent two days on the journey.*
Invierte el vaso. *Turn the glass upside down.*
He invertido mi capital en acciones. *I have invested my capital in shares.*

Invertiremos la marcha. *We'll reverse.*
Pienso invertir las ganancias en el negocio. *I'll plough back the profits into the business.*
No sé en que invierte sus horas libres. *I don't know what he does with his spare time.*
en sentido inverso a las agujas del reloj *anti-clockwise.*

inverso *inverse, inverted*
invertido/a *reversed, upside down*
a la inversa *the other way round*
inversión *reversal, investment*
inversión de capitales *capital investment*
inversionista *investor*

113 investir *to invest, confer* tr.

INDICATIVE

Present	Imperfect	Perfect
invisto	investía	he investido
invistes	investías	has investido
inviste	investía	ha investido
investimos	investíamos	hemos investido
investís	investíais	habéis investido
invisten	investían	han investido
Future	**Pluperfect**	**Past Definite**
investiré	había investido	investí
investirás	habías investido	investiste
investirá	había investido	invistió
investiremos	habíamos investido	investimos
investiréis	habíais investido	investisteis
investirán	habían investido	invistieron
Future Perfect	**Past Perfect**	
habré investido	hube investido	

CONDITIONAL / SUBJUNCTIVE

Present	Present	Imperfect
investiría	invista	invist-iera/iese
investirías	invistas	invist-ieras/ieses
investiría	invista	invist-iera/iese
investiríamos	invistamos	invist-iéramos/iésemos
investiríais	invistáis	invist-ierais/ieseis
investirían	invistan	invist-ieran/iesen
Perfect	**Perfect**	**Pluperfect**
habría investido	haya investido	hub-iera/iese investido

GERUND	PAST PARTICIPLE	IMPERATIVE
invistiendo	investido	inviste, investid invista (Vd), invistan (Vds)

Ha sido investida de Doctor Honoris Causa. *She has had a Doctor Honoris Causa conferred on her.*
Le invistieron en 1938. *He was invested in 1938.*
¿Te investirán este verano con la dignidad del mando? *Will you be invested this summer with the honour of authority?*
Te voy a investir de poderes. *I shall invest you with powers.*

Te investiré una misión. *I shall entrust you with a mission.*
Quiere ser investido con derechos legales. *He wants to be invested with legal rights.*
investir facultades *to invest powers*

investido/a *invested*
investido *conferee*
investido de autoridad *authorised*
investidura *investment*

ir *to go* intr. **114**

INDICATIVE

Present	**Imperfect**	**Perfect**
voy	iba	he ido
vas	ibas	has ido
va	iba	ha ido
vamos	íbamos	hemos ido
váis	ibais	habéis ido
van	iban	han ido
Future	**Pluperfect**	**Past Definite**
iré	había ido	fui
irás	habías ido	fuiste
irá	había ido	fue
iremos	habíamos ido	fuimos
iréis	habíais ido	fuisteis
irán	habían ido	fueron
Future Perfect	**Past Perfect**	
habré ido	hube ido	

CONDITIONAL	SUBJUNCTIVE	
Present	**Present**	**Imperfect**
iría	vaya	fu-era/ese
irías	vayas	fu-eras/eses
iría	vaya	fu-era/ese
iríamos	vayamos	fu-éramos/ésemos
iríais	vayáis	fu-erais/eseis
irían	vayan	fu-eran/esen
Perfect	**Perfect**	**Pluperfect**
habría ido	haya ido	hub-iera/iese ido

GERUND	PAST PARTICIPLE	IMPERATIVE
yendo	ido	ve, id vaya (Vd), vayan (Vds)

Voy a Madrid cada semana. *I go to Madrid every week.*
Fuimos al cine. *We went to the cinema.*
Iremos a la playa. *We'll go to the beach.*
Va en tren hasta Sevilla. *She goes to Seville by train.*

Voy de compras. *I'm going shopping.*
Ni me va ni me viene. *I couldn't care less.*
Va mucho en ello. *A lot depends on it.*
¿Cómo te va? *How are things?*
Va para médico. *He is going to become a doctor.*
¿Me va bien ésto? *Does this suit me?*

¡Qué va! *Rubbish!, Not at all!*
¡Vaya! *Well!, There!, I say!, I never!*
ida *going, departure*
de ida y vuelta *return*

115 jugar *to play* tr./intr.

INDICATIVE

Present	**Imperfect**	**Perfect**
juego	jugaba	he jugado
juegas	jugabas	has jugado
juega	jugaba	ha jugado
jugamos	jugábamos	hemos jugado
jugáis	jugabais	habéis jugado
juegan	jugaban	han jugado
Future	**Pluperfect**	**Past Definite**
jugaré	había jugado	jugué
jugarás	habías jugado	jugaste
jugará	había jugado	jugó
jugaremos	habíamos jugado	jugamos
jugaréis	habíais jugado	juasteis
jugarán	habían jugado	jugaron
Future Perfect	**Past Perfect**	
habré jugado	hube jugado	

CONDITIONAL	SUBJUNCTIVE	
Present	**Present**	**Imperfect**
jugaría	juegue	jug-ara/ase
jugarías	juegues	jug-aras/ases
jugaría	juegue	jug-ara/ase
jugaríamos	juguemos	jug-áramos/ásemos
jugaríais	juguéis	jug-arais/aseis
jugarían	jueguen	jug-aran/asen
Perfect	**Perfect**	**Pluperfect**
habría jugado	haya jugado	hub-iera/iese jugado

GERUND	PAST PARTICIPLE	IMPERATIVE
jugando	jugado	juega, jugad juegue (Vd), jueguen (Vds)

Juega al tenis. *He plays tennis.*
Jugamos al ajedrez. *We play chess.*
Lo jugó todo. *He gambled it all away.*
Hemos jugado £5 a una carta. *We have put £5 on a card.*

¡Me la han jugado! *They've played a trick on me!*
Solamente está jugando contigo. *He is trifling with you.*
Lo hace de jugando. *He does it for fun.*
¿Quién juega? *Whose turn is it?*

jugada *game, play*
hacer una jugada *to make a move*
mala jugada *bad turn*
juego *game*
jugarse *to gamble, bet*
juego sucio *foul play*
juego limpio *fair play*
poner en juego *to set in motion*
juguetón/juguetona *playful*

lavarse *to wash oneself* r. 116

INDICATIVE

Present	Imperfect	Perfect
me lavo	me lavaba	me he lavado
te lavas	te lavabas	te has lavado
se lava	se lavaba	se ha lavado
nos lavamos	nos lavábamos	nos hemos lavado
os laváis	os lavabais	os habéis lavado
se lavan	se lavaban	se han lavado
Future	**Pluperfect**	**Past Definite**
me lavaré	me había lavado	me lavé
te lavarás	te habías lavado	te lavaste
se lavará	se había lavado	se lavó
nos lavaremos	nos habíamos lavado	nos lavamos
os lavaréis	os habíais lavado	os lavasteis
se lavarán	se habían lavado	se lavaron
Future Perfect	**Past Perfect**	
me habré lavado	me hube lavado	

CONDITIONAL	SUBJUNCTIVE	
Present	**Present**	**Imperfect**
me lavaría	me lave	me lav-ara/ase
te lavarías	te laves	te lav-aras/ases
se lavaría	se lave	se lav-ara/ase
nos lavaríamos	nos lavemos	nos lav-áramos/ásemos
os lavaríais	os lavéis	os lav-arais/aseis
se lavarían	se laven	se lav-aran/asen
Perfect	**Perfect**	**Pluperfect**
me habría lavado	me haya lavado	me hub-iera/iese lavado

GERUND	PAST PARTICIPLE	IMPERATIVE
lavándose	lavado	lávate, laváos lávese (Vd), lávense (Vds)

Me lavo las manos antes de comer. *I wash my hands before meals.*
Sara se lava el pelo tres veces por semana. *Sara washes her hair three times a week.*
Nos lavamos la ropa en el jardín. *We wash our clothes in the garden.*
Te lavarás aunque no quieras. *You'll wash whether you like it or not.*

Yo me lavo las manos de esto. *I wash my hands of this.*
Mi vestido es de lavar en seco. *My dress is dry clean only.*
Susanita necesita un lavado de cerebro. *Susanita needs brainwashing.*
Mafalda necesita un lavado de cabeza. *Mafalda needs a shampoo.*

lavable *washable*
lavabo *sink, washbasin, toilet*
lavadero *laundry*
lavadora *washing machine*
lavaplatos *dishwasher*
lavavajillas *dishwasher* (machine)
lavativa *enema*

117 leer *to read* tr./intr.

INDICATIVE

Present	Imperfect	Perfect
leo	leía	he leído
lees	leías	has leído
lee	leía	ha leído
leemos	leíamos	hemos leído
leéis	leíais	habéis leído
leen	leían	han leído
Future	**Pluperfect**	**Past Definite**
leeré	había leído	leí
leerás	habías leído	leíste
leerá	había leído	leyó
leeremos	habíamos leído	leímos
leeréis	habíais leído	leísteis
leerán	habían leído	leyeron
Future Perfect	**Past Perfect**	
habré leído	hube leído	

CONDITIONAL	SUBJUNCTIVE	
Present	**Present**	**Imperfect**
leería	lea	le-yera/yese
leerías	leas	le-yeras/yeses
leería	lea	le-yera/yese
leeríamos	leamos	le-yéramos/yésemos
leeríais	leáis	le-yerais/yeseis
leerían	lean	le-yeran/yesen
Perfect	**Perfect**	**Pluperfect**
habría leído	haya leído	hub-iera/iese leído

GERUND	PAST PARTICIPLE	IMPERATIVE
leyendo	leído	lee, leed lea (Vd), lean (Vds)

Estoy leyendo una novela policíaca. *I'm reading a detective novel.*
Leo todas las noches. *I read every night.*
¿Te gusta leer? *Do you like reading?*
Paqui lee el periódico antes de desayunar. *Paqui reads the paper before breakfast.*

Elvira sabe leer en la boca. *Elvira can lip-read.*
Debes leer entre las líneas. *You ought to read between the lines.*
No te va a leer la mano. *She isn't going to read your palm.*

al que leyere estas líneas *to the reader*
lectura *reading*
dar una lectura *to deliver a lecture*
lector(a) *reader*
lector de fichas *card reader*
lectura de marcas *mark sensing (computing)*
lección *lesson, class*

limpiar *to clean, cleanse* tr. 118

INDICATIVE

Present	Imperfect	Perfect
limpio	limpiaba	he limpiado
limpias	limpiabas	has limpiado
limpia	limpiaba	ha limpiado
limpiamos	limpiábamos	hemos limpiado
limpiáis	limpiabais	habéis limpiado
limpian	limpiaban	han limpiado
Future	**Pluperfect**	**Past Definite**
limpiaré	había limpiado	limpié
limpiarás	habías limpiado	limpiaste
limpiará	había limpiado	limpió
limpiaremos	habíamos limpiado	limpiamos
limpiaréis	habíais limpiado	limpiasteis
limpiarán	habían limpiado	limpiaron
Future Perfect	**Past Perfect**	
habré limpiado	hube limpiado	

CONDITIONAL	SUBJUNCTIVE	
Present	**Present**	**Imperfect**
limpiaría	limpie	limpi-ara/ase
limpiarías	limpies	limpi-aras/ases
limpiaría	limpie	limpi-ara/ase
limpiaríamos	limpiemos	limpi-áramos/ásemos
limpiaríais	limpiéis	limpi-arais/aseis
limpiarían	limpien	limpi-aran/asen
Perfect	**Perfect**	**Pluperfect**
habría limpiado	haya limpiado	hub-iera/iese limpiado

GERUND	PAST PARTICIPLE	IMPERATIVE
limpiando	limpiado	limpia, limpiad
		limpie (Vd), limpien (Vds)

Tenemos que limpiar los cristales. *We have to clean the windows.*
Limpia el suelo. *Mop the floor.*
Se ha limpiado los zapatos. *She has cleaned her shoes.*
Miguel lo limpió ayer. *Miguel cleaned it yesterday.*

Limpia las narices al niño. *Wipe the child's nose.*
La policía quiere limpiar el juego. *The police want to clean out gambling.*
Limpiar en seco. *Dry clean only.*
Leonor está haciendo la limpieza. *Leonor is doing the housework.*
Me limpiaron el bolso en el metro. *I had my bag stolen on the underground.*

limpieza *cleaning*
limpio/a *clean*
limpiacristales *window cleaner*
limpiametales *metal polish*
limpiaplicador *cotton-bud*
limpiaparabrisas *windscreen wiper*

119 llegar *to arrive, reach* tr./intr.

INDICATIVE

Present	Imperfect	Perfect
llego	llegaba	he llegado
llegas	llegabas	has llegado
llega	llegaba	ha llegado
llegamos	llegábamos	hemos llegado
llegáis	llegabais	habéis llegado
llegan	llegaban	han llegado
Future	**Pluperfect**	**Past Definite**
llegaré	había llegado	llegué
llegarás	habías llegado	llegaste
llegará	había llegado	llegó
llegaremos	habíamos llegado	llegamos
llegaréis	habíais llegado	llegasteis
llegarán	habían llegado	llegaron
Future Perfect	**Past Perfect**	
habré llegado	hube llegado	

CONDITIONAL	SUBJUNCTIVE	
Present	**Present**	**Imperfect**
llegaría	llegue	lleg-ara/ase
llegarías	llegues	lleg-aras/ases
llegaría	llegue	lleg-ara/ase
llegaríamos	lleguemos	lleg-áramos/ásemos
llegaríais	lleguéis	lleg-arais/aseis
llegarían	lleguen	lleg-aran/asen
Perfect	**Perfect**	**Pluperfect**
habría llegado	haya llegado	hub-iera/iese llegado

GERUND	PAST PARTICIPLE	IMPERATIVE
llegando	llegado	llega, llegad llegue (Vd), lleguen (Vds)

Llegaremos a las nueve. *We'll arrive at nine.*
Avísame cuando llegue José. *Tell me when José arrives.*
Llegué a Madrid el martes. *I arrived in Madrid on Tuesday.*
No llegan a 40. *There are less than 40.*
No llega el cable. *The cable doesn't reach.*

Llegaron a las manos. *They came to blows.*
Le llegó la hora el mes pasado. *He died last month.*
No me llega el dinero. *I don't have enough money.*
¡Hasta allí podíamos llegar! *What a nerve!*

llegada *arrival*
llegar a un acuerdo *to reach an agreement*
llegar a las armas *to resort to arms*
llegar a una conclusión *to reach a conclusion*
Está al llegar. *She is about to arrive.*
Miguel llegará lejos. *Miguel will go far.*

llorar *to cry, weep* tr./intr. **120**

INDICATIVE

Present	**Imperfect**	**Perfect**
lloro	lloraba	he llorado
lloras	llorabas	has llorado
llora	lloraba	ha llorado
lloramos	llorábamos	hemos llorado
lloráis	llorabais	habéis llorado
lloran	lloraban	han llorado
Future	**Pluperfect**	**Past Definite**
lloraré	había llorado	lloré
llorarás	habías llorado	lloraste
llorará	había llorado	lloró
lloraremos	habíamos llorado	lloramos
lloraréis	habíais llorado	llorasteis
llorarán	habían llorado	lloraron
Future Perfect	**Past Perfect**	
habré llorado	hube llorado	

CONDITIONAL	SUBJUNCTIVE	
Present	**Present**	**Imperfect**
lloraría	llore	llor-ara/ase
llorarías	llores	llor-aras/ases
lloraría	llore	llor-ara/ase
lloraríamos	lloremos	llor-áramos/ásemos
lloraríais	lloréis	llor-arais/aseis
llorarían	lloren	llor-aran/asen
Perfect	**Perfect**	**Pluperfect**
habría llorado	haya llorado	hub-iera/iese llorado

GERUND	PAST PARTICIPLE	IMPERATIVE
llorando	llorado	llora, llorad llore (Vd), lloren (Vds)

Lloro cuando estoy triste. *I cry when I'm sad.*
¡No llores! *Don't cry!*
Mi padre lloró en la guerra. *My father cried in the war.*
Estamos llorando la pérdida de su libertad. *We are crying for their lost freedom.*

Niño que no llora, no mama. *He who doesn't speak up won't get what he wants.*
Ximena lloraba a lágrima viva. *Ximena was crying her eyes out.*
El niño llora a moco tendido. *The child cries uncontrollably.*
Marta llora como una fuente. *Marta weeps buckets.*

el rey llorado *the lamented king*
lloretas *crybaby*
lloriquear *to whimper*
lloro *weeping, crying*
llorón/llorona *weeping, tearful*
llanto *weeping*
llantería *weeping, wailing*
lloroso *tearful*

121 llover *to rain* intr./tr.

INDICATIVE

Present	Imperfect	Perfect
llueve	llovía	ha llovido
Future	**Pluperfect**	**Past Definite**
lloverá	había llovido	llovió
Future Perfect	**Past Perfect**	
habrá llovido	hubo llovido	

CONDITIONAL	SUBJUNCTIVE	
Present	**Present**	**Imperfect**
llovería	llueva	llov-iera/iese
Perfect	**Perfect**	**Pluperfect**
habría llovido	haya llovido	hub-iera/iese llovido

GERUND	PAST PARTICIPLE
lloviendo	llovido

¿Llueve mucho? *Does it rain much?*
Está lloviendo. *It's raining.*
¿Lloverá mañana? *Will it rain tomorrow?*
El mes pasado llovió mucho. *Last month it rained a lot.*

como llovido del cielo *unexpected, godsend*
llueva o no *come what may*
Siempre que llueve escampa. *Every cloud has a silver lining.*
Nos llovieron regalos encima. *We were showered with gifts.*
Llueve a cántaros/cubos/mares/chuzos. *It's raining cats and dogs.*

llovida *shower*
lluvia *rain*
lluvioso/a *rainy, wet*
llovizna *drizzle*
¡Qué llueva! *Let it rain!*
tiempo lluvioso *rainy weather*

medir *to measure* tr. 122

INDICATIVE

Present	Imperfect	Perfect
mido	medía	he medido
mides	medías	has medido
mide	medía	ha medido
medimos	medíamos	hemos medido
medís	medíais	habéis medido
miden	medían	han medido
Future	**Pluperfect**	**Past Definite**
mediré	había medido	medí
medirás	habías medido	mediste
medirá	había medido	midió
mediremos	habíamos medido	medimos
mediréis	habíais medido	medisteis
medirán	habían medido	midieron
Future Perfect	**Past Perfect**	
habré medido	hube medido	

CONDITIONAL	SUBJUNCTIVE	
Present	**Present**	**Imperfect**
mediría	mida	mid-iera/iese
medirías	midas	mid-ieras/ieses
mediría	mida	mid-iera/iese
mediríamos	midamos	mid-iéramos/iésemos
mediríais	midáis	mid-ierais/ieseis
medirían	midan	mid-ieran/iesen
Perfect	**Perfect**	**Pluperfect**
habría medido	haya medido	hub-iera/iese medido

GERUND	PAST PARTICIPLE	IMPERATIVE
midiendo	medido	mide, medid mida (Vd), midan (Vds)

Mide la tela. *Measure the cloth.*
¿Cómo se mide el cariño? *How can one measure love?*
¿Cuánto mide la habitación? *What are the measurements of the room?*
No lo has medido bien. *You haven't measured it properly.*

Le mide con la vista. *He sizes him up.*
a la medida *in proportion*
Bush se medió con Hassan. *Bush tested himself against Hassan.*
Se midieron. *They came to blows.*
a medida *made to measure*

en cierta medida *up to a point*
medida *measurement*
a medida que . . . *as . . ./according . . .*
pesos y medidas *weights and measures*
medición *measurement*
medir un terreno *to survey*
traje a la medida *made-to-measure suit*
medida preventiva *preventive measure*

123 mentir *to lie* intr.

INDICATIVE

Present	Imperfect	Perfect
miento	mentía	he mentido
mientes	mentías	has mentido
miente	mentía	ha mentido
mentimos	mentíamos	hemos mentido
mentís	mentíais	habéis mentido
mienten	mentían	han mentido
Future	**Pluperfect**	**Past Definite**
mentiré	había mentido	mentí
mentirás	habías mentido	mentiste
mentirá	había mentido	mintío
mentiremos	habíamos mentido	mentimos
mentiréis	habíais mentido	mentisteis
mentirán	habían mentido	mintieron
Future Perfect	**Past Perfect**	
habré mentido	hube mentido	

CONDITIONAL	SUBJUNCTIVE	
Present	**Present**	**Imperfect**
mentiría	mienta	mint-iera/iese
mentirías	mientas	mint-ieras/ieses
mentiría	mienta	mint-iera/iese
mentiríamos	mintamos	mint-iéramos/iésemos
mentiríais	mintáis	mint-ierais/ieseis
mentirían	mientan	mint-ieran/iesen
Perfect	**Perfect**	**Pluperfect**
habría mentido	haya mentido	hub-iera/iese mentido

GERUND	PAST PARTICIPLE	IMPERATIVE
mintiendo	mentido	miente, mentid mienta (Vd), mientan (Vds)

No mientas. *Don't tell lies.*
Mentí para salir del apuro. *I lied to avoid embarrassment.*
Mintió para conseguir el empleo. *He lied to get the job.*
Mentiremos para que no se enfade. *We'll lie so that he doesn't get angry.*

Te he cogido en una mentira. *I've caught you in a lie.*
Parece mentira. *It seems impossible.*
Es de mentirijillas. *It's just pretend.*
¡Parece mentira! *Well I never! I don't believe it!*

mentira *lie, falsehood*
mentira piadosa *white lie*
mentirijilla *little lie*
mentiroso/a *liar*
mentirosillo/a *fibber*
mentirosito/a *white liar, little fibber*
mentidero *gossip shop*
mentido/a *deceiving, false*

merendar *to have tea / a snack* tr./intr. 124

INDICATIVE

Present	Imperfect	Perfect
meriendo	merendaba	he merendado
meriendas	merendabas	has merendado
merienda	merendaba	ha merendado
merendamos	merendábamos	hemos merendado
merendáis	merendabais	habéis merendado
meriendan	merendaban	han merendado
Future	**Pluperfect**	**Past Definite**
merendaré	había merendado	merendé
merendarás	habías merendado	merendaste
merendará	había merendado	merendó
merendaremos	habíamos merendado	merendamos
merendaréis	habíais merendado	merendasteis
merendarán	habían merendado	merendaron
Future Perfect	**Past Perfect**	
habré merendado	hube merendado	

CONDITIONAL	SUBJUNCTIVE	
Present	**Present**	**Imperfect**
merendaría	meriende	merend-ara/ase
merendarías	meriendes	merend-aras/ases
merendaría	meriende	merend-ara/ase
merendaríamos	merendemos	meren-áramos/dásemos
merendaríais	merendéis	merend-arais/aseis
merendarían	merienden	merend-aran/asen
Perfect	**Perfect**	**Pluperfect**
habría merendado	haya merendado	hub-iera/iese merendado

GERUND	PAST PARTICIPLE	IMPERATIVE
merendando	merendado	merienda, merendad meriende (Vd), merienden (Vds)

Meriendo a las cinco. *I have a snack at five.*
Merendamos pan y chocolate. *We have bread and chocolate for tea.*
Merendó jamón. *He had ham (as a late-afternoon snack).*
¿Qué quieres merendar? *What do you want for your tea?*

Meriendo lo que escribe Miguel. *I look at what Miguel is writing.*
Merienda las cartas de Daniel. *She is peeping at Daniel's cards.*
Se ha merendado su fortuna. *She has squandered her fortune.*
Piensa merendarse al violador de su hija. *He intends to kill his daughter's rapist.*

merendero *picnic spot*
merienda *tea, afternoon tea, afternoon snack*
merienda cena *early supper (before 8 pm in Spain)*
ir de merienda *to go for a picnic*
juntar meriendas *to join fortunes*

125 moler *to grind, crush, mill* tr.

INDICATIVE

Present	Imperfect	Perfect
muelo	molía	he molido
mueles	molías	has molido
muele	molía	ha molido
molemos	molíamos	hemos molido
moléis	molíais	habéis molido
muelen	molían	han molido
Future	**Pluperfect**	**Past Definite**
moleré	había molido	molí
molerás	habías molido	moliste
molerá	había molido	molió
moleremos	habíamos molido	molimos
moleréis	habíais molido	molisteis
molerán	habían molido	molieron
Future Perfect	**Past Perfect**	
habré molido	hube molido	

CONDITIONAL	SUBJUNCTIVE	
Present	**Present**	**Imperfect**
molería	muela	mol-iera/iese
molerías	muelas	mol-ieras/ieses
molería	muela	mol-iera/iese
moleríamos	molamos	mol-iéramos/iésemos
moleríais	moláis	mol-ierais/ieseis
molerían	muelan	mol-ieran/iesen
Perfect	**Perfect**	**Pluperfect**
habría molido	haya molido	hub-iera/iese molido

GERUND	PAST PARTICIPLE	IMPERATIVE
moliendo	molido	muele, moled muela (Vd), muelan (Vds)

Me gusta moler el café. *I like grinding my own coffee.*
¿Quieres moler las especias? *Will you grind the spices?*
Molerán la aceituna mañana. *They will crush the olives tomorrow.*
¿Cuándo vas a moler el trigo? *When are you going to mill the wheat?*

Le molió a palos. *He gave him a beating.*
Estoy molida. *I'm exhausted.*
Me muele con sus comentarios. *He annoys/bores me with his comments.*
¿Vas a moler la carne? *Are you going to mince the meat?*

moledor *grinder, roller, bore, grinding, crushing*
molido/a *ground, crushed*
molienda *milling, a mill; a nuisance*
molinero/a *miller*
molino de agua *water mill*
molino de viento *windmill*
molinillo de café *coffee mill*
molinillo de carne *mincer*

morder *to bite, nip* tr. 126

INDICATIVE

Present	Imperfect	Perfect
muerdo	mordía	he mordido
muerdes	mordías	has mordido
muerde	mordía	ha mordido
mordemos	mordíamos	hemos mordido
mordéis	mordíais	habéis mordido
muerden	mordían	han mordido
Future	**Pluperfect**	**Past Definite**
morderé	había mordido	mordí
morderás	habías mordido	mordiste
morderá	había mordido	mordió
morderemos	habíamos mordido	mordimos
morderéis	habíais mordido	mordisteis
morderán	habían mordido	mordieron
Future Perfect	**Past Perfect**	
habré mordido	hube mordido	

CONDITIONAL	SUBJUNCTIVE	
Present	**Present**	**Imperfect**
mordería	muerda	mord-iera/iese
morderías	muerdas	mord-ieras/ieses
mordería	muerda	mord-iera/iese
morderíamos	mordamos	mord-iéramos/iésemos
morderíais	mordáis	mord-ierais/ieseis
morderían	muerdan	mord-ieran/iesen
Perfect	**Perfect**	**Pluperfect**
habría mordido	haya mordido	hub-iera/iese mordido

GERUND	PAST PARTICIPLE	IMPERATIVE
mordiendo	mordido	muerde, morded muerda (Vd), muerdan ((Vds)

El niño me ha mordido el dedo. *The boy has bitten my finger.*
Eva mordió la manzana. *Eve bit the apple.*
Este perro no muerde. *This dog doesn't bite.*
Se ha mordido el labio. *He has bitten his lip.*

Estoy que muerdo. *I'm furious.*
Está que muerde. *He is hopping mad.*
Muerde sobre esto. *Bite into this.*
¡Hombre, que no muerde! *Don't be shy!*
Perro que ladra no muerde. *A barking dog does not bite.*

mordedura *bite*
mordisco *bite, nibble*
mordida *bite; bribe*
morder sobre *to bite into*
mordedor(a) *biting*
mordicación *nipping, biting*

127 morir *to die* intr.

INDICATIVE

Present	Imperfect	Perfect
muero	moría	he muerto
mueres	morías	has muerto
muere	moría	ha muerto
morimos	moríamos	hemos muerto
morís	moríais	habéis muerto
mueren	morían	han muerto
Future	**Pluperfect**	**Past Definite**
moriré	había muerto	morí
morirás	habías muerto	moriste
morirá	había muerto	murió
moriremos	habíamos muerto	morimos
moriréis	habíais muerto	moristeis
morirán	habían muerto	murieron
Future Perfect	**Past Perfect**	
habré muerto	hube muerto	

CONDITIONAL / SUBJUNCTIVE

Present	Present	Imperfect
moriría	muera	mur-iera/iese
morirías	mueras	mur-ieras/ieses
moriría	muera	mur-iera/iese
moriríamos	muramos	mur-iéramos/iésemos
moriríais	muráis	mur-ierais/ieseis
morirían	mueran	mur-ieran/iesen
Perfect	**Perfect**	**Pluperfect**
habría muerto	haya muerto	hub-iera/iese muerto

GERUND	PAST PARTICIPLE	IMPERATIVE
muriendo	muerto	muere, morid muera (Vd), mueran (Vds)

Muchos niños mueren de hambre. *Many children die of hunger.*
Jan murió de cáncer. *Jan died of cancer.*
Mi abuelo murió hace diez años. *My grandfather died ten years ago.*
Fredes resultó muerta en el acto. *Fredes died instantly.*

Moría el día. *Night was falling.*
Sara está muerta de hambre. *Sara is starving.*
Joana se moría de vergüenza. *Joana nearly died of shame.*
Paula se murió de risa. *Paula couldn't stop laughing.*
Daniel se muere por el fútbol. *Daniel is mad on football.*

muerte *death*
muerto/a *dead*
Fue muerto a tiros. *He was shot dead.*
hacerse el muerto/a *to play dead*
naturaleza muerta *still-life*
¡Muera el tirano! *Down with the tyrant!*
mortal *fatal, mortal*
mortalidad *mortality*

mover *to move* tr./intr. 128

INDICATIVE

Present	**Imperfect**	**Perfect**
muevo	movía	he movido
mueves	movías	has movido
mueve	movía	ha movido
movemos	movíamos	hemos movido
movéis	movíais	habéis movido
mueven	movían	han movido
Future	**Pluperfect**	**Past Definite**
moveré	había movido	moví
moverás	habías movido	moviste
moverá	había movido	movió
moveremos	habíamos movido	movimos
moveréis	habíais movido	movisteis
moverán	habían movido	movieron
Future Perfect	**Past Perfect**	
habré movido	hube movido	

CONDITIONAL	SUBJUNCTIVE	
Present	**Present**	**Imperfect**
movería	mueva	mov-iera/iese
moverías	muevas	mov-ieras/ieses
movería	mueva	mov-iera/iese
moveríamos	movamos	mov-iéramos/iésemos
moveríais	mováis	mov-ierais/ieseis
moverían	muevan	mov-ieran/iesen
Perfect	**Perfect**	**Pluperfect**
habría movido	haya movido	hub-iera/iese movido

GERUND	PAST PARTICIPLE	IMPERATIVE
moviendo	movido	mueve, moved mueva (Vd), muevan (Vds)

¿Podemos mover la mesa? *Can we move the table?*
Te toca mover. *It's your move.*
No me he movido del sitio. *I've not moved from my place.*
Tenemos que movernos. *We have to get a move on.*

Movió un jaleo tremendo. *He caused a big row.*
Voy a ponerlo en movimiento. *I am going to start it.*
Deja de moverte. *Stop fidgeting.*
¡Muévete! *Hurry up!*

movimiento *movement*
la movida madrileña *the Madrid scene*
móvil *mobile*
movilidad *mobility*
movilización *mobilisation*
movible *changeable, mobile*
movimiento de intercambio *turnover*
tienda de mucho movimiento *very busy shop*

129 mudar *to move, change* tr./intr.

INDICATIVE

Present	Imperfect	Perfect
mudo	mudaba	he mudado
mudas	mudabas	has mudado
muda	mudaba	ha mudado
mudamos	mudábamos	hemos mudado
mudáis	mudabais	habéis mudado
mudan	mudaban	han mudado
Future	**Pluperfect**	**Past Definite**
mudaré	había mudado	mudé
mudarás	habías mudado	mudaste
mudará	había mudado	mudó
mudaremos	habíamos mudado	mudamos
mudaréis	habíais mudado	mudasteis
mudarán	habían mudado	mudaron
Future Perfect	**Past Perfect**	
habré mudado	hube mudado	

CONDITIONAL	SUBJUNCTIVE	
Present	**Present**	**Imperfect**
mudaría	mude	mud-ara/ase
mudarías	mudes	mud-aras/ases
mudaría	mude	mud-ara/ase
mudaríamos	mudemos	mud-áramos/ásemos
mudaríais	mudéis	mud-arais/aseis
mudarían	muden	mud-aran/asen
Perfect	**Perfect**	**Pluperfect**
habría mudado	haya mudado	hub-iera/iese mudado

GERUND	PAST PARTICIPLE	IMPERATIVE
mudando	mudado	muda, mudad mude (Vd), muden (Vds)

Nos mudamos de ciudad. *We are moving to another town.*
Mi hermana se ha mudado de casa. *My sister has moved house.*
Los pollitos mudarán las plumas pronto. *The chicks will shed their feathers soon.*
Lo he mudado de sitio. *I've put it somewhere else.*

A Carlos se le está mudando la voz. *Carlos's voice is breaking.*
Siempre está de mudanza. *She is fickle.*
Peter se ducha antes de mudarse. *Peter has a shower before he changes his clothes.*
He mudado de opinión. *I've changed my opinion.*

muda *change, alteration, change of clothing*
mudar la voz *to change/breaking (a voice)*
mudable *changeable, fickle, inconstant*
mudamente *silently*
mudamiento *change, moving*
mudanza *change, moving, move house*
mudo/a *dumb, mute, silent*

negar *to refuse, deny* tr./intr. 130

INDICATIVE

Present	Imperfect	Perfect
niego	negaba	he negado
niegas	negabas	has negado
niega	negaba	ha negado
negamos	negábamos	hemos negado
negáis	negabais	habéis negado
niegan	negaban	han negado
Future	**Pluperfect**	**Past Definite**
negaré	había negado	negué
negarás	habías negado	negaste
negará	había negado	negó
negaremos	habíamos negado	negamos
negaréis	habíais negado	negasteis
negarán	habían negado	negaron
Future Perfect	**Past Perfect**	
habré negado	hube negado	

CONDITIONAL	SUBJUNCTIVE	
Present	**Present**	**Imperfect**
negaría	niegue	neg-ara/ase
negarías	niegues	neg-aras/ases
negaría	niegue	neg-ara/ase
negaríamos	neguemos	neg-áramos/ásemos
negaríais	neguéis	neg-arais/aseis
negarían	nieguen	neg-aran/asen
Perfect	**Perfect**	**Pluperfect**
habría negado	haya negado	hub-iera/iese negado

GERUND	PAST PARTICIPLE	IMPERATIVE
negando	negado	niega, negad niegue (Vd), nieguen (Vds)

Le niegan todo lo que pide. *They refuse him everything.*
Se negó a devolverme los negativos de mis fotos. *He refused to give me back the negatives of my pictures.*
No creo que se niegue. *I don't think he'll refuse.*
Jacky ne negó a hacerlo. *Jacky refused to do it.*

Me negó la mano. *He refused to shake hands with me.*
Paula les negó el saludo. *Paula would not even speak to them.*
Nos negaron la entrada. *They wouldn't let us in.*
¡No me lo vas a negar! *You aren't going to refuse me!*

negación *negation, refusal, denial*
negado/a *denied, refused, inept, stupid*
negativa *negative, refusal, denial*
negativa rotunda *flat refusal*
negativamente *negatively*
contestar negativamente *to answer in the negative*
negable *deniable*

131 oír *to hear* tr./intr.

INDICATIVE

Present	Imperfect	Perfect
oigo	oía	he oído
oyes	oías	has oído
oye	oía	ha oído
oímos	oíamos	hemos oído
oís	oíais	habéis oído
oyen	aían	han oído
Future	**Pluperfect**	**Past Definite**
oiré	había oído	oí
oirás	habías oído	oíste
oirá	había oído	oyó
oiremos	habíamos oído	oímos
oiréis	habíais oído	oísteis
oirán	habían oído	oyeron
Future Perfect	**Past Perfect**	
habré oído	hube oído	

CONDITIONAL	SUBJUNCTIVE	
Present	**Present**	**Imperfect**
oiría	oiga	o-yera/yese
oirías	oigas	o-yeras/yeses
oiría	oiga	o-yera/yese
oiríamos	oigamos	o-yéramos/yésemos
oiríais	oigáis	o-yerais/yeseis
oirían	oigan	o-yeran/yesen
Perfect	**Perfect**	**Pluperfect**
habría oído	haya oído	hub-iera/iese oído

GERUND	PAST PARTICIPLE	IMPERATIVE
oyendo	oído	oye, oíd oiga (Vd), oigan (Vds)

He oído hablar de tí. *I have heard about you.*
Me gusta oír la radio. *I like to hear the radio.*
Le oí abrir la ventana. *I heard him opening the window.*
Oigo música por las mañanas. *I hear music in the morning.*

Tal y como lo oyes. *Just like I'm telling you.*
Lo oyó como quien oye llover. *He paid no attention to it.*
¡Aguza los oídos! *Prick up your ears!*
Bunny toca el piano de oído. *Bunny plays the piano by ear.*
oir, ver y callar *to mind your own business*

oído *ear, sense of hearing*
oído interno *inner ear*
oídas *by hearsay*
oidor (coloq.) *judge*

dar oídos *to lend an ear, to listen*
oye, oiga Vd *listen, excuse me*
¡Oiga por favor! *Excuse me please!*

oler *to smell* tr./intr. 132

INDICATIVE

Present	Imperfect	Perfect
huelo	olía	he olido
hueles	olías	has olido
huele	olía	ha olido
olemos	olíamos	hemos olido
oléis	olíais	habéis olido
huelen	olían	han olido

Future	Pluperfect	Past Definite
oleré	había olido	olí
olerás	habías olido	oliste
olerá	había olido	olió
oleremos	habíamos olido	olimos
oleréis	habíais olido	olisteis
olerán	habían olido	olieron

Future Perfect	Past Perfect
habré olido	hube olido

CONDITIONAL	SUBJUNCTIVE	
Present	**Present**	**Imperfect**
olería	huela	ol-iera/iese
olerías	huelas	ol-ieras/ieses
olería	huela	ol-iera/iese
oleríamos	olamos	ol-iéramos/iésemos
oleríais	oláis	ol-ierais/ieseis
olerían	huelan	ol-ieran/iesen
Perfect	**Perfect**	**Pluperfect**
habría olido	haya olido	hub-iera/iese olido

GERUND	PAST PARTICIPLE	IMPERATIVE
oliendo	olido	huele, oled huela (Vd), huelan (Vds)

Huele a madreselva. *It smells of honeysuckle.*
Siempre huelen mal. *They always smell bad.*
¿Quieres oler mi perfume? *Do you want to smell my perfume?*
Es inodoro; no tiene olor. *It is odourless; it does not have a smell.*

Ya se ha olido lo que estamos haciendo. *He has already guessed what we are doing.*
Esto me huele a excusa. *I have a feeling that this is just an excuse.*
Huelen todo. *They pry into everything.*
Acude al olor del dinero. *He goes where the money is.*
Huele que apesta. *It stinks.*

olor *smell*
olfato *sense of smell*
oloroso/a = aromático/a *fragrant, sweet smelling*
inodoro *inodorous*
óleo *oil*
oleoso *oily*
olfatear *to sniff*

133 partir *to split, leave* tr./intr.

INDICATIVE

Present	Imperfect	Perfect
parto	partía	he partido
partes	partías	has partido
parte	partía	ha partido
partimos	partíamos	hemos partido
partís	partíais	habéis partido
parten	partían	han partido
Future	**Pluperfect**	**Past Definite**
partiré	había partido	partí
partirás	habías partido	partiste
partirá	había partido	partió
partiremos	habíamos partido	partimos
partiréis	habíais partido	partisteis
partirán	habían partido	partieron
Future Perfect	**Past Perfect**	
habré partido	hube partido	

CONDITIONAL	SUBJUNCTIVE	
Present	**Present**	**Imperfect**
partiría	parta	part-iera/iese
partirías	partas	part-ieras/ieses
partiría	parta	part-iera/iese
partiríamos	partamos	part-iéramos/iésemos
partiríais	partáis	part-ierais/ieseis
partirían	partan	part-ieran/iesen
Perfect	**Perfect**	**Pluperfect**
habría partido	haya partido	hub-iera/iese partido

GERUND	PAST PARTICIPLE	IMPERATIVE
partiendo	partido	parte, partid parta (Vd), partan (Vds)

Vamos a partir la diferencia. *Let's split the difference.*
He partido la naranja en dos. *I have cut the orange in two.*
Paqui partió de Chicago el viernes pasado. *Paqui left Chicago last Friday.*
El avión parte de Ibiza. *The plane departs from Ibiza.*

¡Te voy a partir la cara! *I'll slap you!*
Vamos a echar una partida. *Let's play a hand of cards.*
Felipe piensa formar partido. *Felipe intends to seek aid.*
No pienso tomar partido. *I won't take sides.*

partida *departure, leave*
partida doble *double entry*
partida de nacimiento *birth certificate*
partida de matrimonio *marriage certificate*
partida de defunción *death certificate*
partida de bautismo *Baptism certificate*
partidor *divider, cracker, splitter*
partitura *score*
repartir *to distribute*

pedir *to ask, request* tr. 134

INDICATIVE

Present	Imperfect	Perfect
pido	pedía	he pedido
pides	pedías	has pedido
pide	pedía	ha pedido
pedimos	pedíamos	hemos pedido
pedís	pedíais	habéis pedido
piden	pedían	han pedido
Future	**Pluperfect**	**Past Definite**
pediré	había pedido	pedí
pedirás	habías pedido	pediste
pedirá	había pedido	pidió
pediremos	habíamos pedido	pedimos
pediréis	habíais pedido	pedisteis
pedirán	habían pedido	pidieron
Future Perfect	**Past Perfect**	
habré pedido	hube pedido	

CONDITIONAL	SUBJUNCTIVE	
Present	**Present**	**Imperfect**
pediría	pida	pid-iera/iese
pedirías	pidas	pid-ieras/ieses
pediría	pida	pid-iera/iese
pediríamos	pidamos	pid-iéramos/iésemos
pediríais	pidáis	pid-ierais/ieseis
pedirían	pidan	pid-ieran/iesen
Perfect	**Perfect**	**Pluperfect**
habría pedido	haya pedido	hub-iera/iese pedido

GERUND	PAST PARTICIPLE	IMPERATIVE
pidiendo	pedido	pide, pedid pida (Vd), pidan (Vds)

¿Te puedo pedir un favor? *Can I ask you a favour?*
Me pidió que le comprara un coche. *He asked me to buy him a car.*
¿Cuánto piden por esto? *How much are they asking for this?*
Les pediremos perdón. *We shall ask them to forgive us.*

La pared está pidiendo una mano de pintura. *The wall could do with a coat of paint.*
Ese gris pide un color rosa. *That grey needs a pink.*
¡Te lo pido por Dios! *I beg you!*
El triunfo pide una celebración. *The victory calls for a celebration.*

petición *request, plea*
a petición de . . . *at the request of . . .*
petición de aumento de salarios *demand for higher wages*
pedigüeño/a *insistent, demanding*
pedido *order*
pedidor *petitioner*
pedilón/pedilona *demanding, pest, nuisance*
pedimento *petition*

135 pensar *to think* tr./intr.

INDICATIVE

Present	Imperfect	Perfect
pienso	pensaba	he pensado
piensas	pensabas	has pensado
piensa	pensaba	ha pensado
pensamos	pensábamos	hemos pensado
pensáis	pensabais	habéis pensado
piensan	pensaban	han pensado
Future	**Pluperfect**	**Past Definite**
pensaré	había pensado	pensé
pensarás	habías pensado	pensaste
pensará	había pensado	pensó
pensaremos	habíamos pensado	pensamos
pensaréis	habíais pensado	pensasteis
pensarán	habían pensado	pensaron
Future Perfect	**Past Perfect**	
habré pensado	hube pensado	

CONDITIONAL	SUBJUNCTIVE	
Present	**Present**	**Imperfect**
pensaría	piense	pens-ara/ase
pensarías	pienses	pens-aras/ases
pensaría	piense	pens-ara/ase
pensaríamos	pensemos	pens-áramos/ásemos
pensaríais	penséis	pens-arais/aseis
pensarían	piensen	pens-aran/asen
Perfect	**Perfect**	**Pluperfect**
habría pensado	haya pensado	hub-iera/iese pensado

GERUND	PAST PARTICIPLE	IMPERATIVE
pensando	pensado	piensa, pensad piense (Vd), piensen (Vds)

¿En qué piensas? *What are you thinking about?*
Pensaba en las vacaciones. *I was thinking about the holidays.*
Luis piensa que Francisca es amable. *Luis thinks that Francisca is nice.*
No sé qué pensar de Lola. *I don't know what to think about Lola.*

Mi ropa da que pensar. *My clothes set people thinking.*
¡Ni lo pienses! *Not a bit of it!*
Pensándolo bien . . . *On reflection . . .*
Te voy a dar que pensar. *I'm going to give you food for thought.*

pensamiento *thought*
pensamiento *the mind*
pensador(a) *thinker*
pensado/a *thought out*
pensante *thinking*
pensativo/a *thoughtful, pensive*
sin pensar *without thinking*
pensar mal de *to think ill of*

perder *to lose* tr./intr.

INDICATIVE

Present	**Imperfect**	**Perfect**
pierdo	perdía	he perdido
pierdes	perdías	has perdido
pierde	perdía	ha perdido
perdemos	perdíamos	hemos perdido
perdéis	perdíais	habéis perdido
pierden	perdían	han perdido
Future	**Pluperfect**	**Past Definite**
perderé	había perdido	perdí
perderás	habías perdido	pediste
perderá	había perdido	perdió
perderemos	habíamos perdido	perdimos
perderéis	habíais perdido	perdisteis
perderán	habían perdido	perdieron
Future Perfect	**Past Perfect**	
habré perdido	hube perdido	

CONDITIONAL	SUBJUNCTIVE	
Present	**Present**	**Imperfect**
perdería	pierda	perd-iera/iese
perderías	pierdas	perd-ieras/ieses
perdería	pierda	perd-iera/iese
perderíamos	perdamos	perd-iéramos/iésemos
perderíais	perdáis	perd-ierais/ieseis
perderían	pierdan	perd-ieran/iesen
Perfect	**Perfect**	**Pluperfect**
habría perdido	haya perdido	hub-iera/iese perdido

GERUND	PAST PARTICIPLE	IMPERATIVE
perdiendo	perdido	pierde, perded pierda (Vd), pierdan (Vds)

Sara ha perdido 5 kg. *Sara has lost 5 kg.*
Elena va a perder la costumbre. *Elena is going to lose the habit.*
Daniel no se pierde nada. *Daniel doesn't miss a thing.*
Leonor no pierde un momento. *Leonor doesn't waste a moment.*

Se ha echado a perder. *It has gone to waste.*
Lo doy por perdido. *I give up.*
Romeo estaba perdido por Julieta. *Romeo was crazy about Juliet.*
No tiene pérdida. *You can't miss it.*

pérdida *loss, waste*
perdido/a *lost*
perdidamente enamorado/a *passionately in love*
perdidoso *losing, easily lost*
perdición *ruin, undoing, waste*
perdedor(a) *losing*
perdidizo/a *supposed to be lost, lost on purpose*
perdido *scoundrel*

137 poblar *to populate* tr./intr.

INDICATIVE

Present	Imperfect	Perfect
pueblo	poblaba	he poblado
pueblas	poblabas	has poblado
puebla	poblaba	ha poblado
poblamos	poblábamos	hemos poblado
pobláis	poblabais	habéis poblado
pueblan	poblaban	han poblado
Future	**Pluperfect**	**Past Definite**
poblaré	había poblado	poblé
poblarás	habías poblado	poblaste
poblará	había poblado	pobló
poblaremos	habíamos poblado	poblamos
poblaréis	habíais poblado	poblasteis
poblarán	habían poblado	poblaron
Future Perfect	**Past Perfect**	
habré poblado	hube poblado	

CONDITIONAL	SUBJUNCTIVE	
Present	**Present**	**Imperfect**
poblaría	pueble	pobl-ara/ase
poblarías	puebles	pobl-aras/ases
poblaría	pueble	pobl-ara/ase
poblaríamos	poblemos	pobl-áramos/ásemos
poblaríais	pobléis	pobl-arais/aseis
poblarían	pueblen	pobl-aran/asen
Perfect	**Perfect**	**Pluperfect**
habría poblado	haya poblado	hub-iera/iese poblado

GERUND	PAST PARTICIPLE	IMPERATIVE
poblando	poblado	puebla, poblad pueble (Vd), pueblen (Vds)

Los ingleses poblaron Australia. *The English populated Australia.*
Vamos a poblar la colina de pinos. *We are going to plant pines on the hill.*
Pobló la colmena con abejas importadas. *He filled the hive with imported bees.*
Me gustaría conocer los peces que pueblan el fondo del mar. *I would like to study the fish that live at the bottom of the sea.*

El arbusto se ha poblado. *The bush has come into leaf.*
La acacia está poblada de flores. *The acacia has got a lot of flowers.*
Estas tribus se poblan mucho. *These tribes have many children.*
He poblado la sala de sillas. *I have put a lot of chairs in the room.*

población *population, town, village*
población activa *working population*
poblachón *dump*
poblada *crowd, riot*
poblado/a *inhabited*
poblador *settler*
pueblo *village*
pueblecito *little village*

poder *to be able to, can* tr./intr. 138

INDICATIVE

Present	**Imperfect**	**Perfect**
puedo	podía	he podido
puedes	podías	has podido
puede	podía	ha podido
podemos	podíamos	hemos podido
podéis	podíais	habéis podido
pueden	podían	han podido
Future	**Pluperfect**	**Past Definite**
podré	había podido	pude
podrás	habías podido	pudiste
podrá	había podido	pudo
podremos	habíamos podido	pudimos
podréis	habíais podido	pudisteis
podrán	habían podido	pudieron
Future Perfect	**Past Perfect**	
habré podido	hube podido	

CONDITIONAL	SUBJUNCTIVE	
Present	**Present**	**Imperfect**
podría	pueda	pud-iera/iese
podrías	puedas	pud-ieras/ieses
podría	pueda	pud-iera/iese
podríamos	podamos	pud-iéramos/iésemos
podríais	podáis	pud-ierais/ieseis
podrían	puedan	pud-ieran/iesen
Perfect	**Perfect**	**Pluperfect**
habría podido	haya podido	hub-iera/iese podido

GERUND	PAST PARTICIPLE	IMPERATIVE
pudiendo	podido	puede, poded pueda (Vd), puedan (Vds)

¿Puedes venir un momento? *Can you come for a moment?*
Puede que esté en Burgos. *She may be in Burgos.*
No podemos ir a Pamplona. *We can't go to Pamplona.*
No se puede comer. *It is not fit for human consumption.*

¿Se puede? *May I come in?*
Por lo que pudiera pasar. *Because of what may happen.*
No puedo con él. *I can't deal with him any more.*
¡No puedo más! *I've had enough!*
a más no poder *for all it's worth/to the limit/as much as possible*

poder *power, strength, law*
plenos poderes *full powers*
poderío *power*
poderoso/a *powerful*
poderosamente *powerfully*

139 podrir *to rot* tr.

INDICATIVE

Present	**Imperfect**	**Perfect**
pudro	podría	he podrido
pudres	podrías	has podrido
pudre	podría	ha podrido
podrimos	podríamos	hemos podrido
podrís	podríais	habéis podrido
pudren	podrían	han podrido
Future	**Pluperfect**	**Past Definite**
podriré	había podrido	podrí
podrirás	habías podrido	podriste
podrirá	había podrido	pudrió
podriremos	habíamos podrido	podrimos
podriréis	habíais podrido	podristeis
podrirán	habían podrido	pudrieron
Future Perfect	**Past Perfect**	
habré podrido	hube podrido	

CONDITIONAL	SUBJUNCTIVE	
Present	**Present**	**Imperfect**
podriría	pudra	pudr-iera/iese
podrirías	pudras	pudr-ieras/ieses
podriría	pudra	pudr-iera/iese
podriríamos	pudramos	pudr-iéramos/iésemos
podriríais	pudráis	pudr-ierais/ieseis
podrirían	pudran	pudr-ieran/iesen
Perfect	**Perfect**	**Pluperfect**
habría podrido	haya podrido	hub-iera/iese podrido

GERUND	PAST PARTICIPLE	IMPERATIVE
pudriendo	podrido	pudre, podrid pudra (Vd), pudran (Vds)

Se han podrido las manzanas. *The apples have gone rotten.*
Está podrido por dentro. *It's rotten inside.*
'Algo está podrido en Dinamarca.' *'Something is rotten in the state of Denmark.'*
¡Qué se pudra! *Let him rot!*

Están podridos de dinero. *They are stinking rich.*
Te vas a podrir de aburrimiento. *You'll die of boredom.*
Y mientras se pudría en el exilio. *Meanwhile he was languishing in exile.*
Lleva podrido dos años. *He has been dead and buried for two years.*

podrido/a *rotten*
podredumbre *pus, rot, decay*
pudrición *rotting, rottenness*
pudrición seca *dry rot*
pudrimiento *rotting, rot, rottenness*

poner *to put, place* tr. 140

INDICATIVE

Present	Imperfect	Perfect
pongo	ponía	he puesto
pones	ponías	has puesto
pone	ponía	ha puesto
ponemos	poníamos	hemos puesto
ponéis	poníais	habéis puesto
ponen	ponían	han puesto
Future	**Pluperfect**	**Past Definite**
pondré	había puesto	puse
pondrás	habías puesto	pusiste
pondrá	había puesto	puso
pondremos	habíamos puesto	pusimos
pondréis	habíais puesto	pusisteis
pondrán	habían puesto	pusieron
Future Perfect	**Past Perfect**	
habré puesto	hube puesto	

CONDITIONAL	SUBJUNCTIVE	
Present	**Present**	**Imperfect**
pondría	ponga	pus-iera/iese
pondrías	pongas	pus-ieras/ieses
pondría	ponga	pus-iera/iese
pondríamos	pongamos	pus-iéramos/iésemos
pondríais	pongáis	pus-ierais/ieseis
pondrían	pongan	pus-ieran/iesen
Perfect	**Perfect**	**Pluperfect**
habría puesto	haya puesto	hub-iera/iese puesto

GERUND	PAST PARTICIPLE	IMPERATIVE
poniendo	puesto	pon, poned ponga (Vd), pongan (Vds)

Quiero poner la silla ahí. *I want to put the chair there.*
Elvira se ha puesto pantalones. *Elvira is wearing trousers.*
Pedro está poniendo la mesa. *Pedro is laying the table.*
Frank puso la radio más alta. *Frank turned the radio up.*

Pon un ejemplo. *Quote an example.*
Al bebé le han puesto Javier. *They have called the baby Javier.*
Le he puesto verde. *I have told him off.*
Elena se ha puesto roja. *Elena has gone red.*
Leonor se puso seria. *Leonor became serious.*
¡Paqui, no te pongas así! *Please Paqui, don't be like that!*
La gallina ha puesto un huevo. *The hen has laid an egg.*

ponedero *nesting box*
puesta de sol *sunset*
poner en escena *staging (theatre)*
poner en marcha *launching*

141 preferir *to prefer* tr.

INDICATIVE

Present	Imperfect	Perfect
prefiero	prefería	he preferido
prefieres	preferías	has preferido
prefiere	prefería	ha preferido
preferimos	preferíamos	hemos preferido
preferís	preferíais	habéis preferido
prefieren	preferían	han preferido

Future	Pluperfect	Past Definite
preferiré	había preferido	preferí
preferirás	habías preferido	preferiste
preferirá	había preferido	prefirió
preferiremos	habíamos preferido	preferimos
preferiréis	habíais preferido	preferisteis
preferirán	habían preferido	prefirieron

Future Perfect	Past Perfect
habré preferido	hube preferido

CONDITIONAL	SUBJUNCTIVE	
Present	**Present**	**Imperfect**
preferiría	prefiera	prefir-iera/iese
preferirías	prefieras	prefir-ieras/ieses
preferiría	prefiera	prefir-iera/iese
preferiríamos	prefiramos	prefir-iéramos/iésemos
preferiríais	prefiráis	prefir-ierais/ieseis
preferirían	prefieran	prefir-ieran/iesen
Perfect	**Perfect**	**Pluperfect**
habría preferido	haya preferido	hub-iera/iese preferido

GERUND	PAST PARTICIPLE	IMPERATIVE
prefiriendo	preferido	prefiere, preferid prefiera (Vd), prefieran (Vds)

¿Cuál prefieres? *Which one do you prefer?*
Prefiero el azul. *I prefer the blue one.*
Preferiría ir a casa. *I would rather go home.*
Han preferido ir en taxi. *They have preferred to go by taxi.*

¿Qué prefieres? *What will you have?*
localidad de preferencia *seat in a reserved section*
Muestro preferencia por José. *I am biased in favour of José.*
Paqui y Luis viajan en clase preferente. *Paqui and Luis travel club class.*

preferencia *preference*
preferencia con *preferably*
preferencial *preferential*
preferente *preferential, preferred*
preferible *preferable*
preferentemente *preferably, preferentially*
preferido/a *favourite*
acción preferida *preferred share*
preferiblemente *preferably*

probar *to prove, try (on), taste* tr./intr.

INDICATIVE

Present	Imperfect	Perfect
pruebo	probaba	he probado
pruebas	probabas	has probado
prueba	probaba	ha probado
probamos	probábamos	hemos probado
probáis	probabais	habéis probado
prueban	probaban	han probado

Future	Pluperfect	Past Definite
probaré	había probado	probé
probarás	habías probado	probaste
probará	había probado	probó
probaremos	habíamos probado	probamos
probaréis	habíais probado	probasteis
probarán	habían probado	probaron

Future Perfect	Past Perfect
habré probado	hube probado

CONDITIONAL	SUBJUNCTIVE	
Present	**Present**	**Imperfect**
probaría	pruebe	prob-ara/ase
probarías	pruebes	prob-aras/ases
probaría	pruebe	prob-ara/ase
probaríamos	probemos	prob-áramos/ásemos
probaríais	probéis	prob-arais/aseis
probarían	prueben	prob-aran/asen
Perfect	**Perfect**	**Pluperfect**
habría probado	haya probado	hub-iera/iese probado

GERUND	PAST PARTICIPLE	IMPERATIVE
probando	probado	prueba, probad pruebe (Vd), prueben (Vds)

Prueba el postre, está buenísimo. *Try the dessert, it's very good.*
Está probado que la tierra es redonda. *It has been proved that the earth is round.*
¿Puedo probarme la falda? *Can I try the skirt on?*
No puede probar la máquina. *He can't test the machine.*

¿Probamos? *Shall we try?*
No me prueba bien el café. *Coffee doesn't agree with me.*
Mark no lo prueba nunca. *Mark never touches it.*
No me prueba el verde. *Green doesn't suit me.*

probador *fitting room*
probador(a) *taster (wine, tea)*
probado/a *tasted, proven*
probanza *proof, evidence*
probatorio *convincing*
probeta *test tube*
prueba *proof*

143 quebrar *to break, smash* tr./intr.

INDICATIVE

Present	Imperfect	Perfect
quiebro	quebraba	he quebrado
quiebras	quebrabas	has quebrado
quiebra	quebraba	ha quebrado
quebramos	quebrábamos	hemos quebrado
quebráis	quebrabais	habéis quebrado
quiebran	quebraban	han quebrado
Future	**Pluperfect**	**Past Definite**
quebraré	había quebrado	quebré
quebrarás	habías quebrado	quebraste
quebrará	había quebrado	quebró
quebraremos	habíamos quebrado	quebramos
quebraréis	habíais quebrado	quebrasteis
quebrarán	habían quebrado	quebraron
Future Perfect	**Past Perfect**	
habré quebrado	hube quebrado	

CONDITIONAL	SUBJUNCTIVE	
Present	**Present**	**Imperfect**
quebraría	quiebre	quebr-ara/ase
quebrarías	quiebres	quebr-aras/ases
quebraría	quiebre	quebr-ara/ase
quebraríamos	quebremos	quebr-áramos/ásemos
quebraríais	quebréis	quebr-arais/aseis
quebrarían	quiebren	quebr-aran/asen
Perfect	**Perfect**	**Pluperfect**
habría quebrado	haya quebrado	hub-iera/iese quebrado

GERUND	PAST PARTICIPLE	IMPERATIVE
quebrando	quebrado	quiebra, quebrad quiebre (Vd), quiebren (Vds)

Se ha quebrado un hueso. *He has broken a bone.*
No quiebres el estante. *Don't break the shelf.*
Quebramos la bici. *We broke the bike.*
La compañía ha quebrado. *The company has gone bankrupt.*

Carmen ha quebrado con Pepe. *Carmen has broken up with Pepe.*
Quiebra ese azul. *Make that blue softer.*
Está empezando a quebrar. *She is getting wrinkles.*
No tiene quiebra. *It can't go wrong.*

quiebra *break, loss, bankruptcy*
quebrazón *crushing*
quebrada *gorge, gap, pass*
quebrado *fraction (maths)*
quebradero de cabeza *headache, worry*
quebradizo/a *brittle, fragile*
quebrado/a *rough, bankrupt*
quebrado/a de color *pale*

querer *to like, want* tr. 144

INDICATIVE

Present	Imperfect	Perfect
quiero	quería	he querido
quieres	querías	has querido
quiere	quería	ha querido
queremos	queríamos	hemos querido
queréis	queríais	habéis querido
quieren	querían	han querido
Future	**Pluperfect**	**Past Definite**
querré	había querido	quise
querrás	habías querido	quisiste
querrá	había querido	quiso
querremos	habíamos querido	quisimos
querréis	habíais querido	quisisteis
querrán	habían querido	quisieron
Future Perfect	**Past Perfect**	
habré querido	hube querido	

CONDITIONAL	SUBJUNCTIVE	
Present	**Present**	**Imperfect**
querría	quiera	quis-iera/iese
querrías	quieras	quis-ieras/ieses
querría	quiera	quis-iera/iese
querríamos	queramos	quis-iéramos/iésemos
querríais	queráis	quis-ierais/ieseis
querrían	quieran	quis-ieran/iesen
Perfect	**Perfect**	**Pluperfect**
habría querido	haya querido	hub-iera/iese querido

GERUND	PAST PARTICIPLE	IMPERATIVE
queriendo	querido	quiere, quered quiera (Vd), quieran (Vds)

Te quiero mucho. *I love you a lot.*
¿Quieres pan? *Do you want some bread?*
Ven cuando quieras. *Come whenever you want.*
¿Cuánto quieres por el coche? *How much do you want for the car?*

Lo hizo queriendo. *He did it deliberately.*
Lo hice sin querer. *I didn't mean to do it.*
¿Qué más quieres? *What else do you want?*
Querer es poder. *Where there's a will there's a way.*

No quiero. *I will not.*
querido/a *loved, beloved, lover*
queridongo *lover (pejorative)*
Quiero decir . . . *I mean . . .*
querencia *lair, haunt, favourite spot*
querendón *affectionate, spoiled child, favourite pet*

145 recomendar *to recommend* tr.

INDICATIVE

Present	**Imperfect**	**Perfect**
recomiendo	recomendaba	he recomendado
recomiendas	recomendabas	has recomendado
recomienda	recomendaba	ha recomendado
recomendamos	recomendábamos	hemos recomendado
recomendáis	recomendabais	habéis recomendado
recomiendan	recomendaban	han recomendado
Future	**Pluperfect**	**Past Definite**
recomendaré	había recomendado	recomendé
recomendarás	habías recomendado	recomendaste
recomendará	había recomendado	recomendó
recomendaremos	habíamos recomendado	recomendamos
recomendaréis	habíais recomendado	recomendasteis
recomendarán	habían recomendado	recomendaron
Future Perfect	**Past Perfect**	
habré recomendado	hube recomendado	

CONDITIONAL	SUBJUNCTIVE	
Present	**Present**	**Imperfect**
recomendaría	recomiende	recomend-ara/ase
recomendarías	recomiendes	recomend-aras/ases
recomendaría	recomiende	recomend-ara/ase
recomendaríamos	recomendemos	recomend-áramos/ásemos
recomendaríais	recomendéis	recomend-arais/aseis
recomendarían	recomienden	recomend-aran/asen
Perfect	**Perfect**	**Pluperfect**
habría recomendado	haya recomendado	hub-iera/iese recomendado

GERUND	PAST PARTICIPLE	IMPERATIVE
recomendando	recomendado	recomienda, recomendad recomiende (Vd), recomienden (Vds)

Te recomiendo el helado de mango. *I can recommend the mango ice-cream.*
Nos recomendaron a su hijo. *They entrusted their son to us.*
¿Me recomiendas un dentista? *Can you recommend a dentist?*

Tiene muchas recomendaciones. *He is strongly recommended to us.*
Es poco recomendable. *It is inadvisable.*
Necesito una carta de recomendación. *I need an introductory letter.*

recomendable *recommendable*
recomendación *recommendation, suggestion*
recomendado/a *registered*
recomendatorio/a *recommendatory*
recomendablemente *commendably*
recomendante *recommending; recommender, endorser*

recordar *to remind, remember* tr./intr. 146

INDICATIVE

Present	Imperfect	Perfect
recuerdo	recordaba	he recordado
recuerdas	recordabas	has recordado
recuerda	recordaba	ha recordado
recordamos	recordábamos	hemos recordado
recordáis	recordabais	habéis recordado
recuerdan	recordaban	han recordado
Future	**Pluperfect**	**Past Definite**
recordaré	había recordado	recordé
recordarás	habías recordado	recordaste
recordará	había recordado	recordó
recordaremos	habíamos recordado	recordamos
recordaréis	habíais recordado	recordasteis
recordarán	habían recordado	recordaron
Future Perfect	**Past Perfect**	
habré recordado	hube recordado	

CONDITIONAL	SUBJUNCTIVE	
Present	**Present**	**Imperfect**
recordaría	recuerde	record-ara/ase
recordarías	recuerdes	record-aras/ases
recordaría	recuerde	record-ara/ase
recordaríamos	recordemos	record-áramos/ásemos
recordaríais	recordéis	record-arais/aseis
recordarían	recuerden	record-aran/asen
Perfect	**Perfect**	**Pluperfect**
habría recordado	haya recordado	hub-iera/iese recordado

GERUND	PAST PARTICIPLE	IMPERATIVE
recordando	recordado	recuerda, recordad recuerde (Vd), recuerden (Vds)

Eduardo te recordará siempre. *Eduardo will always remember you.*
No lo recuerdo. *I don't remember it.*
Esto me recuerda a Quevedo. *This reminds me of Quevedo.*
Recuérdale que me debe £20. *Remind him that he owes me £20.*

Que yo recuerde . . . *As far as I can remember . . .*
Si mal no recuerdo . . . *If my memory serves me right . . .*
Creo recordar . . . *I seem to remember . . .*
Da recuerdos a Elvira. *Give my regards to Elvira.*

récord *record*
en un tiempo récord *in record time*
batir el récord *to break a record*
recordable *memorable*
recordación *recollection*
digno de recordar *memorable*
recordativo *reminiscent*
recuerdo *memory, memento, souvenir, regards*

147 **referir** *to refer, relate* tr.

INDICATIVE

Present	Imperfect	Perfect
refiero	refería	he referido
refieres	referías	has referido
refiere	refería	ha referido
referimos	referíamos	hemos referido
referís	referíais	habéis referido
refieren	referían	han referido
Future	**Pluperfect**	**Past Definite**
referiré	había referido	referí
referirás	habías referido	referiste
referirá	había referido	refirió
referiremos	habíamos referido	referimos
referiréis	habíais referido	referisteis
referirán	habían referido	refirieron
Future Perfect	**Past Perfect**	
habré referido	hube referido	

CONDITIONAL	SUBJUNCTIVE	
Present	**Present**	**Imperfect**
referiría	refiera	refir-iera/iese
referirías	refieras	refir-ieras/ieses
referiría	refiera	refir-iera/iese
referiríamos	refiramos	refir-iéramos/iésemos
referiríais	refiráis	refir-ierais/ieseis
referirían	refieran	refir-ieran/iesen
Perfect	**Perfect**	**Pluperfect**
habría referido	haya referido	hub-iera/iese referido

GERUND	PAST PARTICIPLE	IMPERATIVE
refiriendo	referido	refiere, referid refiera (Vd), refieran (Vds)

Me estaba refiriendo a Goya. *I was referring to Goya.*
Te voy a referir la historia. *I'm going to tell you the story.*
Han referido la obra a Cervantes. *They have referred the work to Cervantes.*
¿Te refieres a Leonor de Castilla? *Are you referring to Leonor of Castille?*

Por lo que se refiere a eso . . . *As for that . . .*
En lo que se refiere a su trabajo . . . *As far as his work is concerned . . .*
Esto hace referencia a Hamlet. *This alludes to Hamlet.*
Con referencia a . . . *With reference to . . .*

referencia *reference, allusion*
referéndum *referendum*
referente *referring, relating*
referido/a *related, said, above mentioned*
referí *referee, umpire*
referible *referable*
referencia múltiple *general cross reference*

reforzar *to reinforce, strengthen* tr. 148

INDICATIVE

Present	Imperfect	Perfect
refuerzo	reforzaba	he reforzado
refuerzas	reforzabas	has reforzado
refuerza	reforzaba	ha reforzado
reforzamos	reforzábamos	hemos reforzado
reforzáis	reforzabais	habéis reforzado
refuerzan	refozaban	han reforzado
Future	**Pluperfect**	**Past Definite**
reforzaré	había reforzado	reforcé
reforzarás	habías reforzado	reforzaste
reforzará	había reforzado	reforzó
reforzaremos	habíamos reforzado	reforzamos
reforzaréis	habíais reforzado	reforzasteis
reforzarán	habían reforzado	reforzaron
Future Perfect	**Past Perfect**	
habré reforzado	hube reforzado	

CONDITIONAL	SUBJUNCTIVE	
Present	**Present**	**Imperfect**
reforzaría	refuerce	reforz-ara/ase
reforzarías	refuerces	reforz-aras/ases
reforzaría	refuerce	reforz-ara/ase
reforzaríamos	reforcemos	reforz-áramos/ásemos
reforzaríais	reforcéis	reforz-arais/aseis
reforzarían	refuercen	reforz-aran/asen
Perfect	**Perfect**	**Pluperfect**
habría reforzado	haya reforzado	hub-iera/iese reforzado

GERUND	PAST PARTICIPLE	IMPERATIVE
reforzando	reforzado	refuerza, reforzad refuerce (Vd), refuercen (Vds)

Tengo que reforzar la mesa. *I have to reinforce the table.*
¿Has reforzado la guarnición del libro? *Have you reinforced the book-binding?*
No refuerces el nudo. *Don't reinforce the knot.*
Reforzaron las paredes. *They reinforced the walls.*

¡Pon un refuerzo! *Reinforce it!*
Está reforzado. *It has been reinforced.*
una cerradura reforzada *strengthened lock*
un sonido reforzado *magnified sound*
Está reforzado con hombres. *It is manned.*

reforzador *booster, intensifier*
refuerzo *strengthening, reinforcement, aid*
refuerzos *reinforcements*
reforzado/a *reinforced, tape (to strengthen books, clothes)*
reforzamiento *reinforcement, strengthening*

149 regar *to water, irrigate* tr.

INDICATIVE

Present	Imperfect	Perfect
riego	regaba	he regado
riegas	regabas	has regado
riega	regaba	ha regado
regamos	regábamos	hemos regado
regáis	regabais	habéis regado
riegan	regaban	han regado
Future	**Pluperfect**	**Past Definite**
regaré	había regado	regué
regarás	habías regado	regaste
regará	había regado	regó
regaremos	habíamos regado	regamos
regaréis	habíais regado	regasteis
regarán	habían regado	regaron
Future Perfect	**Past Perfect**	
habré regado	hube regado	

CONDITIONAL	SUBJUNCTIVE	
Present	**Present**	**Imperfect**
regaría	riegue	reg-ara/ase
regarías	riegues	reg-aras/ases
regaría	riegue	reg-ara/ase
regaríamos	reguemos	reg-áramos/ásemos
regaríais	reguéis	reg-arais/aseis
regarían	rieguen	reg-aran/asen
Perfect	**Perfect**	**Pluperfect**
habría regado	haya regado	hub-iera/iese regado

GERUND	PAST PARTICIPLE	IMPERATIVE
regando	regado	riega, regad riegue (Vd), rieguen (Vds)

Riego las plantas con una regadera. *I water the plants with a watering can.*
Peter está regando con la goma. *Peter is watering with the hose.*
Angela no regó los geranios. *Angela didn't water the geraniums.*
¿Has regado las lechugas? *Have you watered the lettuces?*

Angel riega el plato con vino. *Angel has wine with his meal.*
Cele iba regando monedas. *Cele was dropping coins all over the place.*
Nos está regando. *She is having us on.*
Se me han regado los papeles. *I have scattered all my papers.*
Está como una regadera. *She is as mad as a hatter.*

regata *irrigation channel; boat race*
riego *watering, irrigation*
riego por aspersión *watering by spray*
regadura *irrigation*
regador(a) *waterer, irrigator, water sprinkler*
regadío *irrigable, irrigated land*

reír *to laugh* tr./intr. 150

INDICATIVE

Present	**Imperfect**	**Perfect**
río	reía	he reído
ríes	reías	has reído
ríe	reía	ha reído
reímos	reíamos	hemos reído
reís	reíais	habéis reído
ríen	reían	han reído
Future	**Pluperfect**	**Past Definite**
reiré	había reído	reí
reirás	habías reído	reíste
reirá	había reído	rió
reiremos	habíamos reído	reímos
reiréis	habíais reído	reísteis
reirán	habían reído	rieron
Future Perfect	**Past Perfect**	
habré reído	hube reído	

CONDITIONAL	SUBJUNCTIVE	
Present	**Present**	**Imperfect**
reiría	ría	ri-era/ese
reirías	rías	ri-eras/eses
reiría	ría	ri-era/ese
reiríamos	riamos	ri-éramos/ésemos
reiríais	riáis	ri-erais/eseis
reirían	rían	ri-eran/esen
Perfect	**Perfect**	**Pluperfect**
habría reído	haya reído	hub-iera/iese reído

GERUND	PAST PARTICIPLE	IMPERATIVE
riendo	reído	ríe, reíd ría (Vd), rían (Vds)

Nos reímos mucho con Juan. *We laugh a lot with Juan.*
Se ríe mucho de Juan. *He laughs a lot at Juan.*
Pedro nos hace reír siempre. *Pedro always makes us laugh.*
Le ríen los ojos. *His eyes sparkle.*

Fue para reírse. *It was utterly absurd.*
Mi jersey se ríe por los codos. *My jumper is coming apart at the elbows.*
Al freír será el reír. *You'll get your come-uppance.*
¡No es cosa de risa! *It is not a laughing matter!*
Se lo toma a risa. *She takes it as a joke.*

risa *laughter*
risueño/a *smiling*
soltar la risa *to burst out laughing*
risible *risible, ludicrous*
risibilidad *risibility*
risiblemente *laughably*
risica/risita/risilla *giggle*
risotada *guffaw, boisterous laughter*

151 remendar *to mend* tr.

INDICATIVE

Present	Imperfect	Perfect
remiendo	remendaba	he remendado
remiendas	remendabas	has remendado
remienda	remendaba	ha remendado
remendamos	remendábamos	hemos remendado
remendáis	remendabais	habéis remendado
remiendan	remendaban	han remendado
Future	**Pluperfect**	**Past Definite**
remendaré	había remendado	remendé
remendarás	habías remendado	remendaste
remendará	había remendado	remendó
remendaremos	habíamos remendado	remendamos
remendaréis	habíais remendado	remendasteis
remendarán	habían remendado	remendaron
Future Perfect	**Past Perfect**	
habré remendado	hube remendado	

CONDITIONAL	SUBJUNCTIVE	
Present	**Present**	**Imperfect**
remendaría	remiende	remend-ara/ase
remendarías	remiendes	remend-aras/ases
remendaría	remiende	remend-ara/ase
remendaríamos	remendemos	remend-áramos/ásemos
remendaríais	remendéis	remend-arais/aseis
remendarían	remienden	remend-aran/asen
Perfect	**Perfect**	**Pluperfect**
habría remendado	haya remendado	hub-iera/iese remendado

GERUND	PAST PARTICIPLE	IMPERATIVE
remendando	remendado	remienda, remendad remiende (Vd), remienden (Vds)

Peter va a remendar la silla. *Peter is going to mend the chair.*
¿Has remendada la camisa? *Have you mended the shirt?*
Mi abuela remienda calcetines. *My grandmother darns socks.*
Tengo que remendar los errores. *I have to correct the mistakes.*

Lleva un traje muy remendado. *He's wearing a worn-out suit.*
Pili tiene la piel remendada. *Pili has got patchy skin.*
a remiendos *in bits, piecemeal*
Leonor echa un remiendo an los pantalones. *Leonor puts a patch on the trousers.*

remendón *cobbler*
zapatero remendón *shoe repairer*
remendado/a *mended*
remendista *mender*
remiendo *patch, darn; mending, patching*

renegar *to tell off, deny* tr./intr. 152

INDICATIVE

Present	Imperfect	Perfect
reniego	renegaba	he renegado
reniegas	renegabas	has renegado
reniega	renegaba	ha renegado
renegamos	renegábamos	hemos renegado
renegáis	renegabais	habéis renegado
reniegan	renegaban	han renegado
Future	**Pluperfect**	**Past Definite**
renegaré	había renegado	renegué
renegarás	habías renegado	renegaste
renegará	había renegado	renegó
renegaremos	habíamos renegado	renegamos
renegaréis	habíais renegado	renegasteis
renegarán	habían renegado	renegaron
Future Perfect	**Past Perfect**	
habré renegado	hube renegado	

CONDITIONAL	SUBJUNCTIVE	
Present	**Present**	**Imperfect**
renegaría	reniegue	reneg-ara/ase
renegarías	reniegues	reneg-aras/ases
renegaría	reniegue	reneg-ara/ase
renegaríamos	reneguemos	reneg-áramos/ásemos
renegaríais	reneguéis	reneg-arais/aseis
renegarían	renieguen	reneg-aran/asen
Perfect	**Perfect**	**Pluperfect**
habría renegado	haya renegado	hub-iera/iese renegado

GERUND	PAST PARTICIPLE	IMPERATIVE
renegando	renegado	reniega, renegad reniegue (Vd), renieguen (Vds)

Mi madre me renegaba a menudo. *My mother used to tell me off a lot.*
Pedro reniega haberlo dicho. *Pedro vigorously denies having said that.*
Renegó de la religión cristiana y se hizo mahometano. *He abandoned Christianity and became a Moslem.*
Lo niega y reniega. *She denies it categorically.*

Sara reniega del profesorado. *Sara detests the teachers.*
Reniego de tí. *I want nothing more to do with you.*
Bob renegó de su propio hijo. *Bob disowned his own son.*
Renegaremos de su amistad. *We shall break completely with him.*

renegado/a *renegade, cantankerous*
renegón/renegona *grumbling, grouchy, cantankerous*
reniego *curse, grumble, complaint, blasphemy*
renegador(a) *swearing, swearer, blasphemer*
renegado/a *renegade*

153 reñir *to quarrel, scold* tr./intr.

INDICATIVE

Present	Imperfect	Perfect
riño	reñía	he reñido
riñes	reñías	has reñido
riñe	reñía	ha reñido
reñimos	reñíamos	hemos reñido
reñís	reñíais	habéis reñido
riñen	reñían	han reñido
Future	**Pluperfect**	**Past Definite**
reñiré	había reñido	reñí
reñirás	habías reñido	reñiste
reñirá	había reñido	riñó
reñiremos	habíamos reñido	reñimos
reñiréis	habíais reñido	reñisteis
reñirán	habían reñido	riñeron
Future Perfect	**Past Perfect**	
habré reñido	hube reñido	

CONDITIONAL	SUBJUNCTIVE	
Present	**Present**	**Imperfect**
reñiría	riña	riñ-era/ese
reñirías	riñas	riñ-eras/eses
reñiría	riña	riñ-era/ese
reñiríamos	riñamos	riñ-éramos/ésemos
reñiríais	riñáis	riñ-erais/eseis
reñirían	riñan	riñ-eran/esen
Perfect	**Perfect**	**Pluperfect**
habría reñido	haya reñido	hub-iera/iese reñido

GERUND	PAST PARTICIPLE	IMPERATIVE
riñendo	reñido	riñe, riñid riña (Vd), riñan (Vds)

Elena riñe a los niños. *Elena scolds the children.*
No me riñas. *Don't tell me off.*
¿Has reñido a Daniel? *Have you told Daniel off?*
Le reñiré por romperlo. *I shall reprimand him for breaking it.*

Marta ha reñido con Pedro. *Marta has fallen out with Pedro.*
Se pasan le vida riñendo. *They are always quarrelling.*
Riñeron por cuestión de dinero. *They quarrelled over money.*
en lo más reñido de la batalla *in the thick of the battle*

reñidamente *bitterly, hard, stubbornly*
reñidero de gallos *cockpit*
reñidor(a) *quarrelsome*
riña *quarrel, argument, fight, brawl, scuffle*
regañar *to tell off, nag*

repetir *to repeat* tr./intr. 154

INDICATIVE

Present	Imperfect	Perfect
repito	repetía	he repetido
repites	repetías	has repetido
repite	repetía	ha repetido
repetimos	repetíamos	hemos repetido
repetís	repetíais	habéis repetido
repiten	repetían	han repetido
Future	**Pluperfect**	**Past Definite**
repetiré	había repetido	repetí
repetirás	habías repetido	repetiste
repetirá	había repetido	repitió
repetiremos	habíamos repetido	repetimos
repetiréis	habíais repetido	repetisteis
repetirán	habían repetido	repitieron
Future Perfect	**Past Perfect**	
habré repetido	hube repetido	

CONDITIONAL	SUBJUNCTIVE	
Present	**Present**	**Imperfect**
repetiría	repita	repit-iera/iese
repetirías	repitas	repit-ieras/ieses
repitiría	repita	repit-iera/iese
repetiríamos	repitamos	repit-iéramos/iésemos
repetiríais	repitáis	repit-ierais/ieseis
repetirían	repitan	repit-ieran/iesen
Perfect	**Perfect**	**Pluperfect**
habría repetido	haya repetido	hub-iera/iese repetido

GERUND	PAST PARTICIPLE	IMPERATIVE
repitiendo	repetido	repite, repetid repita (Vd), repitan (Vds)

¿Quieres repetir la explicación, por favor? *Can you repeat the explanation, please?*
Repiten que es imposible. *They repeat that it is impossible.*
La paella está muy buena, voy a repetir. *The paella is very good, I am going to have a second helping.*
Lo repitieron muchas veces. *They repeated it over and over again.*

La audiencia pidió que repitieran. *The audience asked for an encore.*
No lo volveré a repetir. *I shall not say it again.*
Los niños repiten lo que hacen los mayores. *Children imitate adults.*
¡Ojalá no se repita eso! *I hope this will not happen again!*

repetición *repetition, recurrence*
fusil de repetición *repeater rifle*
repetidamente *repeatedly*
repetido/a *repeated*
repetidas veces *many times, over and over again*
repetidor *booster, repeater*

155 requerir *to require, need* tr.

INDICATIVE

Present	**Imperfect**	**Perfect**
requiero	requería	he requerido
requieres	requerías	has requerido
requiere	requería	ha requerido
requerimos	requeríamos	hemos requerido
requerís	requeríais	habéis requerido
requieren	requerían	han requerido
Future	**Pluperfect**	**Past Definite**
requeriré	había requerido	requerí
requerirás	habías requerido	requeriste
requerirá	había requerido	requirió
requeriremos	habíamos requerido	requerimos
requeriréis	habíais requerido	requeristeis
requerirán	habían requerido	requirieron
Future Perfect	**Past Perfect**	
habré requerido	hube requerido	

CONDITIONAL	SUBJUNCTIVE	
Present	**Present**	**Imperfect**
requeriría	requiera	requir-iera/iese
requierirías	requieras	requir-ieras/ieses
requeriría	requiera	requir-iera/iese
requeriríamos	requiramos	requir-iéramos/iésemos
requeriríais	requiráis	requir-ierais/ieseis
requerirían	requieran	requir-ieran/iesen
Perfect	**Perfect**	**Pluperfect**
habría requerido	haya requerido	hub-iera/iese requerido

GERUND	PAST PARTICIPLE	IMPERATIVE
requiriendo	requerido	requiere, requerid requiera (Vd), requieran (Vds)

Requiere pericia y experiencia. *It requires skill and experience.*
Esto requiere mucho cuidado. *This requires a lot of care.*
El trabajo requería atención. *The job needed attention.*
¿Requerirás las gafas? *Will you need your glasses?*
Elvira requiere tiempo para eso. *Elvira needs time for that.*

Calixto requiere de amores a Melibea. *Calixto woos Melibea.*
Se requiere experiencia para el trabajo. *Experience is required for the job.*
El Tribunal lo requiere. *The Tribunal demands it.*

requerimiento *request, demand, summons, notification*
requeriente *one who requires/demands*
requisito *requirement*
requiriente *petitioner, process-server*
requisa *levy*
requerimiento de pago *demand for payment*
requerimiento al pago *request for payment*

retemblar *to shake, tremble* intr. **156**

INDICATIVE

Present
retiemblo
retiemblas
retiembla
retemblamos
retembláis
retiemblan

Imperfect
retemblaba
retemblabas
retemblaba
retemblábamos
retemblabais
retemblaban

Perfect
he retemblado
has retemblado
ha retemblado
hemos retemblado
habéis retemblado
han retemblado

Future
retemblaré
retemblarás
retemblará
retemblaremos
retemblaréis
retemblarán

Pluperfect
había retemblado
habías retemblado
había retemblado
habíamos retemblado
habíais retemblado
habían retemblado

Past Definite
retemblé
retemblaste
retembló
retemblamos
retemblasteis
retemblaron

Future Perfect
habré retemblado

Past Perfect
hube retemblado

CONDITIONAL

Present
retemblaría
retemblarías
retemblaría
retemblaríamos
retemblaríais
retemblarían

Perfect
habría retemblado

SUBJUNCTIVE

Present
retiemble
retiembles
retiemble
retemblemos
retembléis
retiemblen

Imperfect
retembl-ara/ase
retembl-aras/ases
retembl-ara/ase
retembl-áramos/ásemos
retembl-arais/aseis
retembl-aran/asen

Perfect
haya retemblado

Pluperfect
hub-iera/iese retemblado

GERUND

retemblando

PAST PARTICIPLE

retemblado

IMPERATIVE

retiembla, retemblad
retiemble (Vd), retiemblen (Vds)

Con el ruido retiemblan las paredas. *The walls shake with the noise.*
Retembló todo el piso. *The whole of the floor trembled.*
Los truenos nos hacían retemblar. *The thunder made us shudder.*
La habitación retiembla cuando pasa un coche por la calle. *The room shakes whenever a car goes by.*
Retiemblo de miedo. *I shake with fear.*
Con ese golpe van a retemblar los muebles. *The furniture will shake with that blow.*
Retemblaron al verle. *They shuddered when they saw him.*
La casa retiembla cuando pasa el tren. *The house shakes every time a train goes by.*
La casa retembló con la explosión. *The house shook with the explosion.*

157 reventar *to burst, explode* tr./intr.

INDICATIVE

Present	**Imperfect**	**Perfect**
reviento	reventaba	he reventado
revientas	reventabas	has reventado
revienta	reventaba	ha reventado
reventamos	reventábamos	hemos reventado
reventáis	reventabais	habéis reventado
revientan	reventaban	han reventado
Future	**Pluperfect**	**Past Definite**
reventaré	había reventado	reventé
reventarás	habías reventado	reventaste
reventará	había reventado	reventó
reventaremos	habíamos reventado	reventamos
reventaréis	habíais reventado	reventasteis
reventarán	habían reventado	reventaron
Future Perfect	**Past Perfect**	
habré reventado	hube reventado	

CONDITIONAL	SUBJUNCTIVE	
Present	**Present**	**Imperfect**
reventaría	reviente	revent-ara/ase
reventarías	revientes	reven-aras/tases
reventaría	reviente	revent-ara/ase
reventaríamos	reventemos	revent-áramos/ásemos
reventaríais	reventéis	revent-arais/aseis
reventarían	revienten	revent-aran/asen
Perfect	**Perfect**	**Pluperfect**
habría reventado	haya reventado	hub-iera/iese reventado

GERUND	PAST PARTICIPLE	IMPERATIVE
reventando	reventado	revienta, reventad reviente (Vd), revienten (Vds)

Reviento de indignación. *I am bursting with indignation.*
Se ha reventado el globo. *The balloon has burst.*
Casi reventé de ira. *I almost exploded with anger.*
Reventamos de risa. *We burst out laughing.*

Tengo una cubierta reventada. *I've got a flat tyre.*
Me revienta hacer eso. *I hate doing that.*
dar un reventón *to peg out (die)*
Les revienta de aburrimiento. *It bores them to tears.*
Reviento por un chocolate. *I crave for a chocolate.*
Elvira está que revienta. *Elvira is full to bursting.*

reventador(a) *noise, disrupter*
reventón *burst, explosion*
reventadero *rough ground, tough job*
reventazón *bursting, explosion, flatulence*

rodar *to roll* tr./intr. 158

INDICATIVE

Present	Imperfect	Perfect
ruedo	rodaba	he rodado
ruedas	rodabas	has rodado
rueda	rodaba	ha rodado
rodamos	rodábamos	hemos rodado
rodáis	rodabais	habéis rodado
ruedan	rodaban	han rodado
Future	**Pluperfect**	**Past Definite**
rodaré	había rodado	rodé
rodarás	habías rodado	rodaste
rodará	había rodado	rodó
rodaremos	habíamos rodado	rodamos
rodaréis	habíais rodado	rodasteis
rodarán	habían rodado	rodaron
Future Perfect	**Past Perfect**	
habré rodado	hube rodado	

CONDITIONAL	SUBJUNCTIVE	
Present	**Present**	**Imperfect**
rodaría	ruede	rod-ara/ase
rodarías	ruedes	rod-aras/ases
rodaría	ruede	rod-ara/ase
rodaríamos	rodemos	rod-áramos/ásemos
rodaríais	rodéis	rod-arais/aseis
rodarían	rueden	rod-aran/asen
Perfect	**Perfect**	**Pluperfect**
habría rodado	haya rodado	hub-iera/iese rodado

GERUND	PAST PARTICIPLE	IMPERATIVE
rodando	rodado	rueda, rodad ruede (Vd), rueden (Vds)

¡Rueda la pelota! *Roll the ball!*
El coche rodó cuesta abajo. *The car rolled downhill.*
El motor lleva rodando toda la mañana. *The engine has been running all morning.*
Va a rodar una película. *She is going to shoot a film.*

Ha rodado medio mundo. *She has travelled over half the world.*
Le quiere rodar a patadas. *He wants to knock him over.*
Lo he echado todo a rodar. *I have spoiled everything.*
Va rodando de aquí para allá. *He drifts from place to place.*

rodada *wheel track, route*
rodadero *cliff, precipice*
rodado/a *on wheels*
rodaja *slice, small wheel, small disc*
ruedo *turn, bullring, arena*
rueda *wheel*
rueda de atrás *rear wheel*
rueda de recambio *spare wheel*
rueda de prensa *press conference*

159 rogar *to beg, ask for* tr.

INDICATIVE

Present	Imperfect	Perfect
ruego	rogaba	he rogado
ruegas	rogabas	has rogado
ruega	rogaba	ha rogado
rogamos	rogábamos	hemos rogado
rogáis	rogabais	habéis rogado
ruegan	rogaban	han rogado
Future	**Pluperfect**	**Past Definite**
rogaré	había rogado	rogué
rogarás	habías rogado	rogaste
rogará	había rogado	rogó
rogaremos	habíamos rogado	rogamos
rogaréis	habíais rogado	rogasteis
rogarán	habían rogado	rogaron
Future Perfect	**Past Perfect**	
habré rogado	hube rogado	

CONDITIONAL	SUBJUNCTIVE	
Present	**Present**	**Imperfect**
rogaría	ruegue	rog-ara/ase
rogarías	ruegues	rog-aras/ases
rogaría	ruegue	rog-ara/ase
rogaríamos	roguemos	rog-áramos/ásemos
rogaríais	roguéis	rog-arais/aseis
rogarían	rueguen	rog-aran/asen
Perfect	**Perfect**	**Pluperfect**
habría rogado	haya rogado	hub-iera/iese rogado

GERUND	PAST PARTICIPLE	IMPERATIVE
rogando	rogado	ruega, rogad ruegue (Vd), rueguen (Vds)

Por favor, te lo ruego. *Please, I beg of you.*
Les rogué que lo hicieran. *I begged them to do it.*
Te ruego que lo hagas. *I ask you to do it.*
Se lo he rogado muchas veces. *I have pleaded with him many a time.*

¡Ruegos y preguntas! *Any other business!*
Se ruega no fumar. *Please do not smoke.*
No se hace de rogar. *You do not have to ask him twice.*

rogación *request, pleading*
rogaciones *rogations*
rogatoria *request, pleading*
ruego *request, plead, entreaty*
a ruego de . . . *at the request of . . .*
rogador/rogadora/rogante *pleader*

saber *to know, know how to* tr./intr. 160

INDICATIVE

Present	Imperfect	Perfect
sé	sabía	he sabido
sabes	sabías	has sabido
sabe	sabía	ha sabido
sabemos	sabíamos	hemos sabido
sabéis	sabíais	habéis sabido
saben	sabían	han sabido
Future	**Pluperfect**	**Past Definite**
sabré	había sabido	supe
sabrás	habías sabido	supiste
sabrá	había sabido	supo
sabremos	habíamos sabido	supimos
sabréis	habíais sabido	supisteis
sabrán	habían sabido	supieron
Future Perfect	**Past Perfect**	
habré sabido	hube sabido	

CONDITIONAL	SUBJUNCTIVE	
Present	**Present**	**Imperfect**
sabría	sepa	sup-iera/iese
sabrías	sepas	sup-ieras/ieses
sabría	sepa	sup-iera/iese
sabríamos	sepamos	sup-iéramos/iésemos
sabríais	sepáis	sup-ierais/ieseis
sabrían	sepan	sup-ieran/iesen
Perfect	**Perfect**	**Pluperfect**
habría sabido	haya sabido	hub-iera/iese sabido

GERUND	PAST PARTICIPLE	IMPERATIVE
sabiendo	sabido	sabe, sabed sepa (Vd), sepan (Vds)

¿Sabes dónde está Sara? *Do you know where Sara is?*
No, no sé. *No, I don't know.*
Yo sí sé, está en la biblioteca. *I do, she's in the library.*
¿Sabes nadar? *Can you swim?*

No sé nada de él. *I haven't heard from him for years.*
Te hago saber . . . *Let me inform you . . .*
¡Yo qué sé! *How should I know!*
Que yo sepa . . . *As far as I know . . .*
Esto sabe a vainilla. *This tastes of vanilla.*

sabedor(a) *one that knows about*
sabelotodo *know-all*
sabio *expert, learned, sensible, wise*
sabihondo/a *self-proclaimed expert*
sabiduría *wisdom*
a sabiendas *in the know, knowing*

161 salir *to go out, leave* intr.

INDICATIVE

Present	**Imperfect**	**Perfect**
salgo	salía	he salido
sales	salías	has salido
sale	salía	ha salido
salimos	salíamos	hemos salido
salís	salíais	habéis salido
salen	salían	han salido
Future	**Pluperfect**	**Past Definite**
saldré	había salido	salí
saldrás	habías salido	saliste
saldrá	había salido	salió
saldremos	habíamos salido	salimos
saldréis	habíais salido	salisteis
saldrán	habían salido	salieron
Future Perfect	**Past Perfect**	
habré salido	hube salido	

CONDITIONAL	SUBJUNCTIVE	
Present	**Present**	**Imperfect**
saldría	salga	sal-iera/iese
saldrías	salgas	sal-ieras/ieses
saldría	salga	sal-iera/iese
saldríamos	salgamos	sal-iéramos/iésemos
saldríais	salgáis	sal-ierais/ieseis
saldrían	salgan	sal-ieran/iesen
Perfect	**Perfect**	**Pluperfect**
habría salido	haya salido	hub-iera/iese salido

GERUND	PAST PARTICIPLE	IMPERATIVE
saliendo	salido	sal, salid salga (Vd), salgan (Vds)

¿Salimos esta noche? *Shall we go out tonight?*
Saldremos el domingo por la mañana. *We'll leave on Sunday morning.*
La sidra sale de las manzanas. *Cider comes from apples.*
Salen juntos desde hace dos años. *They have been going out together for two years.*

¿De dónde has salido? *Where did you spring from?*
Salimos del apuro. *We managed to get out of the jam.*
Cele y Oliva salieron adelante. *Cele and Oliva did well.*
Su respuesta fue una salida de tono. *His answer was inappropriate.*

salida *exit*
salida de tono *unfortunate intervention*
salida de artistas *stage door*
salida de urgencias *emergency exit*
salidero/a *way out, exit*
salido/a *gone, projecting, protuberant; in heat*
saliente *projecting, prominent*

segar *to mow, cut* tr./intr. 162

INDICATIVE

Present	Imperfect	Perfect
siego	segaba	he segado
siegas	segabas	has segado
siega	segaba	ha segado
segamos	segábamos	hemos segado
segáis	segabais	habéis segado
siegan	segaban	han segado
Future	**Pluperfect**	**Past Definite**
segaré	había segado	segué
segarás	habías segado	segaste
segará	había segado	segó
segaremos	habíamos segado	segamos
segaréis	habíais segado	segasteis
segarán	habían segado	segaron
Future Perfect	**Past Perfect**	
habré segado	hube segado	

CONDITIONAL	SUBJUNCTIVE	
Present	**Present**	**Imperfect**
segaría	siegue	seg-ara/ase
segarías	siegues	seg-aras/ases
segaría	siegue	seg-ara/ase
segaríamos	seguemos	seg-áramos/ásemos
segaríais	seguéis	seg-arais/aseis
segarían	sieguen	seg-aran/asen
Perfect	**Perfect**	**Pluperfect**
habría segado	haya segado	hub-iera/iese segado

GERUND	PAST PARTICIPLE	IMPERATIVE
segando	segado	siega, segad siegue (Vd), sieguen (Vds)

Siegan el césped los lunes. *They mow the lawn on Mondays.*
Van a segar el trigo. *They are going to harvest the corn.*
¿Lo segarás mañana? *Will you mow it tomorrow?*
¡No pienso segarlo más! *I shall not cut it again!*

En el 'Cantar de Roldán' se siegan muchas cabezas. *In the 'Song of Roland' many people get killed.*
El accidente le segó la juventud. *The accident cut him off in his prime.*
Ha segado mis esperanzas. *She has ruined my hopes.*

segable *ready to cut*
segadera *sickle*
segador(a) *mower, harvester, reaper*
segadora *mower*
segadora de césped *lawnmower*
segadora-trilladora (cosechadora) *combine harvester*
siega *harvesting, reaping, mowing*

163 sembrar *to sow* tr.

INDICATIVE

Present	Imperfect	Perfect
siembro	sembraba	he sembrado
siembras	sembrabas	has sembrado
siembra	sembraba	ha sembrado
sembramos	sembrábamos	hemos sembrado
sembráis	sembrabais	habéis sembrado
siembran	sembraban	han sembrado
Future	**Pluperfect**	**Past Definite**
sembraré	había sembrado	sembré
sembrarás	habías sembrado	sembraste
sembrará	había sembrado	sembró
sembraremos	habíamos sembrado	sembramos
sembraréis	habíais sembrado	sembrasteis
sembrarán	habían sembrado	sembraron
Future Perfect	**Past Perfect**	
habré sembrado	hube sembrado	

CONDITIONAL	SUBJUNCTIVE	
Present	**Present**	**Imperfect**
sembraría	siembre	sembr-ara/ase
sembrarías	siembres	sembr-aras/ases
sembraría	siembre	sembr-ara/ase
sembraríamos	sembremos	sembr-áramos/ásemos
sembraríais	sembréis	sembr-arais/aseis
sembrarían	siembren	sembr-aran/asen
Perfect	**Perfect**	**Pluperfect**
habría sembrado	haya sembrado	hub-iera/iese sembrado

GERUND	PAST PARTICIPLE	IMPERATIVE
sembrando	sembrado	siembra, sembrad siembre (Vd), siembren (Vds)

Voy a sembrar lechuga. *I am going to plant some lettuce.*
¿Estás sembrando patatas? *Are you sowing potatoes?*
Siembran todo en la primavera. *They sow everything in spring.*
Sembraremos flores y verduras juntas. *We'll sow flowers and vegetables together.*

La idea es sembrar un estrecho de minas. *The idea is to lay mines in a line.*
El que siembra recoge. *One reaps what one has sown.*
Estas semillas son para sembrar en primavera. *These seeds are to be sown in spring.*
Es un sembrador de ideas. *He is an idea-monger.*

sembrar a voleo *to scatter seeds*
sembradera *seed drill*
sembrado *sown field*
sembrío *sown field*
sembrador(a) *sower*
sembradura *sowing*
siembra *sowing time, sowing*

sentarse *to sit down* r. 164

INDICATIVE

Present	Imperfect	Perfect
me siento	me sentaba	me he sentado
te sientas	te sentabas	te has sentado
se sienta	se sentaba	se ha sentado
nos sentamos	nos sentábamos	nos hemos sentado
os sentáis	os sentabais	os habéis sentado
se sientan	se sentaban	se han sentado
Future	**Pluperfect**	**Past Definite**
me sentaré	me había sentado	me senté
te sentarás	te habías sentado	te sentaste
se sentará	se había sentado	se sentó
nos sentaremos	nos habíamos sentado	nos sentamos
os sentaréis	os habíais sentado	os sentasteis
se sentarán	se habían sentado	se sentaron
Future Perfect	**Past Perfect**	
me habré sentado	me hube sentado	

CONDITIONAL	SUBJUNCTIVE	
Present	**Present**	**Imperfect**
me sentaría	me siente	me sent-ara/ase
te sentarías	te sientes	te sent-aras/ases
se sentaría	se siente	se sent-ara/ase
nos sentaríamos	nos sentemos	nos sent-áramos/ásemos
os sentaríais	os sentéis	os sent-arais/aseis
se sentarían	se sienten	se sent-aran/asen
Perfect	**Perfect**	**Pluperfect**
me habría sentado	me haya sentado	me hub-iera/iese sentado

GERUND	PAST PARTICIPLE	IMPERATIVE
sentándose	sentado	siéntate, sentáos siéntese (Vd), siéntense (Vds)

Luis Antonio se sentó a comer. *Luis Antonio sat down to eat.*
Paqui y yo nos sentamos al fuego. *Paqui and I sit by the fire.*
¡Peter, sentémonos aquí! *Peter, let's sit here!*
¡Siéntese usted! *Please, do sit down!*

El sol me sienta bien. *The sun agrees with me.*
Lo damos por sentado. *We take it for granted.*
No me sientan bien los pimientos. *Peppers don't agree with me.*
Ese corte de pelo te sienta mal. *That haircut doesn't suit you.*
Lucidio va a sentar el último ladrillo. *Lucidio is going to tap the last brick into place.*
esperar sentado *wait for ages*
de una sentada *at one sitting*

asiento *seat*
sentadero/a *seat*
sentado/a *seated*
sentador(a) *smart, elegant*

165 sentir *to feel, regret* tr./intr.

INDICATIVE

Present	**Imperfect**	**Perfect**
siento	sentía	he sentido
sientes	sentías	has sentido
siente	sentía	ha sentido
sentimos	sentíamos	hemos sentido
sentís	sentíais	habéis sentido
sienten	sentían	han sentido
Future	**Pluperfect**	**Past Definite**
sentiré	había sentido	sentí
sentirás	habías sentido	sentiste
sentirá	había sentido	sintió
sentiremos	habíamos sentido	sentimos
sentiréis	habíais sentido	sentisteis
sentirán	habían sentido	sintieron
Future Perfect	**Past Perfect**	
habré sentido	hube sentido	

CONDITIONAL	SUBJUNCTIVE	
Present	**Present**	**Imperfect**
sentiría	sienta	sint-iera/iese
sentirías	sientas	sint-ieras/ieses
sentiría	sienta	sint-iera/iese
sentiríamos	sintamos	sint-iéramos/iésemos
sentiríais	sintáis	sint-ierais/ieseis
sentirían	sientan	sint-ieran/iesen
Perfect	**Perfect**	**Pluperfect**
habría sentido	haya sentido	hub-iera/iese sentido

GERUND	PAST PARTICIPLE	IMPERATIVE
sintiendo	sentido	siente, sentid sienta (Vd), sientan (Vds)

Siento ganas de comer. *I feel like eating.*
Siente un dolor en el pecho. *He feels a pain in his chest.*
No sentíamos el frío. *We didn't feel the cold.*
Sentiré no haberlo hecho antes. *I shall regret not having done it before.*

Estaba que ni oía ni sentía. *I was in such a state that I could neither feel nor hear.*
El tiempo pasó sin sentir. *Time went by very quickly.*
Me siento como en mi casa. *I feel at home here.*
Ana me da que sentir. *Ana gives me cause for regret.*

sentimientos *feelings, emotions*
sensiblero/a *sentimental*
aventura sentimental *love affair*
lo siento *I am sorry*
sentimental *sentimental, emotional*
sentimentalismo *sentimentalism, sentimentality*
sentimentalmente *sentimentally*
sensible *sensitive*

ser *to be* intr. (aux.) **166**

INDICATIVE

Present	Imperfect	Perfect
soy	era	he sido
eres	eras	has sido
es	era	ha sido
somos	éramos	hemos sido
sois	erais	habéis sido
son	eran	han sido
Future	**Pluperfect**	**Past Definite**
seré	había sido	fui
serás	habías sido	fuiste
será	había sido	fue
seremos	habíamos sido	fuimos
seréis	habíais sido	fuisteis
serán	habían sido	fueron
Future Perfect	**Past Perfect**	
habré sido	hube sido	

CONDITIONAL	SUBJUNCTIVE	
Present	**Present**	**Imperfect**
sería	sea	fu-era/ese
serías	seas	fu-eras/eses
sería	sea	fu-era/ese
seríamos	seamos	fu-éramos/ésemos
seríais	seáis	fu-erais/eseis
serían	sean	fu-eran/esen
Perfect	**Perfect**	**Pluperfect**
habría sido	haya sido	hub-iera/iese sido

GERUND	PAST PARTICIPLE	IMPERATIVE
siendo	sido	se, sed sea (Vd), sean (Vds)

Soy María. *I am María.*
Es mi hermano Miguel Angel. *This is my brother, Miguel Angel.*
¿Eres española? *Are you Spanish?*
Sí, soy española, soy de Burgos. *Yes, I am, I'm from Burgos.*

Mi padre es granjero. *My father is a farmer.*
¿Quién es? *Who is he?*
Es Rodrigo y es mi secretario. *He's Rodrigo, and he is my secretary.*
Santiago es egoista y tonto. *Santiago is selfish and silly.*
Mi hermana es alta y morena. *My sister is dark and tall.*
Son las cuatro. *It is four o'clock.*

un ser *being, essence*
es decir *ie, that is to say*
los seres vivos *living things*
los seres queridos *loved ones*

167 servir *to serve* tr./intr.

INDICATIVE

Present	**Imperfect**	**Perfect**
sirvo	servía	he servido
sirves	servías	has servido
sirve	servía	ha servido
servimos	servíamos	hemos servido
servís	servíais	habéis servido
sirven	servían	han servido
Future	**Pluperfect**	**Past Definite**
serviré	había servido	serví
servirás	habías servido	serviste
servirá	había servido	sirvió
serviremos	habíamos servido	servimos
serviréis	habíais servido	servisteis
servirán	habían servido	sirvieron
Future Perfect	**Past Perfect**	
habré servido	hube servido	

CONDITIONAL	SUBJUNCTIVE	
Present	**Present**	**Imperfect**
serviría	sirva	sirv-iera/iese
servirías	sirvas	sirv-ieras/ieses
serviría	sirva	sirv-iera/iese
serviríamos	sirvamos	sirv-iéramos/iésemos
serviríais	sirváis	sirv-ierais/ieseis
servirían	sirvan	siev-ieran/iesen
Perfect	**Perfect**	**Pluperfect**
habría servido	haya servido	hub-iera/iese servido

GERUND	PAST PARTICIPLE	IMPERATIVE
sirviendo	servido	sirve, servid sirva (Vd), sirvan (Vds)

Sirvió diez años. *He served ten years.*
No piensa servir a la patria. *He will not serve his country.*
Las monjas sirven a Dios. *Nuns serve God.*
¿Nos servirá vino? *Will he serve us with wine?*

¿En qué puedo servirle? *How can I help you?*
¡Para servirle! *At your service!*
Simón no sirve para nada. *Simón is good for nothing.*
¿Ya le sirven señora? *Are you being served, madam?*

servicio *service*
servicio a domicilio *home delivery*
servicial *helpful, obliging*
servidor(a) *servant, employee*
servidumbre *servitude*
servicialmente *obligingly*
servible *usable, useful, serviceable*
serviciador *tax collector, toll collector*

situar *to put, situate, locate* tr. 168

INDICATIVE

Present	Imperfect	Perfect
sitúo	situaba	he situado
sitúas	situabas	has situado
sitúa	situaba	ha situado
situamos	situábamos	hemos situado
situáis	situabais	habéis situado
sitúan	situaban	han situado

Future	Pluperfect	Past Definite
situaré	había situado	situé
situarás	habías situado	situaste
situará	había situado	situó
situaremos	habíamos situado	situamos
situaréis	habíais situado	situasteis
situarán	habían situado	situaron

Future Perfect	Past Perfect	
habré situado	hube situado	

CONDITIONAL	SUBJUNCTIVE	
Present	**Present**	**Imperfect**
situaría	sitúe	situ-ara/ase
situarías	sitúes	situ-aras/ases
situaría	sitúe	situ-ara/ase
situaríamos	situemos	situ-áramos/ásemos
situaríais	situéis	situ-arais/aseis
situarían	sitúen	situ-aran/asen
Perfect	**Perfect**	**Pluperfect**
habría situado	haya situado	hub-iera/iese situado

GERUND	PAST PARTICIPLE	IMPERATIVE
situando	situado	sitúa, situad sitúe (Vd), sitúen (Vds)

Sitúan la obra en el siglo XVI. *They place the play in the 16th century.*
Han situado Troya en Turquía. *Troy has been placed in Turkey.*
Marcos situó fondos en el extranjero. *Marcos placed money in accounts abroad.*
Nos situaremos en frente de la tienda. *We'll place ourselves opposite the shop.*

Su enemistad me sitúa en una situación embarazosa. *Their quarrel places me in an uncomfortable situation.*
Situaré una pensión para mi sobrina. *I shall settle an income on my niece.*
Quieren crear una buena situación económica. *They wish to attain a position of financial security.*
Estoy en la posición de decir no. *I am in a position to say no.*

situación *situation*
sitio *place, location, siege*
situado/a *located, placed*
sito/a *situated, located, lying*
estar situado/a *to be well placed*

169 soler *to be in the habit of* intr.

INDICATIVE

Present
suelo
sueles
suele
solemos
soléis
suelen

Imperfect
solía
solías
solía
solíamos
solíais
solían

Perfect
he solido
has solido
ha solido
hemos solido
habéis solido
han solido

Future
(not used)

Pluperfect
había solido
habías solido
había solido
habíamos solido
habíais solido
habían solido

Past Definite
solí
soliste
solió
solimos
solisteis
solieron

Future Perfect
(not used)

Past Perfect
hube solido

CONDITIONAL

Present
(not used)

Perfect
(not used)

SUBJUNCTIVE

Present
suela
suelas
suela
solamos
soláis
suelan

Imperfect
sol-iera/iese
sol-ieras/ieses
sol-iera/iese
sol-iéramos/iésemos
sol-ierais/ieseis
sol-ieran/iesen

Perfect
haya solido

Pluperfect
hub-iera/iese solido

GERUND

soliendo

PAST PARTICIPLE

solido

IMPERATIVE

(not used)

Suele pasar por aquí. *He usually comes this way.*
Solíamos ir todos los años. *We used to go every year.*
No suelen beber cerveza. *They don't normally drink beer.*
¿Sueles venir tarde? *Do you normally get here late?*
¿Soléis venir los martes? *Do you normally come on Tuesdays?*

soltar *to loosen, undo, let go of* tr. 170

INDICATIVE

Present	Imperfect	Perfect
suelto	soltaba	he soltado
sueltas	soltabas	has soltado
suelta	soltaba	ha soltado
soltamos	soltábamos	hemos soltado
soltáis	soltabais	habéis soltado
sueltan	soltaban	han soltado
Future	**Pluperfect**	**Past Definite**
soltaré	había soltado	solté
soltarás	habías soltado	soltaste
soltará	había soltado	soltó
soltaremos	habíamos soltado	soltamos
soltaréis	habíais soltado	soltasteis
soltarán	habían soltado	soltaron
Future Perfect	**Past Perfect**	
habré soltado	hube soltado	

CONDITIONAL	SUBJUNCTIVE	
Present	**Present**	**Imperfect**
soltaría	suelte	solt-ara/ase
soltarías	sueltes	solt-aras/ases
soltaría	suelte	solt-ara/ase
soltaríamos	soltemos	solt-áramos/ásemos
soltaríais	soltéis	solt-arais/aseis
soltarían	suelten	solt-aran/asen
Perfect	**Perfect**	**Pluperfect**
habría soltado	haya soltado	hub-iera/iese soltado

GERUND	PAST PARTICIPLE	IMPERATIVE
soltando	soltado	suelta, soltad suelte (Vd), suelten (Vds)

No sueltes la cuerda. *Don't let go of the rope.*
David soltó el globo. *David let go of the balloon.*
Paqui soltó el nudo. *Paqui undid the knot.*
Soltaremos al pájaro la semana que viene. *We'll free the bird next week.*

Franco no suelta el puesto por nada. *Franco will not give up the job for anything.*
Se me soltó un grito. *I let out a yell.*
Me suelto con cada tontería . . . *I come out with such silly ideas . . .*
Se soltó de su gabardina vieja. *He eventually parted with his old raincoat.*
¡Suéltame! *Let go of me!*

soltura de vientre *diarrhoea*
soltero/a *single, unmarried*
apellido de soltera *maiden name*
soltura *looseness, slackness*
Habla árabe con soltura. *She speaks Arabic fluently.*

171 sonar *to ring, sound* tr./intr.

INDICATIVE

Present	Imperfect	Perfect
sueno	sonaba	he sonado
suenas	sonabas	has sonado
suena	sonaba	ha sonado
sonamos	sonábamos	hemos sonado
sonáis	sonabais	habéis sonado
suenan	sonaban	han sonado

Future	Pluperfect	Past Definite
sonaré	había sonado	soné
sonarás	habías sonado	sonaste
sonará	había sonado	sonó
sonaremos	habíamos sonado	sonamos
sonaréis	habíais sonado	sonasteis
sonarán	habían sonado	sonaron

Future Perfect	Past Perfect
habré sonado	hube sonado

CONDITIONAL / SUBJUNCTIVE

Present (Conditional)	Present (Subjunctive)	Imperfect (Subjunctive)
sonaría	suene	son-ara/ase
sonarías	suenes	son-aras/ases
sonaría	suene	son-ara/ase
sonaríamos	sonemos	son-áramos/ásemos
sonaríais	sonéis	son-arais/aseis
sonarían	suenen	son-aran/asen

Perfect (Conditional)	Perfect (Subjunctive)	Pluperfect (Subjunctive)
habría sonado	haya sonado	hub-iera/iese sonado

GERUND	PAST PARTICIPLE	IMPERATIVE
sonando	sonado	suena, sonad suene (Vd), suenen (Vds)

Sonaremos la alarma. *We'll ring the alarm.*
Han sonado las diez. *It has struck ten.*
Esta frase no me suena. *This sentence doesn't sound right to me.*
¡Suena las narices al niño! *Blow the child's nose!*

Me sonaban las tripas. *My tummy was rumbling.*
¿Te suena Rocinante? *Does Rocinante ring a bell with you?*
Angela las da sonadas. *Angela does sensational things.*
Suena a hueco. *It sounds hollow.*

sonado/a *famous, talked about, talked of*
sonaja *little bell, jingle stick*
sonajero *rattle*
sonarse *blow one's nose*
sonante *audible, resounding*
sonata *sonata*
contante y sonante *cash*

soñar *to dream* tr./intr.

INDICATIVE

Present	Imperfect	Perfect
sueño	soñaba	he soñado
sueñas	soñabas	has soñado
sueña	soñaba	ha soñado
soñamos	soñábamos	hemos soñado
soñáis	soñabais	habéis soñado
sueñan	soñaban	han soñado
Future	**Pluperfect**	**Past Definite**
soñaré	había soñado	soñé
soñarás	habías soñado	soñaste
soñará	había soñado	soñó
soñaremos	habíamos soñado	soñamos
soñaréis	habíais soñado	soñasteis
soñarán	habían soñado	soñaron
Future Perfect	**Past Perfect**	
habré soñado	hube soñado	

CONDITIONAL / SUBJUNCTIVE

Present	Present	Imperfect
soñaría	sueñe	soñ-ara/ase
soñarías	sueñes	soñ-aras/ases
soñaría	sueñe	soñ-ara/ase
soñaríamos	soñemos	soñ-áramos/ásemos
soñaríais	soñéis	soñ-arais/aseis
soñarían	sueñen	soñ-aran/asen
Perfect	**Perfect**	**Pluperfect**
habría soñado	haya soñado	hub-iera/iese soñado

GERUND	PAST PARTICIPLE	IMPERATIVE
soñando	soñado	sueña, soñad sueñe (Vd), sueñen (Vds)

Sueño todas las noches. *I dream every night.*
Anoche soñé con Daniel. *Last night I dreamt about Daniel.*
Soñaba con un Rolex. *She dreamed of one day having a Rolex.*
Soñaron lo mismo. *They had the same dream.*

Sueño con una paella. *I fancy a paella.*
Charo sueña despierta. *Charo daydreams.*
Elvira sueña en voz alta. *Elvira talks in her sleep.*
¡Ni lo sueñes! *Not on your life!*

sueño *dream*
la vida es sueño *life is a dream*
soñado/a *dream of, ideal*
soñador(a) *dreamer, dreamy, idealist, romantic*
soñolencia *somnolencia*
soñoliento/a *sleepy, drowsy, somnolent*
tener sueño *be sleepy*
echar un sueño *take a nap*

173 subir *to go up, rise, climb* tr./intr.

INDICATIVE

Present	Imperfect	Perfect
subo	subía	he subido
subes	subías	has subido
sube	subía	ha subido
subimos	subíamos	hemos subido
subís	subíais	habéis subido
suben	subían	han subido
Future	**Pluperfect**	**Past Definite**
subiré	había subido	subí
subirás	habías subido	subiste
subirá	había subido	subió
subiremos	habíamos subido	subimos
subiréis	habíais subido	subisteis
subirán	habían subido	subieron
Future Perfect	**Past Perfect**	
habré subido	hube subido	

CONDITIONAL	SUBJUNCTIVE	
Present	**Present**	**Imperfect**
subiría	suba	sub-iera/iese
subirías	subas	sub-ieras/ieses
subiría	suba	sub-iera/iese
subiríamos	subamos	sub-iéramos/iésemos
subiríais	subáis	sub-ierais/ieseis
subirían	suban	sub-ieran/iesen
Perfect	**Perfect**	**Pluperfect**
habría subido	haya subido	hub-iera/iese subido

GERUND	PAST PARTICIPLE	IMPERATIVE
subiendo	subido	sube, subid suba (Vd), suban (Vds)

Subimos las escaleras corriendo. *We ran upstairs.*
Subí hasta el último piso. *I went up to the top floor.*
Han subido los precios. *Prices have gone up.*
Me subiré a una escalera. *I'll climb a ladder.*

Se le ha subido el vino a la cabeza. *The wine has gone to his head.*
Pedro sube el tono cuando se enfada. *Pedro raises his voice when he gets angry.*
Es un jersey subido de precio. *It is a highly priced jumper.*
Es una de sus subidas de tono. *It's one of his suggestive remarks.*

subida *raise, ascent, going up, climbing*
subidero/a *rising, climbing, way up*
subidor *porter, raiser*
subiente *raising*
subimiento *rise, ascent, hoisting up*
subido/a *strong (smell), high (price), loud (noise), tall (plant)*

sugerir *to suggest, hint* tr. 174

INDICATIVE

Present	Imperfect	Perfect
sugiero	sugería	he sugerido
sugieres	sugerías	has sugerido
sugiere	sugería	ha sugerido
sugerimos	sugeríamos	hemos sugerido
sugerís	sugeríais	habéis sugerido
sugieren	sugerían	han sugerido
Future	**Pluperfect**	**Past Definite**
sugeriré	había sugerido	sugerí
sugerirás	habías sugerido	sugeriste
sugerirá	había sugerido	sugirió
sugeriremos	habíamos sugerido	sugerimos
sugeriréis	habíais sugerido	sugeristeis
sugerirán	habían sugerido	sugirieron
Future Perfect	**Past Perfect**	
habré sugerido	hube sugerido	

CONDITIONAL	SUBJUNCTIVE	
Present	**Present**	**Imperfect**
sugeriría	sugiera	sugir-iera/iese
sugerirías	sugieras	sugir-ieras/ieses
sugeriría	sugiera	sugir-iera/iese
sugeriríamos	sugiramos	sugir-iéramos/iésemos
sugeriríais	sugiráis	sugir-ierais/ieseis
sugerirían	sugieran	sugir-ieran/iesen
Perfect	**Perfect**	**Pluperfect**
habría sugerido	haya sugerido	hub-iera/iese sugerido

GERUND	PAST PARTICIPLE	IMPERATIVE
sugiriendo	sugerido	sugiere, sugerid sugiera (Vd), sugieran (Vds)

Te sugiero el verde. *I suggest the green one.*
El accidente me sugirió el tema del libro. *The accident gave me the idea for the book.*
Se lo sugerimos a Carlos. *We prompted Carlos to do it.*
Sugiero que lo hagas. *I suggest that you do it.*

las sugestiones del corazón *the prompting of the heart*
un lugar de muchas sugestiones *a place rich in associations*
Rodolfo tiene mucha sugestión. *Rodolfo has got a strong hypnotic power.*

sugerencia *suggestion*
sugerente *full of suggestions*
sugerible *suggestive*
sugestionable *suggestive, impressionable, easily influenced*
sugestión *suggestion, hint*
sugestión hipnótica *hypnotic suggestion*
sugeridor(a) *one that suggests, suggestive*
sugestivo/a *suggestive, expressive; interesting, alluring*

175 tapar *to cover, hide* tr.

INDICATIVE

Present	**Imperfect**	**Perfect**
tapo	tapaba	he tapado
tapas	tapabas	has tapado
tapa	tapaba	ha tapado
tapamos	tapábamos	hemos tapado
tapáis	tapabais	habéis tapado
tapan	tapaban	han tapado
Future	**Pluperfect**	**Past Definite**
taparé	había tapado	tapé
taparás	habías tapado	tapaste
tapará	había tapado	tapó
taparemos	habíamos tapado	tapamos
taparéis	habíais tapado	tapasteis
taparán	habían tapado	taparon
Future Perfect	**Past Perfect**	
habré tapado	hube tapado	

CONDITIONAL	SUBJUNCTIVE	
Present	**Present**	**Imperfect**
taparía	tape	tap-ara/ase
taparías	tapes	tap-aras/ases
taparía	tape	tap-ara/ase
taparíamos	tapemos	tap-áramos/ásemos
taparíais	tapéis	tap-arais/aseis
taparían	tapen	tap-aran/asen
Perfect	**Perfect**	**Pluperfect**
habría tapado	haya tapado	hub-iera/iese tapado

GERUND	PAST PARTICIPLE	IMPERATIVE
tapando	tapado	tapa, tapad tape (Vd), tapen (Vds)

Tapa la botella. *Put the top on the bottle.*
¿Has tapado la cazuela? *Have you put the lid on the pan?*
Guille es tímido y se tapa la cara. *Guille is shy and covers his face.*
La valla nos tapa el viento. *The fence protects us from the wind.*

¡Tápate la boca! *Shut your mouth!*
Habla por la tapa de la barriga. *He talks through his hat.*
Le levantó la tapa de los sesos. *He blew his brains out.*
No me tapes la luz. *Don't stand in my light.*

tapar ventanas *to board up windows*
tapa *lid, cap, top*
tapadera *lid*
tapón *plug*
tapia *wall, enclosure*
tapete *rug, table cloth, tapestry*
tapa de libro *book cover*
tapador(a) *covering*

temblar *to tremble, shake* intr. 176

INDICATIVE

Present	Imperfect	Perfect
tiemblo	temblaba	he temblado
tiemblas	temblabas	has temblado
tiembla	temblaba	ha temblado
temblamos	temblábamos	hemos temblado
tembláis	temblabais	habéis temblado
tiemblan	temblaban	han temblado
Future	**Pluperfect**	**Past Definite**
temblaré	había temblado	temblé
temblarás	habías temblado	temblaste
temblará	había temblado	tembló
temblaremos	habíamos temblado	temblamos
temblaréis	habíais temblado	temblasteis
temblarán	habían temblado	temblaron
Future Perfect	**Past Perfect**	
habré temblado	hube temblado	

CONDITIONAL	SUBJUNCTIVE	
Present	**Present**	**Imperfect**
temblaría	tiemble	tembl-ara/ase
temblarías	tiembles	tembl-aras/ases
temblaría	tiemble	tembl-ara/ase
temblaríamos	temblemos	tembl-áramos/ásemos
temblaríais	tembléis	tembl-arais/aseis
temblarían	tiemblen	tembl-aran/asen
Perfect	**Perfect**	**Pluperfect**
habría temblado	haya temblado	hub-iera/iese temblado

GERUND	PAST PARTICIPLE	IMPERATIVE
temblando	temblado	tiembla, temblad tiemble (Vd), tiemblen (Vds)

Los palestinos tiemblan por su vida. *The Palestinians tremble for their lives.*
Mafalda está temblando. *Mafalda is trembling.*
No hace más que temblar. *She can't stop trembling.*
Temblamos de emoción. *We trembled with emotion.*

Carlos tiembla como un azogado. *Carlos trembles like a leaf.*
Tiembla de frío. *She is shivering with cold.*
Dejamos la botella temblando. *We drank most of the bottle.*
Tiemblo ante la esena. *I shudder at the sight.*

tembladera *violent shaking*
temblante *trembling, shaking*
tembleque *shaking, doddering, unstable*
temblor de tierra *earthquake*
temblor *trembling*
tembloroso *trembling, shaking*
temblequera *fear, cowardice*
temblante *trembling, shaking; bangle, bracelet*

177 temer *to fear, dread* tr./intr.

INDICATIVE

Present	Imperfect	Perfect
temo	temía	he temido
temes	temías	has temido
teme	temía	ha temido
tememos	temíamos	hemos temido
teméis	temíais	habéis temido
temen	temían	han temido
Future	**Pluperfect**	**Past Definite**
temeré	había temido	temí
temerás	habías temido	temiste
temerá	había temido	temió
temeremos	habíamos temido	temimos
temeréis	habíais temido	temisteis
temerán	habían temido	temieron
Future Perfect	**Past Perfect**	
habré temido	hube temido	

CONDITIONAL	SUBJUNCTIVE	
Present	**Present**	**Imperfect**
temería	tema	tem-iera/iese
temerías	temas	tem-ieras/ieses
temería	tema	tem-iera/iese
temeríamos	temamos	tem-iéramos/iésemos
temeríais	temáis	tem-ierais/ieseis
temerían	teman	tem-ieran/iesen
Perfect	**Perfect**	**Pluperfect**
habría temido	haya temido	hub-iera/iese temido

GERUND	PAST PARTICIPLE	IMPERATIVE
temiendo	temido	teme, temed tema (Vd), teman (Vds)

Temen a los ladrones. *They are afraid of thieves.*
¿Temes a tu padre? *Are you afraid of your father?*
Teme que vaya a volver. *She is afraid he'll come back.*
No temas. *Don't be afraid.*

sin temor ni favor *without fear or favour*
sin temor a nada *fearless*
por temor al castigo *from fear of punishment*
por temor a su partido *from fear of his party*

temor *fear, dread, apprehension*
temible *frightening, to be feared*
temeroso/a *dreadful, fearful*
temerosamente *timorously, timidly*
temeridad *temerity, boldness, daring*
temerario *bold, imprudent*
temperariamente *rashly, foolhardily*
temoso *persistent*

tender *to spread out, lay* tr./intr. 178

INDICATIVE

Present	Imperfect	Perfect
tiendo	tendía	he tendido
tiendes	tendías	has tendido
tiende	tendía	ha tendido
tendemos	tendíamos	hemos tendido
tendéis	tendíais	habéis tendido
tienden	tendían	han tendido
Future	**Pluperfect**	**Past Definite**
tenderé	había tendido	tendí
tenderás	habías tendido	tendiste
tenderá	había tendido	tendió
tenderemos	habíamos tendido	tendimos
tenderéis	habíais tendido	tendisteis
tenderán	habían tendido	tendieron
Future Perfect	**Past Perfect**	
habré tendido	hube tendido	

CONDITIONAL	SUBJUNCTIVE	
Present	**Present**	**Imperfect**
tendería	tienda	tend-iera/iese
tenderías	tiendas	tend-ieras/ieses
tendería	tienda	tend-iera/iese
tenderíamos	tendamos	tend-iéramos/iésemos
tenderíais	tendáis	tend-ierais/ieseis
tenderían	tiendan	tend-ieran/iesen
Perfect	**Perfect**	**Pluperfect**
habría tendido	haya tendido	hub-iera/iese tendido

GERUND	PAST PARTICIPLE	IMPERATIVE
tendiendo	tendido	tiende, tended tienda (Vd), tiendan (Vds)

Tiende el mantel. *Spread out the tablecloth.*
Grego está tendiendo la ropa. *Grego is hanging the clothes out.*
Se va a tender en la cama. *He is going to lie on the bed.*
Las plantas tienden a la luz. *Plants turn towards the light.*

Lo tendió de un golpe. *He floored him with one blow.*
Susana tiende a exagerar. *Susana tends to exaggerate.*
El color tiende más al verde que al azul. *The colour seems to be more green than blue.*
Pablo tiende al pesimismo. *Pablo is prone to pessimism.*

tendido eléctrico *electric wiring*
tendal *jumble of things in disorder*
tendalera *scattered in disorder*
tendencia *tendency, trend, drift*
tienda *shop*
tendencioso/a *tendentious, slanted*
tendente *tending*
tendedor(a) *spreader*
tendiente *tending*
tendero(a) *shopkeeper*

179 tener *to have, possess* tr./intr.

INDICATIVE

Present	Imperfect	Perfect
tengo	tenía	he tenido
tienes	tenías	has tenido
tiene	tenía	ha tenido
tenemos	teníamos	hemos tenido
tenéis	teníais	habéis tenido
tienen	tenían	han tenido

Future	Pluperfect	Past Definite
tendré	había tenido	tuve
tendrás	habías tenido	tuviste
tendrá	había tenido	tuvo
tendremos	habíamos tenido	tuvimos
tendréis	habíais tenido	tuvisteis
tendrán	habían tenido	tuvieron

Future Perfect	Past Perfect
habré tenido	hube tenido

CONDITIONAL	SUBJUNCTIVE	
Present	**Present**	**Imperfect**
tendría	tenga	tuv-iera/iese
tendrías	tengas	tuv-ieras/ieses
tendría	tenga	tuv-iera/iese
tendríamos	tengamos	tuv-iéramos/iésemos
tendríais	tengáis	tuv-ierais/ieseis
tendrían	tengan	tuv-ieran/iesen
Perfect	**Perfect**	**Pluperfect**
habría tenido	haya tenido	hub-iera/iese tenido

GERUND	PAST PARTICIPLE	IMPERATIVE
teniendo	tenido	ten, tened tenga (Vd), tengan (Vds)

Miguel tiene un piso en Burgos. *Miguel owns a flat in Burgos.*
¿Tienes coche? *Have you got a car?*
No teníamos sitio. *We didn't have room.*
Tengo una reunión mañana. *I've got a meeting tomorrow.*

No las tiene todas consigo. *He is worried about it.*
¿Qué tienes? *What's the matter with you?*
Tenga la bondad de . . . *Be so kind as to . . .*
No tiene nada que ver contigo. *It's got nothing to do with you.*
Leonor tiene prisa. *Leonor is in a hurry.*

Tiene calor. *She's hot.*
Tenemos hambre. *We're hungry.*
Tienes sueño. *You're sleepy.*
Ten cuidado. *Be careful.*

tenencia *holding, tenancy*
tenedor *holder, fork*
teneduría *bookkeeping*
tenedor de acciones *shareholder*

tentar *to touch, try* tr. **180**

INDICATIVE

Present	**Imperfect**	**Perfect**
tiento	tentaba	he tentado
tientas	tentabas	has tentado
tienta	tentaba	ha tentado
tentamos	tentábamos	hemos tentado
tentáis	tentabais	habéis tentado
tientan	tentaban	han tentado
Future	**Pluperfect**	**Past Definite**
tentaré	había tentado	tenté
tentarás	habías tentado	tentaste
tentará	había tentado	tentó
tentaremos	habíamos tentado	tentamos
tentaréis	habíais tentado	tentasteis
tentarán	habían tentado	tentaron
Future Perfect	**Past Perfect**	
habré tentado	hube tentado	

CONDITIONAL	SUBJUNCTIVE	
Present	**Present**	**Imperfect**
tentaría	tiente	tent-ara/ase
tentarías	tientes	tent-aras/ases
tentaría	tiente	tent-ara/ase
tentaríamos	tentemos	tent-áramos/ásemos
tentaríais	tentéis	tent-arais/aseis
tentarían	tienten	tent-aran/asen
Perfect	**Perfect**	**Pluperfect**
habría tentado	haya tentado	hub-iera/iese tentado

GERUND	PAST PARTICIPLE	IMPERATIVE
tentando	tentado	tienta, tentad tiente (Vd), tienten (Vds)

No lo tientes. *Don't touch it.*
El ciego tentaba la pared. *The blind man was touching the wall.*
Hemos tentado todos los remedios. *We've tried all the remedies.*
No me tienta la idea. *The idea doesn't tempt me.*

No le tientes a fumar. *Don't encourage him to smoke.*
Me tienta un vino. *I fancy a glass of wine.*
Resistió la tentación. *She resisted the temptation.*
No tientes al diablo. *Don't look for trouble.*
El café es mi tentación. *I can't resist coffee.*

tentación *temptation*
tentáculo *tentacle, feeler*
tentador(a) *tempting, tempter, temptress, alluring*
tentativa de asesinato *attempted murder*
tentativa *attempt*
tentativo/a *tentative*

181 teñir *to dye, stain* tr.

INDICATIVE

Present	Imperfect	Perfect
tiño	teñía	he teñido
tiñes	teñías	has teñido
tiñe	teñía	ha teñido
teñimos	teñíamos	hemos teñido
teñís	teñíais	habéis teñido
tiñen	teñían	han teñido
Future	**Pluperfect**	**Past Definite**
teñiré	había teñido	teñí
teñirás	habías teñido	teñiste
teñirá	había teñido	tiñó
teñiremos	habíamos teñido	teñimos
teñiréis	habíais teñido	teñisteis
teñirán	habían teñido	tiñeron
Future Perfect	**Past Perfect**	
habré teñido	hube teñido	

CONDITIONAL	SUBJUNCTIVE	
Present	**Present**	**Imperfect**
teñiría	tiña	tiñ-era/ese
teñirías	tiñas	tiñ-eras/eses
teñiría	tiña	tiñ-era/ese
teñiríamos	tiñamos	tiñ-éramos/ésemos
teñiríais	tiñáis	tiñ-erais/eseis
teñirían	tiñan	tiñ-eran/esen
Perfect	**Perfect**	**Pluperfect**
habría teñido	haya teñido	hub-iera/iese teñido

GERUND	PAST PARTICIPLE	IMPERATIVE
tiñendo	teñido	tiñe, teñid tiña (Vd), tiñan (Vds)

He teñido la falda de azul. *I've dyed the skirt blue.*
La toalla ha teñido la camiseta. *The colour of the towel has come out on the T-shirt.*
¿Te tiñes el pelo? *Do you dye your hair?*
Tiñeron todo de color negro. *They dyed everything black.*

Pedro está teñido de amor. *Pedro is love-struck.*
Su pintura está teñida con melancholía. *His paintings have got melancholic tinges.*

teñible *dyeable*
teñido *dyeing, tinting, staining*
teñido/a *dyed, tinted, stained*
teñidura *dyeing, staining*
tintura *tincture, tinge, dye*
tiña *poverty, meanness*
tiñoso/a *scabby, niggardly*
tintorería *dry cleaner's*

tocar *to touch, play* tr./intr. **182**

INDICATIVE

Present	**Imperfect**	**Perfect**
toco	tocaba	he tocado
tocas	tocabas	has tocado
toca	tocaba	ha tocado
tocamos	tocábamos	hemos tocado
tocáis	tocabais	habéis tocado
tocan	tocaban	han tocado
Future	**Pluperfect**	**Past Definite**
tocaré	había tocado	toqué
tocarás	habías tocado	tocaste
tocará	había tocado	tocó
tocaremos	habíamos tocado	tocamos
tocaréis	habíais tocado	tocasteis
tocarán	habían tocado	tocaron
Future Perfect	**Past Perfect**	
habré tocado	hube tocado	

CONDITIONAL	SUBJUNCTIVE	
Present	**Present**	**Imperfect**
tocaría	toque	toc-ara/ase
tocarías	toques	toc-aras/ases
tocaría	toque	toc-ara/ase
tocaríamos	toquemos	toc-áramos/ásemos
tocaríais	toquéis	toc-arais/aseis
tocarían	toquen	toc-aran/asen
Perfect	**Perfect**	**Pluperfect**
habría tocado	haya tocado	hub-iera/iese tocado

GERUND	PAST PARTICIPLE	IMPERATIVE
tocando	tocado	toca, tocad toque (Vd), toquen (Vds)

Toco el piano. *I play the piano.*
Toca el timbre. *Press the bell.*
Te tocaba hablar a tí. *It was your turn to speak.*
Le tocó la lotería. *He won the lottery.*

Puedo tocar el fondo. *I can touch the bottom.*
Tocaremos a diana a las ocho. *We shall sound reveille at eight.*
Por lo que a mí me toca . . . *As far as I'm concerned . . .*
Está tocado. *He is crazy.*

toque *touch*
tocamiento *touching*
tocador *dressing table*
tocador(a) *player, performer*
toca *headdress*
tocado *hair-do; touched*
tocante *with regards to*
tocadiscos *record player*

183 tomar *to take, have* tr./intr.

INDICATIVE

Present	Imperfect	Perfect
tomo	tomaba	he tomado
tomas	tomabas	has tomado
toma	tomaba	ha tomado
tomamos	tomábamos	hemos tomado
tomáis	tomabais	habéis tomado
toman	tomaban	han tomado
Future	**Pluperfect**	**Past Definite**
tomaré	había tomado	tomé
tomarás	habías tomado	tomaste
tomará	había tomado	tomó
tomaremos	habíamos tomado	tomamos
tomaréis	habíais tomado	tomasteis
tomarán	habían tomado	tomaron
Future Perfect	**Past Perfect**	
habré tomado	hube tomado	

CONDITIONAL	SUBJUNCTIVE	
Present	**Present**	**Imperfect**
tomaría	tome	tom-ara/ase
tomarías	tomes	tom-aras/ases
tomaría	tome	tom-ara/ase
tomaríamos	tomemos	tom-áramos/ásemos
tomaríais	toméis	tom-arais/aseis
tomarían	tomen	tom-aran/asen
Perfect	**Perfect**	**Pluperfect**
habría tomado	haya tomado	hub-iera/iese tomado

GERUND	PAST PARTICIPLE	IMPERATIVE
tomando	tomado	toma, tomad tome (Vd), tomen (Vds)

Tomamos unos vinos. *We had a few glasses of wine.*
Tomé la primera calle a la derecha. *I took the first turning on the right.*
Nos tomaremos unas vacaciones en junio. *We'll take a holiday in June.*
Tomaron a Guille por un policía. *They took Guille to be a policeman.*

Más vale un toma que dos te daré. *A bird in the hand is worth two in the bush.*
Te toman por loco. *They think you are mad.*
La tiene tomada conmigo. *He keeps annoying me.*
¡Toma! *Fancy that!/Here you are!*

toma *taking*
toma de aire *air intake*
toma de corriente *power point*
tomada *taking, capture, seizure*
tomar el sol *to sunbathe*
Está tomado. *He is drunk.*
tomadero *handle, tap, outlet*
tomador(a) *taker, drinker*
tomadura de pelo *practical joke*

torcer *to twist, turn* tr./intr. 184

INDICATIVE

Present	Imperfect	Perfect
tuerzo	torcía	he torcido
tuerces	torcías	has torcido
tuerce	torcía	ha torcido
torcemos	torcíamos	hemos torcido
torcéis	torcíais	habéis torcido
tuercen	torcían	han torcido
Future	**Pluperfect**	**Past Definite**
torceré	había torcido	torcí
torcerás	habías torcido	torciste
torcerá	había torcido	torció
torceremos	habíamos torcido	torcimos
torceréis	habíais torcido	torcisteis
torcerán	habían torcido	torcieron
Future Perfect	**Past Perfect**	
habré torcido	hube torcido	

CONDITIONAL	SUBJUNCTIVE	
Present	**Present**	**Imperfect**
torcería	tuerza	torc-iera/iese
torcerías	tuerzas	torc-ieras/ieses
torcería	tuerza	torc-iera/iese
torceríamos	torzamos	torc-iéramos/iésemos
torceríais	torzáis	torc-ierais/ieseis
torcerían	tuerzan	torc-ieran/iesen
Perfect	**Perfect**	**Pluperfect**
habría torcido	haya torcido	hub-iera/iese torcido

GERUND	PAST PARTICIPLE	IMPERATIVE
torciendo	torcido	tuerce, torced tuerza (Vd), tuerzan (Vds)

El coche torció a la izquierda. *The car turned left.*
La cuerda está torcida. *The rope is twisted.*
Quiere torcer la madera. *He wants to bend the wood.*
Torcieron la barra de hierro. *They bent the iron bar.*

Anda torcida con su jefe. *She is on bad terms with her boss.*
Tom no da el brazo a torcer. *Tom is obstinate.*
Me he torcido el pie. *I have sprained my foot.*
Se ha torcido la leche. *The milk has gone sour.*

torcimiento *twisting, sprain*
torcidillo *thick silk thread*
torcedura *sprain*
torcida *wick*
torcido/a *twisted*
torcidamente *crooked*
retorcijón *sudden twist*
torcedero/a *twisted, crooked*

185 tostar *to toast, tan, roast* tr.

INDICATIVE

Present	Imperfect	Perfect
tuesto	tostaba	he tostado
tuestas	tostabas	has tostado
tuesta	tostaba	ha tostado
tostamos	tostábamos	hemos tostado
tostáis	tostabais	habéis tostado
tuestan	tostaban	han tostado
Future	**Pluperfect**	**Past Definite**
tostaré	había tostado	tosté
tostarás	habías tostado	tostaste
tostará	había tostado	tostó
tostaremos	habíamos tostado	tostamos
tostaréis	habíais tostado	tostasteis
tostarán	habían tostado	tostaron
Future Perfect	**Past Perfect**	
habré tostado	hube tostado	

CONDITIONAL	SUBJUNCTIVE	
Present	**Present**	**Imperfect**
tostaría	tueste	tost-ara/ase
tostarías	tuestes	tost-aras/ases
tostaría	tueste	tost-ara/ase
tostaríamos	tostemos	tost-áramos/ásemos
tostaríais	tostéis	tost-arais/aseis
tostarían	tuesten	tost-aran/asen
Perfect	**Perfect**	**Pluperfect**
habría tostado	haya tostado	hub-iera/iese tostado

GERUND	PAST PARTICIPLE	IMPERATIVE
tostando	tostado	tuesta, tostad tueste (Vd), tuesten (Vds)

Tuesta el pan. *Make some toast, please.*
Lo tostó demasiado. *He toasted it too much.*
Nos tostaremos al sol. *We'll get brown in the sun.*
¿Has tostado el café? *Have you roasted the coffee?*

Carlos nos dio el tostón. *Carlos was a bore.*
Le ha dado una tostada a Isabel. *He has cheated on Isabel.*
Fue una visita tostada. *It was a long, interminable visit.*
No van a ver la tostada. *They are not going to understand.*

tostada *piece of toast*
tostado/a *toasted, with a tan, brown*
tostador *toaster*
tostador eléctrico *electric toaster*
tostadero *roasting room*
tostón *crouton; roast suckling pig*
tostación *roasting*
tostadura *toasting, roasting*

trabajar *to work* tr./intr. 186

INDICATIVE

Present	Imperfect	Perfect
trabajo	trabajaba	he trabajado
trabajas	trabajabas	has trabajado
trabaja	trabajaba	ha trabajado
trabajamos	trabajábamos	hemos trabajado
trabajáis	trabajabais	habéis trabajado
trabajan	trabajaban	han trabajado
Future	**Pluperfect**	**Past Definite**
trabajaré	había trabajado	trabajé
trabajarás	habías trabajado	trabajaste
trabajará	había trabajado	trabajó
trabajaremos	habíamos trabajado	trabajamos
trabajaréis	habíais trabajado	trabajasteis
trabajarán	habían trabajado	trabajaron
Future Perfect	**Past Perfect**	
habré trabajado	hube trabajado	

CONDITIONAL	SUBJUNCTIVE	
Present	**Present**	**Imperfect**
trabajaría	trabaje	trabaj-ara/ase
trabajarías	trabajes	trabaj-aras/ases
trabajaría	trabaje	trabaj-ara/ase
trabajaríamos	trabajemos	trabaj-áramos/ásemos
trabajaríais	trabajéis	trabaj-arais/aseis
trabajarían	trabajen	trabaj-aran/asen
Perfect	**Perfect**	**Pluperfect**
habría trabajado	haya trabajado	hub-iera/iese trabajado

GERUND	PAST PARTICIPLE	IMPERATIVE
trabajando	trabajado	trabaja, trabajad trabaje (Vd), trabajen (Vds)

¿Dónde trabajas? *Where do you work?*
Trabajo en un banco. *I work in a bank.*
Trabajaron en un hospital. *They worked in a hospital.*
Trabajaré desde casa. *I'll work from home.*

Me cuesta trabajo entenderlo. *It is hard for me to understand it.*
Angela se tomó el trabajo de venir. *Angela took the trouble to come.*
Trabajo a tiempo parcial. *I work part time.*
Trabajo por horas. *I get paid by the hour.*

trabajo *work, labour*
trabajador(a) *worker, hard working*
trabajado *worked, worn out*
trabajadamente *laboriously, painfully*
trabajillo *slight work, slight trouble*
trabajos forzados *hard labour*
Los Trabajos de Hércules *The Labours of Hercules*

187 traducir *to translate* tr.

INDICATIVE

Present	Imperfect	Perfect
traduzco	traducía	he traducido
traduces	traducías	has traducido
traduce	traducía	ha traducido
traducimos	traducíamos	hemos traducido
traducís	traducíais	habéis traducido
traducen	traducían	han traducido
Future	**Pluperfect**	**Past Definite**
traduciré	había traducido	traduje
traducirás	habías traducido	tradujiste
traducirá	había traducido	tradujo
traduciremos	habíamos traducido	tradujimos
traduciréis	habíais traducido	tradujisteis
traducirán	habían traducido	tradujeron
Future Perfect	**Past Perfect**	
habré traducido	hube traducido	

CONDITIONAL	SUBJUNCTIVE	
Present	**Present**	**Imperfect**
traduciría	traduzca	traduj-era/ese
traducirías	traduzcas	traduj-eras/eses
traduciría	traduzca	traduj-era/ese
traduciríamos	traduzcamos	traduj-éramos/ésemos
traduciríais	traduzcáis	traduj-erais/eseis
traducirían	traduzcan	traduj-eran/esen
Perfect	**Perfect**	**Pluperfect**
habría traducido	haya traducido	hub-iera/iese traducido

GERUND	PAST PARTICIPLE	IMPERATIVE
traduciendo	traducido	traduce, traducid traduzca (Vd), traduzcan (Vds)

Voy a traducir el documento. *I'm going to translate the document.*
Lo traduje al inglés. *I translated it into English.*
Traduce del inglés al español. *He translates from English into Spanish.*
Quiero que traduzcas el contrato. *I want you to translate the contract.*

traductor línea a línea *one-to-one translator*
Lo tradujo erróneamente. *He mistranslated it.*
Es una traducción incorrecta. *It's a loose translation.*
No es una traducción fiel. *It's not a close/accurate translation.*

traducción *translation*
traductor(a) *translator*
traducible *translatable*
traductor de datos *data translator*
traducido/a *translated*

traer *to bring* tr. 188

INDICATIVE

Present	Imperfect	Perfect
traigo	traía	he traído
traes	traías	has traído
trae	traía	ha traído
traemos	traíamos	hemos traído
traéis	traíais	habéis traído
traen	traían	han traído

Future	Pluperfect	Past Definite
traeré	había traído	traje
traerás	habías traído	trajiste
traerá	había traído	trajo
traeremos	habíamos traído	trajimos
traeréis	habíais traído	trajisteis
traerán	habían traído	trajeron

Future Perfect	Past Perfect	
habré traído	hube traído	

CONDITIONAL / SUBJUNCTIVE

Present (Conditional)	Present (Subjunctive)	Imperfect (Subjunctive)
traería	traiga	traj-era/ese
traerías	traigas	traj-eras/eses
traería	traiga	traj-era/ese
traeríamos	traigamos	traj-éramos/ésemos
traeríais	traigáis	traj-erais/eseis
traerían	traigan	traj-eran/esen

Perfect	Perfect	Pluperfect
habría traído	haya traído	hub-iera/iese traído

GERUND	PAST PARTICIPLE	IMPERATIVE
trayendo	traído	trae, traed traiga (Vd), traigan (Vds)

Traigo el pan. *I bring the bread.*
¿Puedes traer el vino? *Can you bring the wine?*
¿Han traído el libro? *Have they brought the book?*
No traigas nada. *Don't bring anything.*

El periódico no trae la noticia. *The newspaper does not carry the news.*
Manolito me trae de cabeza. *Manolito causes me problems.*
Chloe nos trae locos. *Chloe makes us mad.*
Su padre se las trae. *Her father is very severe.*
traer entre manos *to have in mind*

traer a la memoria *to recall (to memory)*
traída *carrying*
traída de aguas *water supply*
traído/a *worn, worn out, old*
traerse algo entre manos *to plot*
traedor(a) *porter, carrier, bearer, bringer*
traedura *bringing, conduction, carrying*
traedizo/a *carried, brought, transported*

189 transferir *to transfer, postpone* tr.

INDICATIVE

Present	**Imperfect**	**Perfect**
transfiero	transfería	he transferido
transfieres	transferías	has transferido
transfiere	transfería	ha transferido
transferimos	transferíamos	hemos transferido
transferís	transferíais	habéis transferido
transfieren	transferían	han transferido

Future	**Pluperfect**	**Past Definite**
transferiré	había transferido	transferí
transferirás	habías transferido	transferiste
transferirá	había transferido	transfirió
transferiremos	habíamos transferido	transferimos
transferiréis	habíais transferido	transferisteis
transferirán	habían transferido	transfirieron

Future Perfect	**Past Perfect**
habré transferido	hube transferido

CONDITIONAL	SUBJUNCTIVE	
Present	**Present**	**Imperfect**
transferiría	transfiera	transfir-iera/iese
transferirías	transfieras	transfir-ieras/ieses
transferiría	transfiera	transfir-iera/iese
transferiríamos	transfiramos	transfir-iéramos/iésemos
transferiríais	transfiráis	transfir-ierais/ieseis
transferirían	transfieran	transfir-ieran/iesen
Perfect	**Perfect**	**Pluperfect**
habría transferido	haya transferido	hub-iera/iese transferido

GERUND	PAST PARTICIPLE	IMPERATIVE
transfiriendo	transferido	transfiere, transferid transfiera (Vd), transfieran (Vds)

Quiere transferir a su hija el derecho de herencia. *He wants to transfer the inheritance rights to his daughter.*
Han transferido sus derechos. *They have transferred their rights.*
Transferiremos la información. *We'll convey the information.*
No transfieras todo el dinero. *Don't transfer all the money.*

transferencia *transference*
transferencia bancaria *banker's order*
transferencia de crédito *credit transfer*
transferible *transferable*
transferidor(a) *transferring*

tronar *to thunder, shoot* tr./intr. 190

INDICATIVE

Present	Imperfect	Perfect
trueno	tronaba	he tronado
truenas	tronabas	has tronado
truena	tronaba	ha tronado
tronamos	tronábamos	hemos tronado
tronáis	tronabais	habéis tronado
truenan	tronaban	han tronado
Future	**Pluperfect**	**Past Definite**
tronaré	había tronado	troné
tronarás	habías tronado	tronaste
tronará	había tronado	tronó
tronaremos	habíamos tronado	tronamos
tronaréis	habíais tronado	tronasteis
tronarán	habían tronado	tronaron
Future Perfect	**Past Perfect**	
habré tronado	hube tronado	

CONDITIONAL	SUBJUNCTIVE	
Present	**Present**	**Imperfect**
tronaría	truene	tron-ara/ase
tronarías	truenes	tron-ases/aras
tronaría	truene	tron-ara/ase
tronaríamos	tronemos	tron-áramos/ásemos
tronaríais	tronéis	tron-arais/aseis
tronarían	truenen	tron-aran/asen
Perfect	**Perfect**	**Pluperfect**
habría tronado	haya tronado	hub-iera/iese tronado

GERUND	PAST PARTICIPLE	IMPERATIVE
tronando	tronado	truena, tronad truene (Vd), truenen (Vds)

Truena mucho. *It thunders a lot.*
Tronó durante toda la tormenta. *It was thundering during all of the storm.*
Tronaron a los prisioneros de guerra. *The prisoners of war were executed.*
El día de la Fiesta de la Hispanidad truenan los cañones como saludo. *They fire the cannons as a salute on Columbus Day.*

por lo que pueda tronar *just in case*
Se tronó. *He became ruined.*
Estoy que trueno. *I'm furious.*
Está que truena con su mujer. *He's fallen out with his wife.*

tronazón *thunderstorm*
tronada *thunderstorm*
trueno *thunder*
tronado/a *broken down, useless*
estar tronado *to be broke*
tronante *thundering, thunderous*

191 valer *to cost, be worth* tr./intr.

INDICATIVE

Present	**Imperfect**	**Perfect**
valgo	valía	he valido
vales	valías	has valido
vale	valía	ha valido
valemos	valíamos	hemos valido
valéis	valíais	habéis valido
valen	valían	han valido
Future	**Pluperfect**	**Past Definite**
valdré	había valido	valí
valdrás	habías valido	valiste
valdrá	había valido	valió
valdremos	habíamos valido	valimos
valdréis	habíais valido	valisteis
valdrán	habían valido	valieron
Future Perfect	**Past Perfect**	
habré valido	hube valido	

CONDITIONAL	SUBJUNCTIVE	
Present	**Present**	**Imperfect**
valdría	valga	val-iera/iese
valdrías	valgas	val-ieras/ieses
valdría	valga	val-iera/iese
vladríamos	valgamos	val-iéramos/iésemos
valdríais	valgáis	val-ierais/ieseis
valdrían	valgan	val-ieran/iesen
Perfect	**Perfect**	**Pluperfect**
habría valido	haya valido	hub-iera/iese valido

GERUND	PAST PARTICIPLE	IMPERATIVE
valiendo	valido	val, valed valga (Vd), valgan (Vds)

¿Cuánto vale? *How much is it?*
Vale £9. *It costs £9.*
La suma vale 90. *The sum comes to 90.*
Valía mucho dinero. *It was worth a lot of money.*

No vale nada. *It is worthless.*
No vale un higo. *It's not worth a brass farthing.*
Vale lo que pesa. *It's worth its weight in gold.*
Más vale así. *It's better this way.*
Más vale tarde que nunca. *Better late than never.*
No vale la pena. *It is not worth it.*

valor *worth, price, value*
valía *worth, value*
valoración *valuation*
vale *coupon, voucher*
valimiento *value*
valioso/a *valuable*

vencer *to defeat, overcome* tr./intr. 192

INDICATIVE

Present	Imperfect	Perfect
venzo	vencía	he vencido
vences	vencías	has vencido
vence	vencía	ha vencido
vencemos	vencíamos	hemos vencido
vencéis	vencíais	habéis vencido
vencen	vencían	han vencido
Future	**Pluperfect**	**Past Definite**
venceré	había vencido	vencí
vencerás	habías vencido	venciste
vencerá	había vencido	venció
venceremos	habíamos vencido	vencimos
venceréis	habíais vencido	vencisteis
vencerán	habían vencido	vencieron
Future Perfect	**Past Perfect**	
habré vencido	hube vencido	

CONDITIONAL	SUBJUNCTIVE	
Present	**Present**	**Imperfect**
vencería	venza	venc-iera/iese
vencerías	venzas	venc-ieras/ieses
vencería	venza	venc-iera/iese
venceríamos	venzamos	venc-iéramos/iésemos
venceríais	venzáis	venc-ierais/ieseis
vencerían	venzan	venc-ieran/iesen
Perfect	**Perfect**	**Pluperfect**
habría vencido	haya vencido	hub-iera/iese vencido

GERUND	PAST PARTICIPLE	IMPERATIVE
venciendo	vencido	vence, venced venza (Vd), venzan (Vds)

Nos han vencido. *They have defeated us.*
El Cid venció a los moros. *El Cid defeated the Moors.*
Venceremos. *We shall win.*
Le venció el sueño. *Sleep overcame him.*

Vence en elegancia. *He is the most elegant.*
No te dejes vencer. *Don't give in.*
Se ha vencido el plazo. *Time is up.*
Me doy por vencido/a. *I give in.*

vencedor(a) *victorious*
vencimiento *breaking, collapsing, time is up*
vencido/a *defeated*
victoria *victory*
pagar vencido *to pay in arrears*

193 vender *to sell* tr.

INDICATIVE

Present	Imperfect	Perfect
vendo	vendía	he vendido
vendes	vendías	has vendido
vende	vendía	ha vendido
vendemos	vendíamos	hemos vendido
vendéis	vendíais	habéis vendido
venden	vendían	han vendido
Future	**Pluperfect**	**Past Definite**
venderé	había vendido	vendí
venderás	habías vendido	vendiste
venderá	había vendido	vendió
venderemos	habíamos vendido	vendimos
venderéis	habíais vendido	vendisteis
venderán	habían vendido	vendieron
Future Perfect	**Past Perfect**	
habré vendido	hube vendido	

CONDITIONAL	SUBJUNCTIVE	
Present	**Present**	**Imperfect**
vendería	venda	vend-iera/iese
venderías	vendas	vend-ieras/ieses
vendería	venda	vend-iera/iese
venderíamos	vendamos	vend-iéramos/iésemos
venderíais	vendáis	vend-ierais/ieseis
venderían	vendan	vend-ieran/iesen
Perfect	**Perfect**	**Pluperfect**
habría vendido	haya vendido	hub-iera/iese vendido

GERUND	PAST PARTICIPLE	IMPERATIVE
vendiendo	vendido	vende, vended venda (Vd), vendan (Vds)

Vende coches. *He sells cars.*
Vamos a vender la casa. *We're going to sell the house.*
He vendido mis libros viejos. *I've sold my old books.*
No vendieron nada. *They didn't sell anything.*

Se venden manzanas. *Apples for sale.*
Venden café al por mayor. *They sell coffee wholesale.*
Vendemos al por menor. *We retail.*
Te lo vendo al contado. *I'll sell it to you for cash.*
Enrique se vende caro. *Enrique plays hard to get.*

se vende *for sale*
venta *sale, selling; country inn*
precio de venta *sale price*
venta a domicilio *door-to-door sale*
vendedor *salesman*
vender a comisión *to sell on commission*

venir *to come, arrive* intr. 194

INDICATIVE

Present	Imperfect	Perfect
vengo	venía	he venido
vienes	venías	has venido
viene	venía	ha venido
venimos	veníamos	hemos venido
venís	veníais	habéis venido
vienen	venían	han venido
Future	**Pluperfect**	**Past Definite**
vendré	había venido	vine
vendrás	habías venido	viniste
vendrá	había venido	vino
vendremos	habíamos venido	vinimos
vendréis	habíais venido	vinisteis
vendrán	habían venido	vinieron
Future Perfect	**Past Perfect**	
habré venido	hube venido	

CONDITIONAL	SUBJUNCTIVE	
Present	**Present**	**Imperfect**
vendría	venga	vin-iera/iese
vendrías	vengas	vin-ieras/ieses
vendría	venga	vin-iera/iese
vendríamos	vengamos	vin-iéramos/iésemos
vendríais	vengáis	vin-ierais/ieseis
vendrían	vengan	vin-ieran/iesen
Perfect	**Perfect**	**Pluperfect**
habría venido	haya venido	hub-iera/iese venido

GERUND	PAST PARTICIPLE	IMPERATIVE
viniendo	venido	ven, venid venga (Vd), vengan (Vds)

Venimos a comer. *We've come for lunch.*
¡Ven acá! *Come over here!*
Vinieron a vernos. *They came to see us.*
Vendrán tarde. *They will come late.*

Le hace venir a su oficina. *He summons him to his office.*
Vino a dar en el cárcel. *He ended up in jail.*
Los planes se vinieron abajo. *The plans collapsed.*
Todo se le viene encima. *Everything gets on top of him.*
Viene a ser lo mismo. *It amounts to the same thing.*

de ahí viene que . . . *hence . . .*
¡Venga! *Come on!*
¡Venga ya! *Come off it!*
venida *coming, arrival*
el mes que viene *next month*
venidero/a *coming, posterity*

195 ver *to see* tr./intr.

INDICATIVE

Present	Imperfect	Perfect
veo	veía	he visto
ves	veías	has visto
ve	veía	ha visto
vemos	veíamos	hemos visto
veis	veíais	habéis visto
ven	veían	han visto
Future	**Pluperfect**	**Past Definite**
veré	había visto	vi
verás	habías visto	viste
verá	había visto	vio
veremos	habíamos visto	vimos
veréis	habíais visto	visteis
verán	habían visto	vieron
Future Perfect	**Past Perfect**	
habré visto	hube visto	

CONDITIONAL	SUBJUNCTIVE	
Present	**Present**	**Imperfect**
vería	vea	vi-era/ese
verías	veas	vi-eras/eses
vería	vea	vi-era/ese
veríamos	veamos	vi-éramos/ésemos
veríais	veáis	vi-erais/eseis
verían	vean	vi-eran/esen
Perfect	**Perfect**	**Pluperfect**
habría visto	haya visto	hub-iera/iese visto

GERUND	PAST PARTICIPLE	IMPERATIVE
viendo	visto	ve, ved vea (Vd), vean (Vds)

La vi en la tienda. *I saw her in the shop.*
No lo veo. *I can't see it.*
Le he visto ya. *I've already seen him.*
Vamos a ver una obra. *We're going to see a play.*

Ver y callar. *It's best to keep your mouth shut about this.*
¡A ver! *Let's see!/Show me!*
Está por ver. *It remains to be seen.*
¡Para que veas! *So there!*

vista *sight, eyesight, vision*
vistazo *look, glance*
vistillas *viewpoint*
una cosa nunca vista *something unheard of*
vistoso/a *colourful*
visto bueno *approval*
Está mal visto. *It is not done.*
Está muy visto. *It is very common.*

verter *to spill, pour* tr./intr.

INDICATIVE

Present	Imperfect	Perfect
vierto	vertía	he vertido
viertes	vertías	has vertido
vierte	vertía	ha vertido
vertemos	vertíamos	hemos vertido
vertéis	vertíais	habéis vertido
vierten	vertían	han vertido
Future	**Pluperfect**	**Past Definite**
verteré	había vertido	vertí
verterás	habías vertido	vertiste
verterá	había vertido	vertió
verteremos	habíamos vertido	vertimos
verteréis	habíais vertido	veristeis
verterán	habían vertido	vertieron
Future Perfect	**Past Perfect**	
habré vertido	hube vertido	

CONDITIONAL	SUBJUNCTIVE	
Present	**Present**	**Imperfect**
vertería	vierta	vert-iera/iese
verterías	viertas	vert-ieras/ieses
vertería	vierta	vert-iera/iese
verteríamos	vertamos	vert-iéramos/iésemos
verteríais	vertáis	vert-ierais/ieseis
verterían	viertan	vert-ieran/iesen
Perfect	**Perfect**	**Pluperfect**
habría vertido	haya vertido	hub-iera/iese vertido

GERUND	PAST PARTICIPLE	IMPERATIVE
vertiendo	vertido	vierte, verted vierta (Vd), viertan (Vds)

Peter ha vertido la sopa sobre el mantel. *Peter has spilled the soup on the tablecloth.*
El río Arlanza vierte en el Duero. *The river Arlanza flows into the Duero.*
Vierte la sopa en la sopera. *Pour the soup into the tureen.*
Vamos a vertir el agua en el jardín. *We're going to pour the water into the garden.*

verter por la vertedera *to put down a chute*
verter alrededor *to circumfuse*
verter a gotas *to drop*

vertedero *rubbish dump*
vertedor *bailer*
vertido/a *spilled*
vertible *spillable*
vertiente *side of a mountain, watershed, slope*
vertedero de presa *dam spillway*
vertedero público *landfill*
vertido accidental de petróleo *accidental oil spill*

197 viajar *to travel* intr.

INDICATIVE

Present	Imperfect	Perfect
viajo	viajaba	he viajado
viajas	viajabas	has viajado
viaja	viajaba	ha viajado
viajamos	viajábamos	hemos viajado
viajáis	viajabais	habéis viajado
viajan	viajaban	han viajado
Future	**Pluperfect**	**Past Definite**
viajaré	había viajado	viajé
viajarás	habías viajado	viajaste
viajará	había viajado	viajó
viajaremos	habíamos viajado	viajamos
viajaréis	habíais viajado	viajasteis
viajarán	habían viajado	viajaron
Future Perfect	**Past Perfect**	
habré viajado	hube viajado	

CONDITIONAL	SUBJUNCTIVE	
Present	**Present**	**Imperfect**
viajaría	viaje	viaj-ara/ase
viajarías	viajes	viaj-aras/ases
viajaría	viaje	viaj-ara/ase
viajaríamos	viajemos	viaj-áramos/ásemos
viajaríais	viajéis	viaj-arais/aseis
viajarían	viajen	viaj-aran/asen
Perfect	**Perfect**	**Pluperfect**
habría viajado	haya viajado	hub-iera/iese viajado

GERUND	PAST PARTICIPLE	IMPERATIVE
viajando	viajado	viaja, viajad viaje (Vd), viajen (Vds)

Me gusta viajar. *I love travelling.*
Viajamos en tren. *We travelled by train.*
Francisca ha viajado mucho. *Francisca has travelled a lot.*
Leonor y Esperanza viajarán por Argentina. *Leonor and Esperanza will travel through Argentina.*

Paqui y Luis Antonio están de viaje. *Paqui and Luis Antonio are travelling/on a trip/on a journey.*
¡Buen viaje! *Bon voyage!*
viaje de ida y vuelta *return journey*
Están haciendo un viaje redondo. *They are on a round trip.*

viaje *journey, trip, tour*
viaje de novios *honeymoon*
viaje de recreo *pleasure trip*
viajero/a *traveller*
viajante de comercio *commercial traveller*

INDICATIVE

Present	Imperfect	Perfect
vivo	vivía	he vivido
vives	vivías	has vivido
vive	vivía	ha vivido
vivimos	vivíamos	hemos vivido
vivís	vivíais	habéis vivido
viven	vivían	han vivido
Future	**Pluperfect**	**Past Definite**
viviré	había vivido	viví
vivirás	habías vivido	viviste
vivirá	había vivido	vivió
viviremos	habíamos vivido	vivimos
viviréis	habíais vivido	vivisteis
vivirán	habían vivido	vivieron
Future Perfect	**Past Perfect**	
habré vivido	hube vivido	

CONDITIONAL	SUBJUNCTIVE	
Present	**Present**	**Imperfect**
viviría	viva	viv-iera/iese
vivirías	vivas	viv-ieras/icses
viviría	viva	viv-iera/iese
viviríamos	vivamos	viv-iéramos/iésemos
viviríais	viváis	viv-ierais/ieseis
vivirían	vivan	viv-ieran/iesen
Perfect	**Perfect**	**Pluperfect**
habría vivido	haya vivido	hub-iera/iese vivido

GERUND	PAST PARTICIPLE	IMPERATIVE
viviendo	vivido	vive, vivid viva (Vd), vivan (Vds)

Vivimos en Burgos. *We live in Burgos.*
Viví en Pamplona en 1974. *I lived in Pamplona in 1974.*
Solía vivir en Berlín. *I used to live in Berlin.*
¿Has vivido en Perú? *Have you ever lived in Peru?*

Quiero vivir en paz. *I want to live in peace.*
Ana vive al día. *Ana lives from day to day.*
Me gustaría vivir para verlo. *I would like to see it happen.*
Viven a lo grande. *They live a grand life.*

vivo/a *living, alive*
lengua viva *living language*
el buen vivir *the good life*
mujer de mal vivir *prostitute*
vivienda *housing, dwelling*
¡Viva el rey! *Long live the king!*
vivero *tree nursery*
viveza *liveliness, smartness*

199 volar *to fly* tr./intr.

INDICATIVE

Present	Imperfect	Perfect
vuelo	volaba	he volado
vuelas	volabas	has volado
vuela	volaba	ha volado
volamos	volábamos	hemos volado
voláis	volabais	habéis volado
vuelan	volaban	han volado
Future	**Pluperfect**	**Past Definite**
volaré	había volado	volé
volarás	habías volado	volaste
volará	había volado	voló
volaremos	habíamos volado	volamos
volaréis	habíais volado	volasteis
volarán	habían volado	volaron
Future Perfect	**Past Perfect**	
habré volado	hube volado	

CONDITIONAL	SUBJUNCTIVE	
Present	**Present**	**Imperfect**
volaría	vuele	vol-ara/ase
volarías	vueles	vol-aras/ases
volaría	vuele	vol-ara/ase
volaríamos	volemos	vol-áramos/ásemos
volaríais	voléis	vol-arais/aseis
volarían	vuelen	vol-aran/asen
Perfect	**Perfect**	**Pluperfect**
habría volado	haya volado	hub-iera/iese volado

GERUND	PAST PARTICIPLE	IMPERATIVE
volando	volado	vuela, volad
		vuele (Vd), vuelen (Vds)

Las aves y los aviones vuelan. *Birds and aeroplanes fly.*
Volaremos el próximo martes. *We'll fly next Tuesday.*
Me gustaría volar en un concorde. *I would love to fly in Concorde.*
Volaremos sobre Cuba. *We'll fly over Cuba.*

El tiempo vuela. *Time flies.*
Id volando. *Go quickly.*
El pájaro alzó el vuelo. *The bird took to the wing.*
El águila se echó a volar. *The eagle took off.*

vuelo *flight*
vuelillo *lace edging*
volada *short flight*
voladizo *projecting*

volcar *to overturn* tr./intr. 200

INDICATIVE

Present	Imperfect	Perfect
vuelco	volcaba	he volcado
vuelcas	volcabas	has volcado
vuelca	volcaba	ha volcado
volcamos	volcábamos	hemos volcado
volcáis	volcabais	habéis volcado
vuelcan	volcaban	han volcado
Future	**Pluperfect**	**Past Definite**
volcaré	había volcado	volqué
volcarás	habías volcado	volcaste
volcará	había volcado	volcó
volcaremos	habíamos volcado	volcamos
volcaréis	habíais volcado	volcasteis
volcarán	habían volcado	volcaron
Future Perfect	**Past Perfect**	
habré volcado	hube volcado	

CONDITIONAL	SUBJUNCTIVE	
Present	**Present**	**Imperfect**
volcaría	vuelque	volc-ara/ase
volcarías	vuelques	volc-aras/ases
volcaría	vuelque	volc-ara/ase
volcaríamos	volquemos	volc-áramos/ásemos
volcaríais	volquéis	volc-arais/aseis
volcarían	vuelquen	volc-aran/asen
Perfect	**Perfect**	**Pluperfect**
habría volcado	haya volcado	hub-iera/iese volcado

GERUND	PAST PARTICIPLE	IMPERATIVE
volcando	volcado	vuelca, volcad
		vuelque (Vd), vuelquen (Vds)

El coche volcó en la curva. *The car turned over on the bend.*
Volcamos en el kilómetro 40. *We overturned at kilometre 40.*
El barco ha volcado. *The ship capsized.*
Se volcó el vaso. *The glass tipped over.*

Volcamos a Sara. *We made Sara dizzy.*
Pienso volcar a Elena. *I'm going to make Elena change her mind.*
Miguel se vuelca para conseguirlo. *Miguel does the utmost to get it.*
Miguel se vuelca por complacerte. *Miguel bends over backwards to satisfy you.*

vuelco *overturning, upset, spill*
dar un vuelco *to overturn*
volquete *dumper, dumptruck*
volquetero/a *dump driver*

201 volver *to return, do again* tr./intr.

INDICATIVE

Present	**Imperfect**	**Perfect**
vuelvo	volvía	he vuelto
vuelves	volvías	has vuelto
vuelve	volvía	ha vuelto
volvemos	volvíamos	hemos vuelto
volvéis	volvíais	habéis vuelto
vuelven	volvían	han vuelto
Future	**Pluperfect**	**Past Definite**
volveré	había vuelto	volví
volverás	habías vuelto	volviste
volverá	había vuelto	volvió
volveremos	habíamos vuelto	volvimos
volveréis	habíais vuelto	volvisteis
volverán	habían vuelto	volvieron
Future Perfect	**Past Perfect**	
habré vuelto	hube vuelto	

CONDITIONAL	SUBJUNCTIVE	
Present	**Present**	**Imperfect**
volvería	vuelva	volv-iera/iese
volverías	vuelvas	volv-ieras/ieses
volvería	vuelva	volv-iera/iese
volveríamos	volvamos	volv-iéramos/iésemos
volveríais	volváis	volv-ierais/ieseis
volverían	vuelvan	volv-ieran/iesen
Perfect	**Perfect**	**Pluperfect**
habría vuelto	haya vuelto	hub-iera/iese vuelto

GERUND	PAST PARTICIPLE	IMPERATIVE
volviendo	vuelto	vuelve, volved vuelva (Vd), vuelvan (Vds)

Vuelve la hoja del libro. *Turn the page of the book.*
Volvió tarde a casa. *He returned home late.*
Volveremos mañana. *We'll return tomorrow.*
Ha vuelto a hacerlo. *He has done it again.*

Volvió a decirlo. *He said it again.*
Se desmayó, pero enseguida volvió en sí. *He fainted, but he soon came to.*
El ruido me vuelve loco. *Noise makes me mad.*
Se ha vuelto atrás. *He has gone back on his word.*

vuelta *other side; tour*
dar una vuelta *to go for a short walk*
vueltas *change*
volvible *reversible*

votar *to vote, pass, approve* tr. 202

INDICATIVE

Present	**Imperfect**	**Perfect**
voto	votaba	he votado
votas	votabas	has votado
vota	votaba	ha votado
votamos	votábamos	hemos votado
votáis	votabais	habéis votado
votan	votaban	han votado
Future	**Pluperfect**	**Past Definite**
votaré	había votado	voté
votarás	habías votado	votaste
votará	había votado	votó
votaremos	habíamos votado	votamos
votaréis	habíais votado	votasteis
votarán	habían votado	votaron
Future Perfect	**Past Perfect**	
habré votado	hube votado	

CONDITIONAL	SUBJUNCTIVE	
Present	**Present**	**Imperfect**
votaría	vote	vot-ara/ase
votarías	votes	vot-aras/ases
votaría	vote	vot-ara/ase
votaríamos	votemos	vot-áramos/ásemos
votaríais	votéis	vot-arais/aseis
votarían	voten	vot-aran/asen
Perfect	**Perfect**	**Pluperfect**
habría votado	haya votado	hub-iera/iese votado

GERUND	PAST PARTICIPLE	IMPERATIVE
votando	votado	vota, votad vote (Vd), voten (Vds)

¿Vas a votar en las próximas elecciones? *Are you going to vote in the next elections?*
Votaron por unanimidad. *They voted unanimously.*
No han votado nunca. *They have never voted.*
Peter vota al partido conservador. *Peter votes Conservative.*

No tengo ni voz ni voto en ello. *I don't have a say in it.*
La reina Margaret echaba votos. *Queen Margaret used to curse.*
Hamlet hacía votos. *Hamlet kept wishing.*
Tenemos voto activo. *We have the right to vote.*

voto femenino *the female vote*
voto de confianza *vote of confidence*
voto secreto *secret ballot*
votación *voting, balloting*
votante *voter, one who votes*
votador(a) *voter, voting*
voto solemne *solemn vow*
voto de castidad *chastity vow*

VERB LIST

On the following pages you will find approximately 3000 Spanish verbs, with their meanings and the number, or numbers, of the model verb they follow. If the number is in **bold print**, the verb is one of the 200 modelled in full.

abajar *to go down* tr. 10
abalanzar *to balance* tr. (r.) 31
abalar *to move, shake* tr. (r.) 10
abaldonar *to vilify, offend* tr. 10
abalear *to separate, fire on, shoot at* tr. 10
abalizar *to mark with buoys, take bearings* tr. 31
aballar *to move* tr. 10
aballestar *to haul, make taut* tr. 10
abanar *to cool* tr. 10
abanderar *to register under a flag, join* tr./intr. 10
abandonar *to abandon, give up* tr./intr. (r.) 10
abanicar *to fan* tr. (r.) 24
abaratar *to make cheaper* tr./intr. 10
abarcar *to encompass, embrace, contain* tr. 24
abarrotar *to secure; fill, crowd* tr. 10
abastar *to supply, provision* tr. (r.) 10
abastecer *to supply, provide* tr. 47
abatanar *to fill, beat* tr. 10
abatar *to frighten* tr. (r.) 10
abatir *to knock down, overthrow, demolish* tr./intr. 133
abdicar *to abdicate* tr./intr. 24
abducir *to abduct* tr. 45
abellacar *to make / become vile* tr. (r.) 24
aberrar *to err, be mistaken* intr. 10
abetunar *to blacken* tr. 10
abigarrar *to crowd* tr. 10
abismar *to overwhelm, confuse* tr. (r.) 10
abjurar *to abjure* tr. 10
ablandar *to soften, pacify, improve* tr./intr. 10
ablandecer *to soften* tr. 47
abnegarse *to go without* r. 30, 116
abobar *to bewilder, make stupid* tr. (r.) 10
abocar *to bite; pour* tr./intr. (r.) 24
abocetar *to sketch* tr. 10
abochornar *to embarrass, wilt, wither* tr. (r.) 10
abofetear *to slap* tr. 10
abogar *to plead, defend, plead for* intr. 30
abolir *to abolish* tr. 133
abollar *to dent, bruise* tr. (r.) 10
abombar *to make convex* tr./intr. (r.) 10
abominar *to abominate* tr./intr. 10
abonar *to subscribe* tr./intr. (r.) 10
abordar *to board* tr./intr. 10
aborrascarse *to become stormy* r. 24, 116
aborrecer *to abhor, detest* tr. 47
abortar *to abort, miscarry* tr./intr. 10
abotijarse *to get bloated* r. 116
abotonar *to button; bud* tr./intr. (r.) 10
abovedar *to vault, arch* tr. 10
abozalar *to muzzle* tr. 10
abrasar *to burn, fire* tr./intr. (r.) 10
abrazar *to embrace, hug* tr. (r.) 31
abrevar *to water, provide a drink* tr. 10
abreviar *to shorten, reduce* tr. (r.) 10
abrigar *to shelter, protect* tr. (r.) 30
abrillantar *to polish, make glitter* tr. 10
abrir *to open* (past participle: **abierto**) tr. (r.) 133
abrochar *to button up, fasten* tr. 10
abrogar *to repeal, abolish, annul* tr. 30
abroncar *to annoy, irritate* tr. (r.) 24
abrumar *to overwhelm, crush; embarrass* tr. (r.) 10
absolver *to absolve* tr. 2
absortar *to engross* tr. (r.) 10
abstenerse *to abstain* r. 179
abstraer *to abstract* tr./intr. (r.) 188
abuenar *to calm, improve* tr. 10
abullonar *to emboss, embroider* tr. 10
abultar *to augment, enlarge, be bulky* tr./intr. 10
abundar *to abound* tr./intr. 10
abuñolar *to make fritters (of / with* sth.) tr. 2
aburar *to burn, scorch* tr. 10
aburguesarse *to become bourgeois* r. 116
aburrarse *to become stupid* r. 116
aburrir *to bore, annoy* tr. 133
aburrirse *to be bored, get bored* r. 133
abusar *to abuse* intr. 10

acaballerar *to be / behave like a gentleman* tr. (r.) 10
acabar *to finish, end* tr. (r.) 10
acachetear *to slap in the face* tr. 10
academizar *to academize* tr. 31
acaecer *to happen* intr. (imp.) 54
acalambrarse *to get a cramp* r. 116
acallar *to silence, pacify* tr. 10
acalorar *to heat, warm up, get hot* tr. 10
acamar *to flatten, be flattened* tr./intr. (r.) 10
acamastronarse *to become artful* r. 116
acampanar *to shape (be shaped) like a bell* tr. 10
acampar *to camp* tr./intr. (r.) 10
acanalar *to striate, channel* tr. 10
acanallar *to corrupt, become base* tr. (r.) 10
acantalear *to hail, rain very hard* intr. 10
acantear *to throw stones at, stone* tr. 10
acantilar *to run aground, dredge* tr. (r.) 10
acantonar *to quarter, billet, limit* tr. (r.) 10
acaparar *to buy up, hoard, monopolise* tr. 10
acaparrarse *to come to terms with* r. 116
acapillar *to capture, trap* tr. 10
acapuchar *to shape into a hood* tr. 10
acaramelar *to cover with caramel; get carried away* tr. (r.) 10
acarar *to confront, face* tr. 10
acardenalar *to bruise* tr. (r.) 10
acarear *to confront, face* tr. 10
acariciar *to caress, fondle* tr. 10
acariciarse *to fondle oneself / each other* tr. (r.) 116
acariñar *to treat lovingly* tr. 10
acarminar *to dye red, redden* tr. 10
acarralar *to skip a thread; wither* tr. (r.) 10
acarrear *to transport, carry, incur* tr. (r.) 10
acarroñar *to intimidate, become intimidated* tr. (r.) 10
acartonar *to become like cardboard; wither* tr. (r.) 10
acaserarse *to become fond of* r. 116
acatar *to obey, respect, observe* tr. 10
acatarrar *to catch a cold; annoy* tr. (r.) 10
acaudalar *to amass, accumulate* tr. 10
acaudillar *to lead, command, elect a leader* tr. (r.) 10
acceder *to acceed, agree* intr. 23
accidentar *to have an accident, injure* tr. (r.) 10
accionar *to put in motion, gesticulate* tr./intr. 10
acechar *to lie in wait for, observe, spy on* tr. 10
acecinar *to cure meat by salting and smoking* tr. 10
acecinarse *to become thin or lean with age* r. 116
acedar *to sour, make bitter* tr. (r.) 10
aceitar *to oil, smear with oil* tr. 10
acelerar *to accelerate, speed* tr./intr. 10
acemilar *to deal with mules* tr. 10
acendrar *to purify, refine* tr. 10
acensuar *to take the census, assess, tax* tr. 10
acentuar *to stress, accent, mark with an accent* tr. 10
acepar *to take root* intr. 10
acepillar *to plane, brush, polish* tr. 10
aceptar *to accept* tr. 10
acequiar *to dig irrigation ditches* tr./intr. 10
acerar *to make pavements / sidewalks* tr. 10
acerar *to steel, turn into steel, strengthen* tr. 10
acercar *to bring near* tr. 24
acercarse *to approach* r. 24, 116
acerrojar *to lock, bolt* tr. 10
acertar *to guess, be right* tr./intr. 1
acetrinar *to turn greenish* tr. (r.) 10
acezar *to pant, gasp* intr. 31
achacar *to impute, attribute* tr. 24
achanchar *to check* tr. (r.) 10
achantarse *to hide, conform* r. 116
achaparrarse *to become chubby, grow*

stunted r. 116
acharolar *to varnish* tr. 10
achatar *to flatten* tr. 10
achicar *to diminish, bale out (a boat), lessen, reduce* tr. 24
achicharrar *to scorch, burn, sizzle* tr. (r.) 10
achinar *to intimidate, scare* tr. 10
achirlar *to thin down* tr. 10
achispar *to brighten up, make tipsy* tr. (r.) 10
achocar *to hurl, injure* tr./intr. 24
achocharse *to become senile, dote* r. 116
achubascarse *to cloud over and threaten rain* r. 24, 116
achuchar *to crush, crumple, squeeze* tr. 10
achularse *to become uncouth/rude/caddish* r. 116
achurar *to gut, knife* tr. 10
achurrar *to flatten* tr. 10
achurruscar *to burn, scorch, squeeze* tr. 24
acibarar *to make bitter, embitter* tr. 10
acicalar *to dress up, make oneself smart* tr. (r.) 10
acicatear *to incite, spur on* tr. 10
acidificar *to acidify* tr. 24
aciguatar *to watch, observe* tr. 10
aciguatarse *to get fish poisoning* r. 116
aclamar *to acclaim, hail* tr. 10
aclarar *to clarify, explain, clear* tr./intr. 10
aclararse *to rinse, clarify, clear* r. 116
aclimatar *to acclimatise* tr. 10
aclimatizarse *to acclimatise* r. 116
aclocarse *to go broody* r. 2, 24, 116
acobardar *to intimidate, become frightened* tr./intr. 10
acobijar *to mulch* tr. 10
acocarse *to become worm-ridden (fruit)* r. 24, 116
acocear *to kick, maltreat* tr. 10
acocharse *to crouch, duck* r. 116
acochinar *to make dirty* tr. 10
acodalar *to prop, shore* tr. 10
acodar *to lean; layer* tr. 10
acodarse *to lean (on elbow)* r. 116
acoderar *to bring the broad side, bear* tr. 10
acodiciar *to covet, long for, desire* tr. 10
acoger *to welcome, shelter* tr. 35
acogollar *to cover up tender plants, sprout, bud* tr./intr. 10
acogotar *to kill, intimidate* tr. 10
acohombrar *to bank, hill, earth up* tr. 10
acojinar *to make cushions* tr. 10
acolar *to unite* tr. 10
acolchar *to pad, stuff, quilt* tr. 10
acollar *to bank up with earth, caulk* tr. 2
acollarar *to put a collar on* tr. 10
acollonar *to scare, frighten* tr. (r.) 10
acomedirse *to volunteer, oblige* r. 122
acometer *to attack, undertake* tr. 23
acomodar *to accommodate, suit* tr./intr. 10
acompañar *to accompany, escort, go with* tr. 10
acompasar *to measure, divide into bars* tr. 10
acomplejar *to cause inhibitions, suffer from complexes* tr. 10
acomunarse *to unite, confederate* r. 116
aconchar *to push to safety, run aground, go to a safe place* tr. 10
acondicionar *to condition, prepare* tr. (r.) 10
acongojar *to anguish, be anguished* tr. (r.) 10
aconsejar *to advise, counsel* tr. 10
acontecer *to happen, come to pass* intr. (imp.) 192
acopar *to trim, shape* tr./intr. 10
acopiar *to gather, classify, collect* tr. 10
acoplar *to couple, join, mate* tr. (r.) 10
acoquinar *to intimidate, scare* tr. (r.) 10
acorar *to anguish, wither, wilt* tr. (r.) 10
acorazar *to armour, armourplate* tr. (r.) 31

acorchar *to line with cork* tr. 10
acordar *to agree* tr. **2**
acordarse *to recollect, remember* r. 2, 116
acordonar *to fasten with a cord, tie* tr. 10
acornear *to gore, butt* tr. 10
acorralar *to pen, corner, intimidate* tr. 10
acorrer *to help, turn to the aid of* tr./intr. 23
acortar *to shorten,reduce, cut down* tr. (r.) 10
acosar *to harass, pursue, pester* tr. 10
acosijar *to overwhelm, oppress* tr. 10
acostar *to put to bed* tr./intr. 3
acostarse *to go to bed, lie down* r. **3**
acostumbrar *to get used to, be accustomed to* tr./intr. 10
acostumbrarse *to get used to* r. 116
acotar *to annotate, choose, select* tr. 10; *to survey, fix, prune, trim* tr. (r.) 10
acotejar *to make oneself comfortable* tr. (r.) 10
acrecentar *to increase* tr. (r.) **4**
acrecer *to augment, be transferred* tr./intr. (r.) 54
acreditar *to credit* tr. (r.) 10
acrianzar *to raise, rear, bring up* tr. 31
acribar *to riddle, sift* tr. 10
acribillar *to riddle with bullets, harass* tr. 10
acriminar *to incriminate, impute* tr. 10
acriollarse *to adopt Spanish American ways* r. 116
acrisolar *to refine, purify* tr. 10
acristianar *to make Christian, Christianise* tr. 10
activar *to activate* tr. 10
actuar *to act, perform, bring an action* tr. 168
acuadrillar *to band together, get together* tr. (r.) 10
acuantiar *to assess the value or the quantity* tr. 10
acuartelar *to quarter, billet* tr. (r.) 10
acuartillar *to make into quarters* tr. 10
acuatizar *to land on water* intr. 31
acuchamarse *to become sad / languid* r. 116
acuchillar *to cut, knife, slash* tr. 10
acuchucar *to squeeze, squash* tr. 24
acuciar *to hasten, urge, yearn for* tr. 10
acuclillarse *to squat* r. 116
acudir *to attend, assist* intr. 133
acuerpar *to support, defend* tr. 10
acuidarse *to be preoccupied with* r. 116
acuilmarse *to grieve* r. 116
acular *to back, back up* tr. (r.) 10
acullicar *to chew cocoa leaves* tr. 24
acumuchar *to accumulate, heap* tr. 10
acumular *to accumulate, amass* tr. 10
acunar *to cradle, rock* tr. 10
acuñar *to wedge, coin, seal* tr. 10
acurrucarse *to curl up, get cosy* r. 24, 116
acusar *to accuse* tr. (r.) 10
adamar *to become effeminate* tr. (r.) 10
adaptar *to adapt, adjust* tr. (r.) 10
adatar *to credit* tr. 10
adecenar *to divide into tens* tr. 10
adecentar *to make presentable, smarten* tr. 33
adecuar *to adapt, fit* tr. 10
adehesar *to convert land into pasture* tr. 10
adelantar *to overtake, advance, progress* tr./intr. 10
adelantarse *to go ahead, go forward* r. 116
adelgazar *to lose weight* tr./intr. (r.) 31
adensar *to thicken, condense* tr. 10
adentellar *to bite* tr. 10
adentrar *to go deeper into* tr. 10
aderezar *to adorn, mend, get ready* tr. 31
adestrar *to direct* tr. **5**
adeudar *to owe, go into debt, debit* tr. (r.) 10
adherir *to adhere* tr. (r.) 108

adiamantar *to set diamonds* tr. 10
adicionar *to add, prolong* tr. 10
adiestrar *to train, teach* tr. (r.) 10
adietar *to put on a diet, go on a diet* tr. (r.) 10
adinerar *to convert into money, become rich* tr. (r.) 10
adivinar *to guess, foretell* tr. 10
adjudicar *to award, judge* tr. (r.) 24
adjuntar *to enclose* tr. 10
administrar *to manage* tr. 10
admirar *to admire* tr. (r.) 10
admitir *to admit, grant* tr. 133
adobar *to season, marinate* tr. 10
adocenar *to divide into dozens* tr. 10
adoctrinar *to indoctrinate, instruct* tr. 10
adolecer *to fall sick* intr. (r.) 47
adolorar *to ache* tr. 10
adomiciliar *to live* (somewhere), *have an address* tr. (r.) 10
adonizarse *to adorn oneself, beautify* r. 31, 116
adoptar *to adopt* tr. 10
adoquinar *to pave* tr. 10
adorar *to adore, worship* tr./intr. 10
adormecer *to put to sleep* tr. (r.) 47
adornar *to adorn* tr. 10
adosar *to place near* tr. 10
adquirir *to acquire* tr. **6**
adscribir *to attach, ascribe* tr. 98
aducir *to provide, quote* tr. 45
adueñarse *to take possession* r. 116
adular *to adulate, flatter* tr. 10
adulterar *to adulterate, commit adultery* tr./intr. (r.) 10
adulzar *to sweeten, soften* tr. 31
adulzorar *to become sweet* tr. 10
adurir *to burn* tr. (r.) 133
advenir *to come, arrive* intr. 194
adverar *to attest, authenticate* tr. 10
advertir *to warn, advise* tr. **7**
afamar *to make famous, become famous* tr. (r.) 10
afanar *to press, hurry, steal* tr. (r.) 10
afear *to make ugly, deform* tr. 10
afectar *to affect, have an effect on* tr. 10
afeitarse *to shave oneself* tr. (r.) 116
afeminar *to make or become effeminate* tr. (r.) 10
aferrar *to grapple* tr./intr. (r.) 33
afianzar *to fasten, hold on fast* tr. (r.) 31
aficionar *to inspire affection* tr. (r.) 10
afijar *to affix, secure* tr. 10
afilar *to sharpen, grow thin / pointed* tr. (r.) 10
afiliar *to join, affiliate* tr. (r.) 10
afillar *to adopt* tr. 10
afinar *to tune, perfect* tr./intr. (r.) 10
afincar *to settle down, buy estate* intr. (r.) 24
afirmar *to state, assure, affirm* tr. (r.) 10
afligir *to afflict, grieve* tr. (r.) 84
aflojar *to loosen, slacken* tr./intr. (r.) 10
aflorar *to show, emerge* tr./intr. 10
aflotar *to loosen, pay up, slacken* tr./intr. 10
afluir *to flow, congregate* intr. 110
afollar *to blow at* tr. (r.) 2
afondar *to sink, submerge, touch the bottom* tr./intr. (r.) 10
aforar *to rent* tr. 2
aforrar *to line* tr. (r.) 10
afortunar *to make happy* tr. 10
afrentar *to affront, insult* tr. (r.) 10
afrontar *to face, defy, confront* tr./intr. 10
afufar *to escape* intr. (r.) 10
afumarse *to get drunk* r. 116
agachar *to lower, bend* tr. (r.) 10
agañotar *to choke, strangle* tr. 10
agarbar *to crouch, stoop* r. 10
agarrar *to grasp, catch* tr. 10
agarrotar *to choke, stiffen* tr. 10
agasajar *to pamper, shower with gifts* tr. 10
agaucharse *to become a gaucho* r. 116
agazapar *to catch, stalk, crouch* tr. (r.) 10
agenciar *to get, obtain, procure* tr./intr. (r.) 10
agestarse *to make gestures, make faces* r. 116
agigantar *to make or become enormous* tr. (r.) 10
agilitar *to set in motion* tr. (r.) 10

agilitarse *to limber up* tr. (r.) 10
agitar *to shake, agitate* tr. (r.) 10
aglomerar *to gather* tr. (r.) 10
aglutinar *to join* tr. (r.) 10
agobiar *to overwhelm, oppress* tr. (r.) 10
agonizar *to be in agony, annoy* tr./intr. 31
agorar *to augur, predict* tr. 2
agostar *to wither* tr./intr. (r.) 10
agotar *to exhaust, use up* tr. (r.) 10
agraciar *to grace, adorn, award* tr. 10
agradar *to be pleasing, please* intr. 10
agradarse *to please* intr. 116
agradecer *to be grateful* tr. 54
agrandar *to enlarge, increase* tr. (r.) 10
agravar *to aggravate, make worse* tr. (r.) 10
agraviar *to wrong, injure* tr. (r.) 10
agredir *to attack* tr. 133
agregar *to collate, collect, add* tr. 30
agregarse *to add, collect* r. 30, 116
agremiar *to unite, become a union / syndicate* tr. (r.) 10
agriar *to make sour* tr. (r.) 10
agrietar *to split, crack* tr. (r.) 10
agrumar *to curdle, clot* tr. (r.) 10
agrupar *to group* tr. (r.) 10
agruparse *to group* r. 116
aguachar *to flood* tr. (r.) 10
aguachinarse *to flood, get waterlogged* tr. (r.) 116
aguantar *to bear, endure* tr./intr. (r.) 10
aguar *to dilute* tr. (r.) 10
aguardar *to await, expect* tr./intr. 10
aguardarse *to expect, wait for* r. 116
aguerrir *to instruct (military)* tr. (r.) 133
aguijonear *to prick, goad, incite* tr. 10
aguzar *to sharpen, grind* tr. 31
ahijar *to adopt* tr./intr. 10
ahilar *to go in single file, line up* tr./intr. (r.) 10
ahitar *to surfeit, bloat* tr. (r.) 10
ahogarse *to drown* tr. (r.) 30, 116
ahondar *to deepen, go down* tr./intr. (r.) 10
ahorcar *to hang* tr. (r.) 10
ahormar *to mould, fit* tr. (r.) 10
ahornar *to put in the oven* tr. 10
ahorrar *to economise, save* tr. 10
ahorrarse *to save, economise* r. 116
ahuecar *to soften, fluff up, become vain* tr./intr. (r.) 24
ahumar *to smoke, cure in smoke* tr. (r.) 10
ahuyentar *to drive away, banish* tr. 10
aislar *to isolate* tr. (r.) 10
ajetrear *to bustle about, tire, fatigue* tr. (r.) 10
ajornalar *to hire by the day* tr. (r.) 10
ajuarar *to furnish* tr. 10
ajuiciar *to judge, become sensible* tr./intr. 10
ajumarse *to get drunk* r. 116
ajustar *to adjust, fit, adapt* tr./intr. 10
ajustarse *to conform* r. 116
alabar *to praise, sing* tr./intr. 10
aladrar *to plough* tr. 10
alambicar *to distill* tr. 24
alambrar *to fence with wire* tr. 10
alampar *to yearn, crave for* intr. (r.) 10
alardear *to show off, boast, brag* intr. 10
alargar *to lengthen, extend* tr. (r.) 30
alarmar *to alarm, call to arms, be alarmed* tr. (r.) 10
albear *to turn white; get up at dawn* intr. 10
albergar *to give shelter, take lodging* tr./intr. (r.) 30
alborear *to dawn* intr. (imp.) 10
alborotar *to stir up, agitate, make noise* tr./intr. (r.) 10
alborozar *to delight, feel elated* tr. (r.) 31
albuminar *to emulsify* tr. 10
alcahazar *to keep / put in a cage* tr. 31
alcahuetear *to procure, pimp* tr./intr. 10
alcalizar *to alkalise* tr. 31
alcantarillar *to provide drains* tr. 10
alcanzar *to attain* tr./intr. (r.) 31

alcoholizar *to make alcohol, drink heavily* tr. (r.) 31
alcorzar *to coat with sugar icing* tr. 31
alear *to flutter / flap; recover* tr./intr. 10
alebrar *to cower, be scared* intr. (r.) 33
alebrarse *to throw oneself flat on the ground* r. 116
aleccionar *to instruct, teach* tr. 10
alegamar *to fertilise with mud or silt* tr. 10
alegar *to allege, contend, declare* tr. 30
alegrar *to make happy; stir up* tr. 10
alegrarse *to rejoice, be glad* r. 116
alejar *to remove, go far away* tr. (r.) 10
alentar *to encourage, breathe* tr./intr. (r.) **8**
alertar *to alert, sound the alarm* tr. 10
alfombrar *to carpet* tr. 10
alforzar *to pleat, tuck* tr. 10
algodonar *to cover / fill / work with cotton* tr. 10
alhajar *to bejewel, adorn with jewels* tr. 10
alheñar *to dye with henna* tr. (r.) 10
aliar *to join, ally* tr. (r.) 10
alicatar *to tile* tr. 10
alienar *to alienate, transfer, become alienated* tr. (r.) 10
alifar *to polish* tr. 10
aligar *to tie, bind* tr. 30
aligerar *to lighten, relieve, make lighter* tr./intr. 10
alimentar *to feed* tr./intr. (r.) 10
alimonarse *to turn yellowish* r. 116
alindar *to adorn, make pretty; mark the limits, border* tr./intr. (r.) 10
alinear *to align, line up* tr. (r.) 10
aliñar *to season, put salad dressing on* tr. 10
aliquebrarse *to break a wing, be crestfallen* r. 116, 143
alisar *to smooth, sleek* tr. (r.) 10
alistar *to recruit, enlist, enrol* tr./intr. (r.) 10
aliviar *to lessen, lighten, relieve* tr. (r.) 10
allanar *to make flat, level* tr. (r.) 10
allegar *to gather, arrive* tr./intr. 119
almacenar *to store* tr. 10
almadiar *to get sea sick* tr. (r.) 10
almagrar *to colour with red ochre; defame* tr. 10
almibarar *to cover with syrup* tr. 10
almidonar *to starch* tr. 10
almizclar *to perfume with musk* tr. 10
almorzar *to have lunch / a late breakfast* tr./intr. **9**
alocar *to make mad* tr. (r.) 24
alojar *to lodge, give accommodation* tr. (r.) 10
alongar *to lengthen* tr. (r.) 2, 30
aloquecerse *to become mad* r. 92
alorarse *to become tanned from the sun and the wind* r. 116
alquilar *to rent, hire* tr. (r.) 10
alquitranar *to tar, coat with tar* tr. 10
alterar *to alter, change* tr. (r.) 10
altercar *to disagree* intr. (r.) 24
alternar *to alternate* tr./intr. 10
altivar *to become proud* tr. (r.) 10
altivecer *to become arrogant* tr. (r.) 47
alucinar *to hallucinate, delude* tr. (r.) 10
alumbrar *to illuminate* tr./intr. 10
alumbrarse *to be / get high / tipsy, become lively (from drink); illuminate, enlighten* r. 116
alzar *to lift, elevate, pick up* tr. 31
alzarse *to raise, lift, pick up* r. 31, 116
amaestrar *to train, coach, tame* tr. 10
amagar *to simulate, appear* tr. (r.) 30
amainar *to lower, calm, lessen* tr./intr. 10
amalgamar *to amalgamate, mix* tr. 10
amamantar *to suckle, nurse* tr. 10
amancebarse *to cohabit, live together* r. 116
amancillar *to stain, defame* tr. 10
amanecer *to dawn* intr. (imp.) 47
amanerarse *to become mannered, act*

affectedly r. 116
amanojar *to bundle, bunch* tr. 10
amansar *to tame* tr. (r.) 10
amañar *to fake; get the knack of doing things* tr. (r.) 10
amar *to love, be fond of* tr. **10**
amarar *to land on water* intr. 10
amarecer *to mate* tr. 47
amargar *to make bitter, embitter* tr. (r.) 30
amarrar *to tie, moor, bind* tr. (r.) 10
amartelar *to drive mad, fall deeply in love* tr. (r.) 10
amartillar *to hammer* tr. 10
amasar *to knead, mix, amass* tr. 10
ambicionar *to desire, yearn* tr. 10
ambular *to walk, stroll* intr. 10
amedrantar *to frighten* tr. 10
amelonarse *to fall madly in love* tr. 116
amenazar *to threaten* tr. 31
amenguar *to reduce* tr./intr. 12
amigar *to bring together* tr. (r.) 30
amilanar *to intimidate, scare* tr. (r.) 10
aminorar *to diminish* tr. 10
amnistiar *to grant amnisty* tr. 10
amoblar *to furnish* tr. 2
amodorrarse *to become drowsy, grow sleepy* r. 116
amojonar *to delimit, mark* tr. 10
amolar *to grind* tr. 2
amoldar *to model, fashion* tr. 10
amollar *to yield, ease off, give in* tr./intr. 10
amonestar *to reprove, warn* tr. 10
amontonar *to pile together* tr. 10
amoratar *to turn blue / purple* tr. (r.) 10
amorrar *to sulk, hang, pitch* tr./intr. 10
amortajar *to shroud, lay out* tr. 10
amortecer *to dull, dim, soften* tr. (r.) 47
amortiguar *to muffle, soften, cushion* tr. 12
amortizar *to pay off, amortise* tr. 31
amoscarse *to get angry* r. 116
amotinar *to mutiny* tr. 10
amparar *to protect* tr. 10
ampliar *to amplify* tr. 10
amplificar *to amplify, enlarge* tr. 24
amputar *to amputate* tr. 10
amustiar *to wither* tr. 10
analizar *to analyse* tr. 31
anclar *to anchor* intr. 10
andar *to walk* tr./intr. (r.) **11**
anegar *to drown, become flooded* tr. 30
anestesiar *to anaesthetise* tr. 10
anexar *to anex* tr. 10
angostar *to narrow* tr./intr. (r.) 10
anhelar *to wish, desire, yearn for* tr. 10
anillar *to form into rings* tr. 10
animar *to animate, enlighten* tr. (r.) 10
aniquilar *to wipe out, annihilate* tr. (r.) 10
anochecer *to get dark* intr. (imp.) 47
anotar *to annotate, make notes* tr. 10
ansiar *to yearn for* tr. 10
anteponer *to place in front, prefer* tr. (r.) 140
antevenir *to precede* intr. 194
antever *to foresee* tr. 195
anticipar *to anticipate, advance, be early* tr. (r.) 10
antojarse *to feel like, fancy* r. 116
anublar *to cloud, dim, darken* tr. (r.) 10
anudar *to tie knots* tr. (r.) 10
anular *to cancel, make null and void* tr. 10
anularse *to annul, make void* r. 116
anunciar *to announce, foretell, proclaim* tr. 10
anunciarse *to announce, proclaim* r. 116
añadir *to add, pad* tr. 133
añorar *to pine for, miss* tr./intr. 10
apabullar *to crush, overwhelm* tr. 10
apacentar *to graze, feed* tr. 33
apaciguar *to pacify, soothe* tr. (r.) **12**
apadrinar *to sponsor* tr. (r.) 10
apagar *to turn off, put out* tr. 30
apagarse *to turn off* r. 30, 116
apalabrar *to come to an agreement* tr. (r.) 10
apalear *to beat* tr. 10
apañar *to pick up, manage* tr. (r.) 10
aparar *to prepare* tr. 10

aparcar *to park* tr. 24
aparecer *to appear, show up* intr. 47
aparecerse *to appear, show up* r. 47, 116
aparentar *to feign, simulate, seem* tr. 10
apartar *to separate, sort* tr./intr. (r.) 10
apasionar *to incite, excite, be mad about* tr. (r.) 10
apear *to dismount, get off, lodge* tr. (r.) 10
apedrear *to stone* tr. 10
apelar *to appeal* intr. 10
apellidar *to call by the surname* tr. (r.) 10
apercibir *to provide, prepare, warn* tr. 133
apercibirse (de) *to became aware of* r. 133
apercollar *to seize by the collar or neck* tr. 2
apernar *to tackle* tr. 33
aperrear *to annoy, pester* tr. 10
apestar *to be infected, stink* tr./intr. (r.) 10
apetecer *to fancy, crave for* tr. 47
apiadar *to feel with pity* tr. (r.) 10
apiñar *to crowd* tr. 10
apiparse *to gorge food* r. 116
aplacar *to placate* tr. 24
aplacer *to please* tr./intr. 47
aplacerse *to please* r. 47, 116
aplanar *to flatten* tr. (r.) 10
aplastar *to squash, crush* tr. (r.) 10
aplaudir *to applaud, clap* tr. (r.) 133
aplazar *to postpone* tr. 31
aplicar *to apply* tr. (r.) 24
apodar *to nickname* tr. 10
apoderarse *to take possession* r. 116
aporcar *to cover with earth* tr. 2, 24
aportar *to arrive at a port* intr. 2
aportarse *to bring* r. 2, 116
apostar *to bet, post* tr./intr. (r.) **13**
apoyar *to rest, lean* tr./intr. (r.) 10
apreciar *to appreciate* tr. 10
apreciarse *to appreciate, appraise* r. 116
aprender *to learn* tr. (r.) 23
apresurar *to hurry, hasten* tr. (r.) 10
apresurarse *to hasten, hurry, rush* r. 116
apretar *to grip, press together* tr./intr. (r.) **14**
aprobar *to approve, pass* tr./intr. **15**
aprovechar *to take advantage of* tr./intr. (r.) 10
aprovecharse *to take advantage, avail oneself* r. 116
apuñalar *to slash, stab* tr. 10
apuñar *to grasp, clench the fist* tr./intr. 10
apurar *to grieve; hurry, finish* tr. 10
apurarse *to fret, grieve, worry* r. 116
aquejar *to afflict, worry* tr. 10
arañar *to scratch* tr. (r.) 10
arar *to plough* tr. 10
arbitrar *to referee, judge* tr./intr. (r.) 10
archivar *to file* tr. 10
arder *to burn* intr. 23
argüir *to argue, reason* tr./intr. **16**
armar *to arm* tr. (r.) 10
arrancar *to snatch, pull out, start (engines)* tr./intr. 24
arrancarse *to start, pull up, root out* r. 24, 116
arrastrar *to drag, pull along* tr./intr. (r.) 10
arreciar *to make stronger* tr./intr. 10
arrecirse *to become numb* r. 134
arreglar *to arrange, fix, repair* tr. (r.) 10
arreglarse *to settle, make one look one's best; get ready, manage* r. 116
arrendar *to rent, lease, hire* tr. **17**
arrepentir *to repent, regret* tr. (r.) 108
arriesgar *to risk* tr. (r.) 30
arrimar *to bring near* tr. (r.) 10
arrojar *to fling, hurl* tr. 10
arrojarse *to throw, hurl, fling* r. 116
arropar *to clothe, wrap up* tr. (r.) 10
arrugar *to wrinkle, crease, crumple* tr. (r.) 30
articular *to articulate, pronounce distinctly* tr. 10
asaltar *to assail, assault* tr. 10
asar *to roast* tr. (r.) 10
ascender *to ascend* tr./intr. (r.) 136
asear *to clean, tidy* tr. (r.) 10

asegurar *to assure, assert, insure* tr. 10
asegurarse *to affirm, insure* r. 116
asentar *to fix, set down* tr. **18**
asentir *to assent, agree* intr. **19**
aserrar *to saw* tr. 33
asestar *to aim, deal, deliver* tr. 33
asir *to grasp, seize* tr./intr. **20**
asistir *to be present at, attend; assist* tr./intr. (r.) 133
asolar *to devastate* tr. (r.) 2
asoldar *to pay troops* tr. (r.) 53
asomar *to show, appear* tr./intr. (r.) 10
asombrar *to amaze, astonish* tr. (r.) 10
asonar *to sound* intr. 2
aspirar *to inhale, suck in, aspirate* tr./intr. 10
asquear *to be nauseated* tr./intr. (r.) 10
asumir *to assume, command* tr. 133
asustarse *to be frightened* r. 116
atacar *to attack* tr. (r.) 24
atañer *to concern, appertain* intr. (r.) 23
atar *to bind, tie* tr. (r.) 10
atardecer *to draw towards evening, get dark* intr. (imp.) 47
atarear *to give work* tr. 10
atascar *to get stuck* tr. (r.) 24
ataviar *to attire, adorn, deck* tr. (r.) 10
atender *to attend, pay attention* tr./intr. (r.) **21**
atenderse *to depend on, rely on, abide by* r. 116
atentar *to attempt* tr./intr. 33
aterirse *to become numb with cold* tr. (r.) 133
aterrar *to terrorise* tr./intr. 33
atestar *to cram* tr. 33
atestarse *to pack, attest, stuff, testify* r. 33, 116
atraer *to allure, attract, charm* tr. 188
atraerse *to attract, allure* r. 188
atrancar *to lock* tr./intr. (r.) 24
atrapar *to trap, catch* tr. 10
atravesar *to cross, go through* tr. **22**
atravesarse *to cross, go through* r. 22, 116
atreverse *to dare, venture* r. 23
atribuir *to attribute to* tr. (r.) 110
atronar *to thunder* tr. (r.) 2
atropellar *to trample / knock down* tr. (r.) 10
aturdir *to daze, stun, bewilder* tr. (r.) 133
aullar *to howl* tr. 10
aumentar *to increase* tr./intr. (r.) 10
ausentarse *to be absent* r. 116
autorizar *to authorise* tr. 31
avanzar *to advance* tr./intr. (r.) 31
avenir *to reconcile* tr. (r.) 194
aventar *to fan* tr. (r.) 33
avergonzar *to shame, embarrass* tr. 2, 31
avergonzarse *to be ashamed* r. 2, 31, 116
averiar *to go wrong* tr. (r.) 10
averiguar *to find out* tr./intr. 12
avisar *to inform, (give) notice, warn* tr. 10
avivar *to enliven* tr./intr. (r.) 10
ayudar *to help, aid, assist* tr. (r.) 10
ayunar *to fast* intr. 10
azolar *to chop with an axe* tr. 2
azotar *to beat, thrash* tr. (r.) 10

babear *to dribble* intr. 10
bailar *to dance* tr. 10
bajar *to descend, go down* tr./intr. 10
bajarse *to go down, descend* r. 116
baladrar *to shout, whoop* intr. 10
balancear *to sway, balance, rock* intr./tr. (r.) 10
balar *to bleat* intr. 10
balbucear *to hesitate (in speech), stammer* intr. 10
balbucir *to stammer, stutter* intr. 187
baldar *to cripple, maim* tr. (r.) 10
bandear *to chase, wound* tr./intr. 10
bañar *to bathe* tr. 10
bañarse *to bathe oneself, take a bath* r. 116
barajar *to shuffle cards, quarrel* tr./intr. (r.) 10
barbar *to grow a beard* intr. 10
barbotar *to mumble, mutter* tr./intr. 10

barnizar *to varnish* tr. 31
barquear *to cross in a boat* tr./intr. 10
barrenar *to drill* tr. 10
barrer *to sweep* tr./intr. (r.) 23
barruntar *to guess, surmise* tr. 10
bartolear *to idle* intr. 10
basar *to base, support* tr. (r.) 10
bastar *to be enough* intr. (imp.) 10
bastardear *to degenerate, debase* tr./intr. 10
bastarse *to be sufficient, suffice* r. 116
bastonear *to cane* tr. 10
batallar *to fight, battle* intr. 10
batir *to beat, whip* tr./intr. (r.) 133
bautizar *to baptise, christen* tr. 31
beber *to drink* tr./intr. (r.) **23**
becar *to grant, award* tr. 24
bendecir *to bless* tr. 57
beneficiar *to benefit* tr. (r.) 10
berrear *to bleat, bellow, shriek* intr. 10
besar *to kiss* tr. (r.) 10
bestializarse *to become beast-like* r. 116
besuquear *to lavish kisses on* tr. 10
betunar *to polish* tr. 10
bichar *to spy on* tr. 10
bieldar *to winnow* tr. 10
bienquerer *to like, to be fond of* tr. 144
bienquistar *to reconcile* tr. (r.) 10
bienvivir *to live well* intr. 198
bifurcarse *to branch off, bifurcate* r. 24, 116
bigardear *to lead an aimless life* intr. 10
bilocarse *to be in two places, go mad* r. 24, 116
binar *to hoe, dig over* tr./intr. 10
biografiar *to write a biography* tr. 10
birlar *to throw, cheat, rob, filch* tr. 10
bisar *to repeat* tr. 10
bizarrear *to act gallantly* intr. 10
bizcochar *to bake* tr. 10
bizcornear *to squint* intr. 10
bizmar *to apply a poultice* tr. 10
bizquear *to squint* intr. 10
blandear *to soften* tr./intr. (r.) 10
blandir *to brandish, swing* tr./intr. (r.) 133
blanquear *to whiten, bleach, whitewash* tr./intr. 10
blanquecer *to blanch, whiten* tr. 54
blasfemar *to blaspheme, curse, swear* intr. 10
blasonar *to emblazon, boast, brag* tr./intr. 10
blindar *to armour* tr. 10
bloquear *to block, obstruct* tr. 10
bobear *to play the fool* intr. 10
bobinar *to wind, reel, coil* tr. 10
bocadear *to divide into bits / mouthfuls* tr. 10
bocartear *to crush* tr. 10
bochar *to hit and move* tr. 10
bocinar *to blow a horn* intr. 10
bofarse *to sag, grow spongy* tr. 116
bogar *to row* tr. 30
bombardear *to bombard* tr. 10
bonificar *to increase production* tr. 24
borbotar (=borboritar) *to bubble, boil* tr. 10
bordar *to embroider* tr. 10
bordear *to skirt, go round* tr./intr. 10
bornear *to twist* tr. 10
borrar *to cross out, erase* tr. 10
borrarse *to erase, delete* r. 116
borronear *to scribble, scrawl* tr. 10
bostezar *to yawn, gape* intr. 31
botar *to launch (a boat), bounce* tr./intr. 10
botar *to fling, cast away* tr. 10
bramar *to bellow, roar* intr. 10
bravear *to bluster, bully* intr. 10
brear *to maltreat, annoy, vex* tr. 10
bregar *to fight, brawl* tr./intr. 30
bregarse *to struggle* r. 30, 116
brillar *to shine* intr. 10
brincar *to skip, jump, bounce* tr./intr. 24
brindar *to toast, offer* tr./intr. (r.) 10
bromear *to joke, jest* intr. (r.) 10
broncear *to bronze, tan* tr. (r.) 10
brotar *to sprout, bud* intr. 10
brumar *to crash, oppress* tr. 10
bruñir *to polish, buff* tr. 198
bucear *to dive, swim under water* intr. 10
bufar *to snort, puff* intr. (r.) 10

bufonear *to jest, joke, act the buffoon* intr. (r.) 10
bullir *to boil, bustle, budge, bubble* tr./intr. 198
burbujear *to bubble* intr. 10
burlar *to mock, dodge, make fun* tr./intr. 10
burlarse *to ridicule, make fun* r. 116
buscar *to look for* tr. **24**

cabalgar *to ride a horse* tr./intr. 30
cabecear *to nod, shake / toss the head* intr. 10
caber *to fit, have enough room* intr. **25**
caberse *to be contained, fit into* r. 25
cabrearse *to annoy, bother* tr./intr. (r.) 116
cacarear *to crow, cackle, brag, boast* tr./intr. 10
cachar *to break into pieces* tr. 10
caer *to fall, drop* intr. **26**
caerse *to fall down, tumble* r. 26
cagar *to defecate, soil, spoil* (vulg.) tr./intr. (r.) 30
calar *to soak, drench* tr./intr. (r.) 10
calaverear *to lead a wild / dissolute life* intr. 10
calcar *to trace, copy* tr. 24
calcular *to calculate* tr. 10
caldear *to heat up, warm* tr. (r.) 10
calentar *to warm, heat (up)* tr. **27**
calentarse *to get warm, get angry, become excited* r. 27, 116
calificar *to assess, rate, rank* tr. (r.) 24
callar *to shut up, be silent* tr./intr. 10
callarse *to be / remain silent, keep quiet* r. 116
callejear *to be (always) in the streets* intr. 10
calmar *to calm, soothe, grow calm* tr./intr. (r.) 10
calumniar *to slander, defame* tr. 10
calzarse *to shoe, put on shoes* r. 31, 116
cambiar *to change* tr./intr. (r.) 10
camelar *to woo, use flattery to achieve something* tr. 10
caminar *to walk* tr./intr. **28**
camochar *to trim, prune* tr. 10
camorrear *to quarrel* intr. 10
canalizar *to make channels, pipe* tr. 31
cancelar *to cancel, strike out* tr. 10
cancerar *to make cancerous, reprove* tr. (r.) 10
canchar *to toast, roast* tr./intr. 10
canchear *to clamber, shirk* intr. 10
candar *to lock* tr. 10
canecer *to grow grey hair, go grey* tr./intr. 47
canillar *to wind on a spool* tr. 10
canjear *to exchange* tr. 10
cansar *to be tired, get tired* tr. 10
cansarse *to get tired, become weary* r. 116
cantalear *to sing softly, hum* intr. 10
cantar *to sing, chant* tr./intr. (r.) **29**
cantonear *to idle, wander about* intr. 10
capar *to castrate* tr. 10
capitular *to capitulate, surrender* tr./intr. 10
capotar *to turn over* intr. 10
captar *to win, capture* tr. 10
caracterizar *to characterise* tr. (r.) 31
carbonizar *to carbonise, char* tr. (r.) 31
carcajear *to laugh heartily, guffaw* intr. (r.) 10
carcomer *to gnaw, decay* tr. (r.) 39
carear *to confront, face* tr./intr. (r.) 10
carecer *to lack* intr. 47
cargar *to burden, load* tr./intr. (r.) 30
cargarse *to load, burden* r. 30, 116
carpintear *to work as a carpenter* intr. 10
carrasquear *to crackle, crunch* intr. 10
cartear *to write letters to one another, correspond* intr. (r.) 10
casar *to get married, marry* tr./intr. (r.) 10
casarse *to get married, marry* r. 116
cascar *to break, crack* tr./intr. (r.) 24
castigar *to punish, chastise* tr. **30**
castrar *to castrate, dry, prune* tr. (r.) 10
catalogar *to list, catalogue* tr. 30

catar *to sample, taste* tr. 10
catear *to seek, search for* tr. 10
categorizar *to categorise* tr. 31
catonizar *to censure severely* intr. 31
caucionar *to bond, pledge, caution* tr. 10
causar *to cause* tr. 10
cautelar *to prevent, take precautions* tr. (r.) 10
cautivar *to capture, captivate* tr. 10
cavar *to dig, excavate* tr./intr. 10
cavilar *to ponder, meditate, reflect upon* tr./intr. 10
cayapear *to gang up on and attack* intr. 10
cazar *to hunt, chase* tr. **31**
cazoletear *to meddle* intr. 10
cebar *to fatten* tr./intr. (r.) 10
ceder *to yield, surrender* tr./intr. 23
cegar *to dazzle, blind* tr./intr. (r.) **32**
cejar *to back up, withdraw* intr. 10
celar *to supervise, watch out for* tr./intr. 10
celebrar *to celebrate* tr./intr. 10
cellisquear *to sleet* intr. 10
cenar *to have supper* tr. 10
cencerrear *to jingle, clang* intr. 10
censar *to census, take a census of* tr. 10
censurar *to censure, criticise, judge* tr. 10
centellar *to sparkle, twinkle* intr. 10
centellear *to flicker, sparkle, shimmer* intr. 10
centrar *to centre* tr. 10
centuplicar *to increase hundredfold* tr. (r.) 24
ceñir *to gird* tr. (r.) 134
cepillar *to brush* tr. (r.) 10
cepillarse *to brush oneself, finish* r. 116
cercar *to fence, enclose, lay siege* tr. 24
cerner *to sift, bolt* tr./intr. (r.) 136
cernir *to sift* tr. 165
cerrar *to close, shut, lock* tr./intr. (r.) **33**
certificar *to certify, register (letters)* tr. 24
certificarse *to certify, attest* r. 24, 116
cesar *to cease, stop* intr. 10
cicatrizar *to scar* tr./intr. (r.) 31
cifrar *to cipher, code* tr. (r.) 10
cimbrar *to bend, beat* tr./intr. (r.) 10
cimentar *to cement* tr. 33
cincar *to galvanise* tr. 24
cincelar *to chisel, carve, engrave* tr. 10
cinchar *to slog, work hard* tr./intr. 10
circular *to move, circulate* tr./intr. 10
circuncidar *to circumcise, trim* tr. 10
circundar *to encircle* tr. 10
circunferir *to circumscribe, limit, confine* tr. 108
circunvalar *to surround, encircle* tr. 10
circunvolar *to fly around, circumnavigate* tr. 199
ciscar *to soil, make dirty* tr. (r.) 24
citar *to make an appointment, quote* tr. 10
civilizar *to civilise, become civilised* tr. (r.) 31
cizañar *to create enmity* tr. 10
clamar *to cry out, implore* intr. 10
clamorear *to clamour, wail* tr./intr. 10
clarear *to make clear, make lighter, dawn* tr./intr. (r.) 10
clasificar *to classify, sort out* tr. (r.) 24
claudicar *to limp, give up* intr. 24
clausurar *to close, close up* tr. 10
clavar *to nail, fix* tr. 10
clisar *to stereotype* tr. 10
clocar (= cloquear) *to cluck, cackle* intr. 24
clorar *to chlorinate* tr. 10
coagular *to coagulate, curdle* tr. (r.) 10
coartar *to limit, restrain* tr. 10
cobardear *to be a coward* tr. 10
cobijar *to cover, shelter* tr. (r.) 10
cobrar *to charge, get paid, collect* tr. (r.) 10
cocer *to boil, cook* tr./intr. (r.) **34**
cocinar *to cook* tr./intr. (r.) 10
codear *to nudge* tr./intr. (r.) 10
coger *to take, pick up, catch* tr./intr. **35**

confiscar *to confiscate* tr. 24
confitar *to coat with sugar* tr. 10
conformar *to conform* tr. (r.) 10
conformarse (con) *to put up with, resign* r. 10
confortar *to comfort* tr. 10
confrontar *to confront,border* tr./intr. (r.) 10
confundir *to confound, mix up, muddle up* tr. (r.) 133
congelar *to freeze, get / become frozen* tr. (r.) 10
congeniar *to be compatible* intr. 10
conglomerar *to conglomerate* tr. (r.) 10
congraciar *to adulate, flatter* tr. (r.) 10
congratular *to congratulate* tr. (r.) 10
congregar *to assemble, congregate* tr. (r.) 10
conjugar *to conjugate* tr. 115
conjurar *to swear, entreat* tr./intr. (r.) 10
conmemorar *to commemorate* tr. 10
conmover *to excite emotion* tr. (r.) 128
conocer *to know, be acquainted with* tr./intr. (r.) **47**
conocerse *to know oneself* r. 47
conseguir *to obtain, achieve* tr. **48**
conseguirse *to achieve, attain, get, obtain* r. 48
consentir *to consent, allow* tr./intr. (r.) **49**
conservar *to preserve* tr. (r.) 10
considerar *to consider, examine, think over* tr. (r.) 10
consignar *to write in, consign, deposit* tr. 10
consistir *to consist, be composed of* intr. 133
consolar *to console* tr. (r.) 2
consonar *to harmonise* intr. 2
constar *to be clear, consist, be composed* intr. 10
constatar *to verify, prove* tr. 10
constipar *to give a cold, catch a cold* tr. (r.) 10
constituir *to constitute, make up* tr. (r.) 110
constreñir *to constrain* tr. 134
construir *to construct* tr. (r.) 110
consultar *to ask for advice* tr./intr. 10
consumar *to consummate* tr. 10
consumir *to consume* tr. (r.) 133
contactar *to contact* tr. 10
contagiar *to infect, transmit* tr. 10
contar *to count, tell* **50**
contender *to contend, compete* intr. (r.) 136
contener *to contain, hold* tr. 179
contenerse *to restrain oneself* r. 179
contentar *to please, gratify* tr. (r.) 10
contestar *to reply, answer* tr./intr. (r.) 10
continuar *to continue, proceed* tr./intr. 168
contradecir *to contradict* tr. (r.) 57
contraer *to contract* tr. (r.) 188
contrahacer *to imitate, copy* tr. (r.) 106
contramarcar *to countermark* tr. 24
contraponer *to compare, contrast* tr. (r.) 140
contratar *to contract, engage, hire* tr. 10
contravenir *to contravene, violate* tr. 194
contribuir *to contribute* tr./intr. 110
controlar *to monitor, control* tr. 10
controvertir *to argue* tr./intr. 108
contundir *to bruise* tr. (r.) 133
convalecer *to convalesce, recover* intr. 47
convencer *to convince* tr. (r.) 192
convenir *to agree, be convenient* intr. (r.) 194
conversar *to converse, have a conversation* intr. 10
convertir *to convert, change* tr. (r.) **51**
convidar *to invite* tr. 10
convocar *to call together, summon* tr. 24
convocarse *to convoke, call, summon* r. 24, 116
coordinar *to coordinate* tr. 10
copiar *to copy* tr. 10
coquetear *to flirt* tr. 10
coronar *to crown* tr. (r.) 10

corregir *to correct, put right* tr. **52**
corregirse *to correct oneself* r. 52
correr *to run, race, flow* tr./intr. (r.) 23
correrse *to run, hurry, move, come* r. 23
corresponder *to correspond* intr. (r.) 23
corretar *to run around, chase* tr./intr. 10
corroer *to erode, corrode* tr. (r.) 23
corromper *to corrupt* tr./intr. (r.) 23
cortar *to cut, cut off, cut out (eliminate)* tr./intr. 10
cortarse *to cut oneself* r. 116
cosechar *to harvest* tr./intr. 10
coser *to sew* tr./intr. 23
cosquillear *to tickle* tr. 10
costar *to cost, be difficult* intr. **53**
costear *to pay for* tr. (r.) 10
cotejar *to tally, check* tr. 10
cotizar *to quote, contribute* tr. 31
cotorrear *to chatter, prattle* tr. 10
crear *to create, establish* tr. 10
crecer *to grow, increase* intr. **54**
creer *to believe* tr./intr. (r.) 117
criar *to breed, bring up, rear* tr. 10
cribar *to sieve, bolt* tr. 10
crispar *to put on edge, twitch* tr. (r.) 10
criticar *to criticise* tr. 24
croar *to croak* tr. 10
cruzar *to cross* (r.) (r.) 31
cruzarse *to cross* (r.) 31, 116
cubrir *to cover* (past participle: **cubierto**) tr. (r.) 133
cubrirse *to cover oneself* (past participle: **cubierto**) r. 133
cucar *to wink, mock* tr./intr. 24
cuidar *to care for* tr./intr. (r.) 10
cuidarse *to take care of oneself* r. 116
culpar *to blame, accuse* tr. (r.) 10
cultivar *to grow, cultivate* tr. 10
cumplir *to fulfil, keep, reach (years)* tr./intr. (r.) 133
curar *to cure* tr./intr. (r.) 10
curtir *to tan, harden* tr. (r.) 133
curvar *to curve, bend* tr. (r.) 10
custodiar *to guard, take care of* tr. 10

chafar *to crease, crumple* tr. (r.) 10
chafarse *to flatten* r. 116
chamuscar *to singe, scorch* tr. (r.) 24
chapar *to cover, plate* tr. 10
chaparrear *to rain heavily, pour* intr. 10
chapucear *to botch, bungle* tr. 10
chapuzar *to duck, dip under water* tr./intr. (r.) 31
charlar *to chat, prattle* intr. 10
chascar *to click, crack, crunch* tr./intr. 24
chasquear *to play a practical joke, crackle* tr./intr. (r.) 10
chequear *to check, inspect* tr. 10
chiflar *to whistle, jeer, trim* intr./tr. (r.) 10
chillar *to scream, shriek* intr. 10
chinchar *to annoy, irritate* tr. 10
chingar *to drink; annoy, bother* tr. (r.) 30
chirriar *to squeak, sizzle, creak, spatter* intr. 10
chismear *to gossip* intr. 10
chispear *to throw sparks, sparkle* tr. 10
chistar *to mumble, mutter* intr. 10
chocar *to collide, clash* tr./intr. 24
chochear *to be doddering* intr. 10
chorrear *to gush, spurt, jet* intr. 10
chuchear *to whisper* intr. 10
chupar *to lick, suck* tr./intr. (r.) 10
churruscar *to burn* tr. (r.) 24

danzar *to dance* tr./intr. 31
dañar *to damage* tr. 10
dañarse *to get damaged / hurt* r. 116
dar *to give* tr. (r.) **55**
debatir *to debate* tr. 133
deber *to owe, must, ought to* tr. (r.) **56**
decaer *to decay, weaken* intr. 26
decentar *to cut into* tr. (r.) 33
decepcionar *to disappoint* tr. 10
decidir *to decide, determine* tr./intr. (r.) 133
decir *to say, tell* tr. (r.) **57**
declamar *to recite, declaim* tr./intr. 10
declarar *to state, declare, admit* tr./intr. (r.) 10

declinar *to decline, refuse, decay* tr./intr. 10
decorar *to decorate* tr. 10
decretar *to decree, give judgement on* tr. 10
dedicar *to dedicate, address* tr. 24
decicarse *to devote oneself* r. 24, 116
deducir *to deduce* tr. 45
defecar *to defecate* tr./intr. 24
defender *to defend* tr. **58**
defenderse *to defend* r. 58
defenecer *to close* tr. 47
deferir *to defer, delegate* tr./intr. **59**
deferirse *to pay deference* r. 59
definir *to define, clarify* tr. 133
deflagrar *to burn with sudden and sparkling combustion* intr. 30
deformar *to deform, become deformed* tr. (r.) 10
defraudar *to defraud, cheat, disappoint* tr. 10
degenerar *to degenerate* intr. 10
deglutir *to swallow* tr./intr. 133
degollar *to behead* tr. 2
degradar *to demote, degrade* tr. (r.) 10
degustar *to taste, sample* tr. 10
dejar *to allow, let, leave* tr. (r.) 10
dejarse *to let, allow, leave, permit* r. 116
delatar *to denounce, accuse* tr. 10
delegar *to delegate* tr. 30
deleitar *to delight, please* tr. (r.) 10
deletrear *to spell, decipher* tr. 10
deliberar *to deliberate, ponder, consider* tr./intr. 10
delinquir *to break the law* intr. **60**
delirar *to be delirious, rave* intr. 10
demacrar *to emaciate, waste away* tr. (r.) 10
demandar *to sue, crave, demand* tr. 10
demarcar *to delimit, mark* tr. 24
demediar *to divide in halves* tr. (r.) 10
demoler *to demolish, pull down* tr. **61**
demorar *to delay, remain* tr./intr. (r.) 10
demostrar *to prove, demonstrate* tr. **62**
demostrarse *to demonstrate, prove* r. 62, 116
demudar *to change, alter, disguise* tr. (r.) 10
denegar *to deny, refuse* tr. 130
denigrar *to slander, defame* tr. 10
denominar *to denominate, designate* tr. 10
denostar *to revile, insult* tr. 62
denotar *to denote, indicate* tr. 10
densar *to condense* tr. 10
dentar *to indent* tr./intr. **63**
denunciar *to denounce, accuse* tr. (r.) 10
departir *to converse* intr. 133
depender *to depend* intr. 23
depilar *to remove hair* tr. (r.) 10
deponer *to depose, lay aside, vomit* tr./intr. 140
deportar *to deport, exile* tr. 10
depositar *to store, place* tr. (r.) 10
depreciar *to depreciate* tr. 10
deprimir *to depress, humiliate* tr. (r.) 133
depurar *to purify* tr. (r.) 10
derivar *to derive* tr./intr. (r.) 10
derogar *to abolish, derogate* tr. 30
derramar *to spill* tr. (r.) 10
derrengar *to strain, sprain* tr. (r.) 30, 33
derretir *to melt, thaw* tr. (r.) **64**
derribar *to demolish, knock down, throw down* tr. 10
derribarse *to fall down, overthrow* r. 116
derrocar *to hurtle, cast, overthrow* tr. (r.) 24
derrochar *to waste, squander* tr. 10
derrotar *to defeat* tr. (r.) 10
derrumbar *to demolish, tear down* tr. (r.) 10
derrumbarse *to demolish* r. 116
desabrigar *to uncover* tr. (r.) 10
desabrochar *to unfasten* tr. (r.) 10
desacertar *to err* intr. 1
desacordar *to be in discord* tr. (r.) 2
desaferrar *to unfasten* tr. (r.) 33
desafinar *to be / play out of tune* intr. (r.) 10
desaforar *to encroach* tr. (r.) 2
desagradecer *to be ungrateful* tr. 47

desguar *to drain, dissipate* tr./intr. (r.) 12
desahogar *to comfort, alleviate* tr. (r.) 10
desairar *to rebuff, upset, disregard* tr. 10
desalentar *to discourage, make breathless* tr. (r.) **65**
desaliñar *to disarrange, make untidy* tr. (r.) 10
desalmar *to weaken* tr. (r.) 10
desalojar *to move out, vacate* tr./intr. 10
desamoblar *to unfurnish* tr. 2
desandar *to go back, retrace* tr. 11
desanimar *to discourage* tr. (r.) 10
desaparecer *to disappear, make disappear* tr./intr. 47
desapretar *to loosen* tr. (r.) 33
desaprobar *to disapprove of, condemn* tr. 15
desarbolar *to strip, clear trees* tr. 10
desarmar *to disarm* tr. (r.) 10
desarrendarse *to shake off the bridle* r. 17, 116
desarrollar *to develop* tr. (r.) 10
desasentar *not to suit, move* tr./intr. (r.) 33
desasir *to let go, get loose, disengage* tr. (r.) 20
desasonar *to make tasteless* tr. (r.) 171
desasosegar *to disturb* tr. 30, 33
desatender *to disregard* tr. 178
desatentar *to perturb* tr. (r.) 180
desavenir *to bring discord, disagree* tr. (r.) 194
desaviar *to deprive, mislead* tr. (r.) 10
desayunar *to have breakfast* intr. (r.) 10
desayunarse *to breakfast, have breakfast* r. 116
desbaratar *to wreck, ruin* tr./intr. (r.) 10
desbordar *to overflow* intr. (r.) 10
descalzarse *to take off ones shoes* r. 31, 116
descansar *to rest, get rest* tr./intr. (r.) 10
descararse *to behave impudently* r. 116
descargar *to unload, free* tr./intr. (r.) 30
descarriar *to misguide, lead astray* tr. (r.) 10
descender *to descend, go down* tr./intr. **66**
descerrajar *to remove, fire* tr. 10
descogollar *to strip, remove the core (from vegetables)* tr. 10
descolgar *to take down, unhook* tr. (r.) **67**
descollar *to protrude* intr. (r.) 2
descomedir *to to be rude* intr. 134
descomer *to defecate* intr. 23
descomponer *to disarrange, disturb* tr. 140
descomponerse *to decompose* r. 140
desconcertar *to disconcert* tr. **68**
desconcertarse *to disconcert, disarrange* r. 68, 116
desconectar *to switch off, disconnect* tr. (r.) 10
desconfiar *to distrust, doubt, suspect* intr. 10
desconocer *to be ignorant, not to know* tr. (r.) 47
desconsentir *to dissent* tr. 165
desconsolar *to discourage* tr. (r.) 2
descontar *to discount, take away* tr. **69**
descontarse *to discount, deduct* r. 69, 116
descontinuar *to discontinue* tr. 10
desconvenir *to disagree, not to fit* intr. (r.) 194
descornarse *to dehorn, rack one's brains* r. 2, 116
describir *to delineate, describe* tr. 98
describirse *to describe, sketch* r. 98
descubrir *to discover* (past participle: **descubierto**) tr. (r.) 133
descuidar *to neglect* tr./intr. 10
descuidarse *to neglect, not to bother* r. 116
desdecir *to degenerate, retract* intr. (r.) 57
desdentar *to pull teeth* tr. 33
desdentarse *to extract teeth, break one's teeth* r. 33, 116
desdeñar *to disdain, scorn* tr. (r.) 10

desear *to desire, wish, want* tr. (r.) 10
desecar *to dessicate* tr. (r.) 24
desechar *to reject* tr. 83
desembarcar *to disembark, go ashore* tr./intr. (r.) 24
desembragar *to declutch, disengage gears* tr. 30
desempedrar *to unpave* tr. 33
desempedrarse *to remove stone; rush along* r. 33, 116
desempeñar *to take out of pawn, discharge, play, perform, play a part in* tr. (r.) 10
desencajar *to take apart* tr. (r.) 10
desencantar *to disenchant, disillusion* tr. (r.) 29
desencerrar *to let loose* tr. 33
desencordar *to disentangle* tr. 2
desenfadar *to make up, soothe, calm down* tr. (r.) 10
desengrosar *to make thinner* tr./intr. 2
desenredar *to disentangle* tr. (r.) 10
desentablar *to break up* tr. 10
desentender *to ignore* tr. 91
desentenderse *to pay no attention to* r. 92
desenterrar *to exhume, dig up* tr. 93
desentonar *to be out of tune, not to fit, humble* tr./intr. (r.) 10
desenvolver *to unroll, unwrap* tr. (r.) 95
desertar *to desert* tr. (r.) 10
deservir *to be disobliging* tr. 134
desesperar *to despair* tr./intr. (r.) 10
desfallecer *to weaken, become weak* tr./intr. 47
desferrar *to free from irons* 33
desflocar *to unravel* tr. (r.) 2
desfogar *to make a vent to allow fire to escape* tr./intr. (r.) 2
desfogarse *to get in a passion* r. 2, 116
desgajar *to rip, tear off* tr. (r.) 10
desganar *to dissuade* tr. (r.) 10
desganarse *to lose one's appetite, be bored* r. 116
desgarrar *to split, rip, tear* tr. (r.) 10
desgastar *to wear out* tr. (r.) 10
desgobernar *to misgovern* tr. (r.) 103
desgraciar *to deprive, make ungraceful* tr. 10
desguarnecer *to remove, disarm* tr. 47
deshacer *to destroy, take apart, undo* tr. (r.) 106
deshechar *to destroy, waste* tr. 83
deshelar *to thaw* tr. (r.) 107
desherbar *to remove weeds* tr. 33
desherrar *to unshoe horses* tr. (r.) 33
deshonrar *to dishonour* tr. 10
designar *to designate, appoint* tr. 10
desinflar *to deflate* tr. (r.) 10
desinteresarse *to disinterest* r. 116
desleír *to dilute, dissolve* tr. (r.) 150
deslendrar *to clean the hair* tr. 33
desliar *to untie* tr. (r.) 94
desligar *to untie, undo* tr. (r.) 30
deslizar *to slide* tr. (r.) 31
deslucir *to tarnish* tr. (r.) 45
deslumbrar *to dazzle, blind* tr. (r.) 10
desmandar *to stray* tr. (r.) 10
desmatar *to clear shrubs/plants* tr. 10
desmayar *to faint, dismay, lose heart* tr./intr. (r.) 10
desmejorar *to deteriorate, get worse* tr./intr. (r.) 10
desmelar *to harvest honey* tr. 33
desmembrar *to dismember* tr. (r.) 33
desmentir *to deny, refute* tr./intr. 123
desmenuzar *to crumble, break into pieces* tr. 31
desmerecer *to be unworthy, deteriorate* tr./intr. 47
desmigajar *to crumble* tr. (r.) 10
desmochar *to top, cut, cut off the top* tr. 10
desmoler *to digest, wear out* tr. 125
desmoronar *to fall to pieces* tr. (r.) 10
desnatar *to skim* tr. 10
desnevar *to remove snow, thaw* intr. 33
desnucar *to break the neck* tr. (r.) 182
desnudar *to undress, strip* tr. 10
desnudarse *to get undressed* r. 116
desobedecer *to disobey* tr. 47

desocupar *to vacate, clear* tr. (r.) 10
desoír *to ignore, be deaf to* tr. 131
desolar *to desolate, destroy* tr. (r.) 2
desollar *to flay, skin* tr. 2
desordenar *to disarrange, disorder* tr. (r.) 10
desorganizar *to disorganise* tr. (r.) 31
desosar *to remove bones* tr. 2
desovar *to spawn* intr. (r.) 2
despabilar *to liven up, sharpen* tr. (r.) 10
despachar *to finish, send, hurry* tr./intr. (r.) 10
despachurrar *to squash, crush, smash* tr. 10
despampanar *to prune, let off steam* tr./intr. (r.) 10
desparramar *to scatter, sprinkle* tr. (r.) 10
despavorir *to be aghast* intr. (r.) 133
despechar *to spite* tr. (r.) 10
despedazar *to shred, tear to pieces* tr. (r.) 31
despedir *to dismiss, say goodbye* tr. (r.) **70**
despedirse *to take leave, say goodbye* r. 70
despedrar *to clear, remove rubble* tr. 33
despegar *to unglue, take off* tr./intr. 30
despegarse *to unstick, unglue, detach* r. 30, 116
despeinarse *to dishevel, to let one's hair down* r. 116
desperdiciar *to waste, miss* tr. 10
desperezarse *to stretch oneself* r. 31, 116
despernar *to cut off a leg* tr. (r.) 33
despertar *to awake, wake up* tr. **71**
despertarse *to wake up* r. 71, 116
despilfarrar *to waste, squander* tr. (r.) 10
despistar *to mislead* tr. (r.) 10
desplacer *to displease, annoy* tr. 54
desplazar *to displace* tr. 31
desplegar *to unfold, spread* tr. (r.) **72**
despoblar *to depopulate* tr. (r.) 137
despojar *to strip off* tr. (r.) 10
despreciar *to despise, scorn* tr. 10
desprender *to detach* tr. (r.) 23
desquiciar *to disjoint, deprive* tr. (r.) 10
destacar *to stand out, emphasise* tr./intr. (r.) 24
destellar *to twinkle, sparkle* intr. 10
destemplar *to disturb, lose control* tr. (r.) 10
destentar *to free from temptation* tr. 33
desteñir *to lose colour* tr./intr. (r.) 181
desterrar *to exile, banish* tr. **73**
destinar *to destine* tr. 10
destituir *to discharge, dismiss* tr. 110
destorcer *to untwist* tr. (r.) 184
destrocar *to re-exchange* tr. 182
destruir *to destroy, ruin* tr. (r.) **74**
destruirse *to destroy, cancel* r. 74
desusar *to disuse, go out of use* tr. (r.) 10
desvalijar *to rob, swindle* tr. 10
desvanecer *to make vanish, disappear* tr. 47
desvanecerse *to vanish, disappear* r. 47
desventar *to let out air* tr. 33
desvergonzarse *to be impudent* r. 2, 31, 116
desvestirse *to undress oneself* r. 133
desviar *to divert, lead away* tr. (r.) 10
desvivirse *to be very eager* r. 198
detallar *to itemise, detail* tr. 10
detener *to stop, detain* tr. (r.) 179
detenerse *to stop oneself* r. 179
determinar *to determine* tr. (r.) 10
devengar *to produce (interest)* tr. 30
devenir *to happen, become* intr. 194
devolver *to return, give back* tr. (r.) **75**
devolverse *to restore, give back* r. 201
devorar *to devour* tr. (r.) 10
dezmar *to diminish* tr. 33
dialogar *to converse, speak* 30
dibujar *to sketch* tr. 10
dictar *to dictate, prescribe* tr. 10
difamar *to defame, discredit* tr. 10
diferenciar *to distinguish,*

embalar *to pack* tr./intr. 10
embarazar *to hamper; make pregnant* tr. (r.) 31
embarcar *to board, go on board* tr. (r.) 24
embargar *to impede, obstruct* tr. 30
embarrar *to splash with mud* tr. (r.) 10
embaucar *to deceive, cheat* tr. 24
embeber *to soak in, soak up, shrink* tr./intr. (r.) 23
embelesar *to fascinate, captivate* tr. (r.) 10
embellecer *to beautify, embellish* tr. (r.) 47
embestir *to assail* tr./intr. 134
embobar *to stupefy, fascinate* tr. (r.) 10
embobecer *to make foolish* tr. (r.) 47
emborrachar *to intoxicate, get drunk* tr. (r.) 10
emborronar *to scribble* tr. 10
embravecer *to infuriate, enrage, become furious* tr./intr. 47
embrollar *to mix up, muddle* tr. (r.) 10
embromar *to tease, loiter* tr./intr. (r.) 10
embrutecer *to brutalise, become brutal* tr. (r.) 47
embustear *to lie, fib* intr. 10
emitir *to emit* tr. (r.) 133
emocionar *to move, touch* tr. (r.) 10
empachar *to give / get indigestion* tr. (r.) 10
empalmar *to join, couple* tr./intr. (r.) 10
empañar *to mist, blur* tr. 10
empapar *to soak* tr. (r.) 10
emparejar *to match, pair off* tr./intr. (r.) 10
emparentar *to become related by marriage* intr. 33
empedernir *to become petrified, harden* tr. (r.) 133
empedrar *to pave* tr. 33
empeller (= empellar) *to push, shove* tr. 23
empeñar *to pawn, pledge* tr. (r.) 10
empequeñecer *to make smaller, reduce, diminish* tr. (r.) 47
empezar *to begin, start* tr./intr. (r.) **85**
empezarse *to begin, start* r. 85, 116
emplear *to employ, use* tr. (r.) 10
emplumecer *to fledge, grow feathers* intr. 47
empobrecer *to impoverish, become poorer* tr./intr. (r.) 47
emporcar *to soil, stain* tr. (r.) 2, 24
emprender *to undertake, star* tr. 23
empujar *to push, shove* tr. 10
enaltecer *to extol, praise* tr. 47
enamorar *to inspire love in, fall in love, flirt* tr. (r.) 10
enardecer *to kindle, get worked up* tr. (r.) 47
encabezar *to lead, register, bestow the title* tr. (r.) 31
encabronar *to enrage* tr. 10
encajar *to fit in* tr. (r.) 10
encallecer *to harden, become hardened* intr. 47
encalvecer *to become bald* intr. 47
encanecer *to grow grey, become grey* tr./intr. (r.) 47
encantar *to enchant* tr. (r.) 10
encañar *to channel; form stalks* tr./intr. 10
encarar *to face* tr./intr. (r.) 10
encarecer *to raise, praise* tr. (r.) 47
encargar *to entrust, ask for in advance* tr. (r.) 30
encargarse (de) *to take charge of* r. 30, 116
encender *to light* tr. (r.) **86**
encensar *to perfume* 33
encerrar *to shut in, lock up* tr. (r.) **87**
enchapar *to veneer, plate* tr. 10
enchufar *to connect, plug in* tr. (r.) 10
enclocar *to cluck* intr. (r.) 2, 24
encobar *to brood, sit on eggs* intr. 2
encoger *to shrink* tr./intr. (r.) 35
encojar *to lame, cripple* tr. (r.) 10
encomendar *to entrust* tr./intr. (r.) **88**
encontrar *to find, meet* tr./intr. **89**
encontrarse *to come across / upon, meet* r. 89, 116
encorar *to cover with leather* tr./intr. (r.) 2

encorarse *to heal* intr. (r.) 2, 116
encordar *to string instruments* tr. 2
encorvar *to curve, bend* tr. (r.) 10
encostrar *to coat, form a crust* tr./intr. (r.) 10
encovar *to put in a cellar* tr. (r.) 2
encrespar *to curl, enrage* tr. (r.) 10
encrudecer *to make rough / raw, irritate* tr. 54
encruelecer *to incite to cruelty* tr. 47
encubertar *to cover* tr. (r.) 33
encubrir *to conceal* (past participle: **encubierto**) tr. 133
endentar *to enrage* tr. 33
endentecer *to teethe, cut teeth* intr. 47
enderezar *to straighten, make straight* tr./intr. (r.) 31
endeudarse *to get into debt* r. 116
endorsar *to endorse* tr. 10
endulzar *to sweeten* tr. (r.) 31
endurecer *to harden, become hard* tr./intr. (r.) 47
enemistar *to make enemies* tr. (r.) 10
enfadar *to anger, irritate* tr. (r.) 10
enfadarse *to become angry* r. 116
enfermar *to make sick, become ill* tr./intr. (r.) 10
enflaquecer *to make / become thin* tr./intr. 47
enfocar *to focus* tr. 24
enfrascar *to bottle up, put into bottles* tr. 24
enfrascarse *to become entangled, become involved* r. 24, 116
enfrentar *to face, confront* tr./intr. (r.) 10
enfrentarse *to face, confront* r. 116
enfriar *to cool, chill* tr./intr. (r.) 94
enfriarse *to get cold* r. 94, 116
enfurecer *to infuriate, make furious* tr. 47
enfurecerse *to become furious* r. 47
engaitar *to trick, deceive* tr. 10
engañar *to deceive, mislead* tr. 10
engañarse *to lie to oneself* r. 116
engatusar *to inveigle, swindle, take in, beguile* tr. 10
engendrar *to beget, engender* tr. (r.) 10
engomar *to glue, gum* tr. 10
engorar *to confuse* tr./intr. (r.) 2
engordar *to put on weight, fatten, become fat* tr./intr. (r.) 10
engorrar *to irritate, bother, annoy* tr. (r.) 10
engrandecer *to enlarge, increase* tr. (r.) 47
engrasar *to grease, oil* tr. (r.) 10
engreír *to make vain or conceited* tr. 134
engreírse *to become haughty* r. 134
engrosar *to make thick, put on weight* tr./intr. (r.) 2
engullir *to gulp down, bolt, gobble* tr. 198
enhestar *to hoist, rise up* tr. 33
enhestarse *to set upright* r. 33, 116
enjabonar *to soap, wash with soap* tr. 10
enjalbegar *to whitewash* tr. (r.) 30
enjambrar *to swarm, multiply* tr./intr. 10
enjaular *to put in a cage, confine* tr. 10
enjuagar *to rinse* tr. (r.) 30
enjugar *to dry, wipe* tr. (r.) 115
enjuiciar *to examine, judge a case* tr. 10
enlazar *to join, connect* tr. (r.) 31
enloquecer *to drive insane, go mad* tr./intr. (r.) 47
enlucir *to plaster, polish* tr. 187
enmelar *to smear with honey* tr./intr. 33
enmendar *to correct, amend* tr. (r.) **90**
enmohecer *to make mouldy, mildew, go rusty* tr. 47
enmudecer *to silence, hush, become speechless* tr./intr. (r.) 47
ennegrecer *to blacken, turn black* tr. 47
ennoblecer *to ennoble, embellish* tr. 47
ennoblecerse *to become noble* r. 47
enojar *to annoy, irritate, vex* tr. (r.) 10
enojarse *to become angry* r. 116
enorgullecer *to make proud, become proud* tr. (r.) 47
enrabiar *to anger* tr. (r.) 10

enrarecer *to thin out, become scarce* tr./intr. 47
enredar *to entangle, cause trouble / mischief* tr./intr. (r.) 10
enripiar *to fill with gravel* tr. 10
enriquecer *to enrich, get rich* tr./intr. (r.) 47
enrodar *to wheel* tr. 2
enrojecer *to make red, blush* tr./intr. (r.) 47
enronquecer *to make / become hoarse* tr. (r.) 47
enroscar *to curl, twist* tr. (r.) 24
ensacar *to bag* tr. 24
ensalzar *to glorify, praise* tr. (r.) 31
ensanchar *to widen* tr./intr. (r.) 10
ensangrentar *to stain with blood* tr. (r.) 33
ensartar *to string, thread* tr. (r.) 10
ensayar *to practise, rehearse, test* tr. (r.) 10
enseñar *to teach, point out, show* tr. (r.) 10
ensillar *to saddle* tr. 10
ensolver *to include, reduce* tr. 2
ensorbecer *to make arrogant / proud* tr. (r.) 47
ensordecer *to deafen, become deaf* tr./intr. (r.) 47
ensuciar *to dirty, stain, soil* tr./intr. (r.) 10
entablar *to start, board* tr. (r.) 10
entallecer *to grow shoots* tr. 47
entender *to understand* tr./intr. (r.) **91**
entenderse *to be understood* r. **92**
enterar *to inform* tr. (r.) 10
enterarse *to find out* r. 116
enternecer *to make tender, move, touch* tr. (r.) 47
enterrar *to bury, forget* tr. (r.) **93**
entonar *to intone, sing in tune, put on airs* tr. (r.) 10
entontar *to stupefy* tr. (r.) 10
entontecer *to make / become silly* tr./intr. (r.) 47
entorpecer *to dull, stupefy, obstruct* tr. 47
entortar *to make tortuous* tr. 2
entortar *to make crooked, make blind in one eye* tr. 2
entrar *to enter, come in, go in* tr./intr. (r.) 10
entregar *to deliver, hand over, give* tr. (r.) 30
entregarse *to surrender, give in* r. 30, 116
entrelazar *to interweave, interlace* tr. 31
entrelucir *to show, shine* intr. 187
entremorir *to burn out, flicker* intr. (r.) 127
entrenar *to train* tr. (r.) 10
entreoír *to half hear, hear vaguely* tr. 131
entrepernar *to cross one's legs* intr. (r.) 33
entretener *to entertain, make bearable* tr. (r.) 179
entretenerse *to amuse oneself* r. 179
entrever *to descry, surmise, catch a glimpse* tr. 195
entrevistar *to interview* tr./intr. (r.) 10
entristecer *to sadden, become sad* tr. (r.) 47
entullecer *to stop, become crippled* tr./intr. 47
entumecer *to numb, become numb, become swollen* tr. 47
entumecerse *to become numb* r. 47
enunciar *to state, enunciate* tr. (r.) 10
envanecer *to make conceited* tr. (r.) 47
envasar *to bottle, pack* tr. 10
envejecer *to age, become old* tr. (r.) 47
envenenar *to poison* tr. (r.) 10
enverdecer *to turn green* intr. 47
envestir *to clothe* tr. 134
enviar *to send* tr. (r.) **94**
enviciar *to corrupt; grow too much foliage* tr./intr. (r.) 10
cnvidiar *to envy, covet* tr. 10
envilecer *to debase, vilify, degrade* tr. (r.) 47
envolver *to wrap up* tr. (r.) **95**
envolverse *to have an affair, become involved* r. 95
enyesar *to plaster* tr. 10
enzarzar *to cover with brambles; get*

evacuar *to evacuate* tr. **100**
evadir *to evade* tr. (r.) 133
evaluar *to evaluate* tr. (r.) 10
evaporar *to evaporate, vanish* tr. (r.) 10
evitar *to avoid* tr. (r.) 10
evolucionar *to evolve, develop* intr. 10
examinar *to examine* tr. 10
examinarse *to sit an exam* r. 116
exasperar *to irritate, exasperate* tr. (r.) 10
exceder *to exceed, surpass* tr. (r.) 23
exceptuar *to exclude, exempt* tr. 10
excitar *to excite, stimulate* tr. (r.) 10
excluir *to exclude, expel* tr. (r.) 110
excusar *to excuse, apologise* tr. (r.) 10
exhibir *to exhibit, display, show* tr. 133
exigir *to demand, urge, require* tr. (r.) 84
exiliar *to exile* tr. (r.) 10
eximir *to exempt, free* tr. (r.) 133
existir *to exist, be* intr. 133
expedir *to forward, expedite* 134
expedirse *to expedite, dispatch* tr. (r.) 134
expeler *to expel, eject* tr. 23
experimentar *to try, experiment* tr./intr. (r.) 10
explicar *to explain* tr. (r.) 24
explorar *to explore, investigate* tr. 10
explotar *to exploit, explode* tr./intr. (r.) 10
exponer *to expose, jeopardise* tr. (r.) 140
expresar *to express, express oneself* tr. (r.) 10
extender *to extend* tr. (r.) 136
extenuar *to debilitate, weaken* tr. (r.) 10
exterminar *to eradicate, exterminate* tr. (r.) 10
extinguir *to extinguish, become extinct* tr. (r.) 110
extraer *to draw out, remove, extract* tr. (r.) 188
extraviar *to lose, lead astray* tr. (r.) 10

fabricar *to fabricate, manufacture* tr. (r.) 24
facilitar *to facilitate* tr. 10
fallar *to judge, find, fail* tr./intr. (r.) 10
fallecer *to expire, die* intr. 47
falsear *to falsify, misrepresent* tr. 10
falsificar *to falsify, forge* tr. 24
faltar *to be missing, lack* intr. (r.) 10
fantasear *to daydream, fancy* tr./intr. 10
farfullar *to gabble, do hastily* tr./intr. 10
farolear *to brag, boast, show off* intr. 10
fascinar *to fascinate, enchant* tr. (r.) 10
fastidiar *to annoy, irritate* tr. (r.) 10
fatigar *to tire, exhaust* tr. (r.) 30
favorecer *to favour, support* tr./intr. (r.) 47
fecundar(= fecundizar) *to fertilise* tr. 10
felicitar *to congratulate* tr. (r.) 10
fenecer *to finish, die, end* tr./intr. 47
fermentar *to ferment, be agitated* tr./intr. 10
ferrarse *to trim* r. 33, 116
fertilizar *to fertilise, enrich* tr. 31
festejar *to feast, entertain, celebrate* tr. (r.) 10
fiar *to confide, trust, guarantee* tr./intr. (r.) 10
fichar *to register, clock in* tr. 10
figurar *to figure, depict, draw, appear* tr./intr. 10
figurarse *to figure, imagine* r. 116
fijar *to fix, fasten, clinch, set* tr. 10
fijarse *to notice, settle, pay attention* r. 116
filiar *to take personal data, join* tr. (r.) 10
filmar *to film* tr. 10
filtrar *to filter, leak* tr./intr. (r.) 10
finalizar *to end, conclude* tr./intr. 31
financiar *to finance* tr. 10
fingir *to feign, pretend* tr. (r.) 52
firmar *to sign* tr. 10
fisgar *to snoop, pry on, mock* tr./intr. (r.) 30
flamear *to blaze, flame* tr. 10
flaquear *to weaken* intr. 10

fletar *to charter a ship, hire* tr. (r.) 10
flirtear *to flirt* intr. 10
flojear *to weaken, grow weak* intr. 10
florecer *to flower* intr. (r.) 47
flotar *to float* intr. 10
fluctuar *to fluctuate* intr. 10
fluir *to flow* intr. 110
fomentar *to encourage, promote* tr. 10
forjar *to forge, shape* tr. 10
formar *to form, shape* tr./intr. (r.) 10
formular *to formulate* tr. 10
forrar *to line, cover* tr. (r.) 10
fortalecer *to fortify, strengthen* tr. (r.) 47
fortificar *to strengthen* tr. 24
forzar *to compel, force* tr. (r.) 2
fotocopiar *to photocopy, make photocopies* tr. 10
fotografiar *to photograph, take photographs* tr. 10
fracasar *to fail* intr. 10
fraccionar *to break up, divide* tr. (r.) 10
fraguar *to forge, set, plan* tr./intr. (r.) 12
franquear *to free, liberate* tr. (r.) 10
frecuentar *to frequent, do again and again* tr. 10
fregar *to wash up, scrub,* tr. **101**
freír *to fry* tr. **102**
frenar *to break, restrain* tr./intr. 10
frisar *to frizz; approach* tr./intr. 10
frotar *to rub* tr. (r.) 10
fruncir *to pleat, knit* tr. (r.) 45
frustrar *to frustrate* tr. (r.) 10
fulminar *to strike* tr. 10
fumar *to smoke* tr./intr. (r.) 10
funcionar *to function, run/work (machinery)* intr. 10
fundar *to found* tr. (r.) 10
fundir *to melt, cast* tr. (r.) 133
fusionar *to combine, merge, amalgamate* tr. (r.) 10
fustigar *to whip, lash* tr. 30

galantear *to woo, court* tr. 10
galardonar *to recompense, reward* tr. 10
gallear *to tread, cover, shout and threaten* tr./intr. 10
galopar *to gallop* intr. 10
galvanizar *to galvanise* tr. 31
ganar *to gain, earn, win* tr./intr. (r.) 10
gansear *to say/do stupid things* tr. 10
garabatear *to scribble* tr./intr. 10
garantir *to guarantee* tr. 133
garantizar *to guarantee, answer for* tr. (r.) 31
garbear *to put on airs, show off* intr. 10
gastar *to waste, use up, spend* tr. (r.) 10
gatear *to crawl* tr./intr. 10
gemiquear *to whine* intr. 10
gemir *to groan, grieve, moan, howl* intr. 134
generalizar *to generalise* tr./intr. (r.) 31
generar *to generate* tr. 10
gestionar *to negotiate* tr. 10
gibar *to bend, annoy, bother* tr. 10
gimotear *to whine, wail* intr. 10
girar *to turn round, spin* tr./intr. 10
glorificar *to glorify* tr. (r.) 24
glosar *to gloss, censure* tr. 10
gobernar *to govern, rule* tr./intr. (r.) **103**
golfear *to waste time* intr. 10
golosear *to nibble at delicacies* intr. 10
golpear *to crush, blow, hit* tr./intr. (r.) 10
gorgoritear *to trill, quaver* intr. 10
gorjear *to warble, gurgle* intr. (r.) 10
gorrear *to live parasitically, sponge* intr. 10
gorronear *to cadge, sponge* intr. 10
gotear *to drip* intr. 10
gozar *to enjoy, be happy* tr./intr. (r.) 31
grabar *to engrave, record* tr. (r.) 10
graduar *to graduate, grade* tr. (r.) 10
grajear *to caw, gurgle, chatter* intr. 10
gramar *to knead* tr. 10
granar *to seed* intr. 10
granear *to sow seeds, granulate* tr. 10
granizar *to hail, hurl* tr./intr.

(imp.) 31
granjear *to earn, get, gain* tr. (r.) 10
gratificar *to reward, recompense* tr. 24
gravar *to burden, tax* tr. 10
gravitar *to gravitate* intr. 10
graznar *to crow, croak, squawk* intr. 10
grietarse *to crack, split* r. 116
grillarse *to escape* r. 116
gritar *to shout, yell, scream, shriek* tr./intr. (r.) 10
groar *to croak* intr. 10
gruñir *to creak (door hinges, etc.); grunt, growl, snarl* intr. (r.) 198
guadañar *to mow, scythe* tr. 10
guardar *to keep, guard, save* tr./intr. (r.) 10
guarecer *to shelter, hide* tr. (r.) 47
guarnecer *to garnish, decorate* tr. 47
guasearse *to joke, jest* r. 116
guerrear *to wage war, fight* intr. 10
guiar *to guide, lead, sprout* tr./intr. (r.) 94
guipar *to notice, see* tr. 10
guisar *to cook, prepare (food)* tr. 10
gustar *to be pleasing, like, enjoy* tr./intr. (r.) 10

haber *to have* tr. (aux.) **104**
habitar *to inhabit, reside, dwell* tr./intr. 10
habituar *to accustom, get used to* tr. (r.) 10
hablar *to speak, talk* tr./intr. (r.) **105**
hacendar *to transfer, own (property)* tr. (r.) 33
hacer *to do, make* tr./intr. **106**
halagar *to flatter* tr. 30
halar *to haul, pull* tr./intr. 10
hallar *to find, locate, discover* tr. 10
hallarse *to find, be (location)* r. 116
hamacar (= hamaquear) *to rock, swing* tr. 24
hambrear *to starve, hunger* tr./intr. 10
hartar *to satiate, fill, bore* tr. (r.) 10
hastiar *to bore, tire* tr. 10
hechizar *to bewitch, charm* tr. 31
heder *to stink* intr. 136
helar *to freeze, chill* tr./intr. **107**
henchir *to fill* tr. (r.) 134
hender *to split* 136
hendir *to split, crack* tr. (r.) 108
heñir *to knead* tr. 134
heredar *to inherit* tr. 10
herir *to wound, hurt, harm* tr. (r.) **108**
hermanar *to join, harmonise* tr. (r.) 10
hermosear *to beautify, embellish* tr. 10
herrar *to shoe a horse* tr. 33
hervir *to boil* intr. **109**
hidratar *to hydrate* tr. (r.) 10
hidrogenar *to hydrogenate* tr. 10
higienizar *to make hygienic* tr. 31
hilar *to spin* tr. 10
hilvanar *to baste, tack, hem* tr. 10
hincar *to prick, drive into* tr. (r.) 24
hinchar *to fill with air, inflate, swell* tr./intr. (r.) 10
hipar *to hiccup, have hiccups* intr. 10
hipnotizar *to hypnotise* tr. 31
hipotecar *to mortgage, take out a mortgage* tr. 24
historiar *to record history* tr. 10
hojear *to leaf through, glance, flake* tr./intr. 10
holgar *to rest* intr. (r.) 2
hollar *to trample on* tr. 2
homenajear *to pay homage to* tr. 10
hondear *to sound, sling* tr./intr. 10
honrar *to honour, accept, pay* tr. 10
hornear *to bake* intr. 10
horripilar *to horrify, become terrified* tr. (r.) 10
hospedar *to lodge* tr. (r.) 10
hospitalizar *to hospitalise* tr. 31
hostigar *to lash, whip, trouble* tr. 30
hostilizar *to antagonise, harass* tr. 31
huir *to run away, escape* tr./intr. (r.) **110**
humear *to smoke, fumigate* tr./intr. 10
humedecer *to dampen, humidify* tr. 47
humillar *to humiliate, humble* tr. (r.) 10
hundir *to sink* tr. (r.) 133
hurgar *to poke* tr. 30

hurtar *to rob, steal, pinch* tr. (r.) 10
husmear *to snoop on, smell out, nose* tr./intr. (r.) 10

idealizar *to idealise* tr. 31
idear *to plan, think up, conceive* tr. 10
identificar *to identify* tr. (r.) 24
ignorar *to be ignorant of, ignore, not to know* tr. (r.) 10
igualar *to make equal, equal* tr./intr. (r.) 10
iluminar *to illuminate* tr. 10
ilusionar *to fascinate, have illusions, hope* tr. (r.) 10
ilustrar *to enlighten* tr. (r.) 10
imaginar *to imagine, fancy, suppose* tr. (r.) 10
imbuir *to imbue, infuse* tr. 110
imitar *to imitate* tr. 10
impacientar *to make / become impatient* tr. (r.) 10
impartir *to grant, impart* tr. 133
impedir *to impede, hinder, prevent* tr. (r.) **111**
impeler *to push, incite, urge* tr. 23
imperar *to rule, prevail* intr. 10
implantar *to implant, introduce* tr. 10
implicar *to implicate, imply* tr./intr. (r.) 24
implorar *to entreat, beg, implore* tr. 10
imponer *to impose, dominate* tr. (r.) 140
importar *to import, cost; be important, matter, mind* tr./intr. (r.) (imp.) 10
importunar *to bother, pester, importune* tr. 10
imposibilitar *to prevent, stop, make impossible* tr. 10
impregnar *to impregnate* tr. 10
impresionar *to impress, make an impression* tr. (r.) 10
imprimir *to print, imprint, impress; fix in the mind* tr. (past participle: **impreso**) 133
improbar *to disapprove, condemn* tr. 2
improvisar *to improvise* tr. 10
impugnar *to contradict, refute* tr. 10
impulsar *to encourage, impel* tr. 10
imputar *to impute, charge with* tr. 10
inaugurar *to open, initiate* tr. 10
incapacitar *to disable, incapacitate* tr. 10
incendiar *to set on fire* tr. 10
incendiarse *to catch fire* r. 116
incensar *to perfume* tr. 33
incidir *to fall, cut, influence* tr./intr. 133
inclinar *to incline, bow, tilt* tr. (r.) 10
incluir *to include, enclose* tr. (r.) 110
incomodar *to inconvenience, bother* tr. (r.) 10
incomunicar *to isolate, confine* tr. (r.) 24
incordiar *to annoy, inconvenience* tr. 10
incorporar *to incorporate* tr. (r.) 10
incorporarse *to sit up* r. 116
inculcar *to instill, inculcate, implant* tr. (r.) 24
incumbir *to be incumbent, concern* tr./intr. (r.) 133
incumplir *to fail, fulfil* tr. 133
incurrir *to incur, become liable* intr. 133
indagar *to investigate* tr. 30
indemnizar *to compensate* tr. 31
independizar *to emancipate, liberate* tr. (r.) 31
indicar *to indicate, point out* tr. 24
indignar *to irritate, make indignant* tr. (r.) 10
indisponer *to indispose, become ill* tr. (r.) 140
inducir *to induce, persuade* tr. (r.) 45
indultar *to pardon* tr. 10
inebriar *to intoxicate, make drunk* tr. 10
infamar *to defame, slander* tr. (r.) 10
infectar *to infect* tr. (r.) 10
inferir *to infer* tr. 108
infernar *to damn* tr. 33
infestar *to infest, become infested* tr. (r.) 10
inflamar *to inflame, burst into flame* tr. (r.) 10
inflar *to inflate, become inflated / proud* tr. (r.) 10
influir *to influence, have influence*

jurar *to swear, take an oath* tr./intr. (r.) 10
justificar *to justify, be justified* tr. (r.) 24
juzgar *to judge* tr. (r.) 30

labrar *to farm; make a lasting impression* tr./intr. 10
lacrar *to seal* tr. (r.) 10
ladear *to tilt* tr./intr. (r.) 10
ladrar *to bark* tr./intr. 10
ladronear *to steal, shoplift* intr. 10
lamentar *to lament* tr./intr. (r.) 10
lamer *to lick* tr. (r.) 23
languidecer *to languish* intr. 47
lanzar *to hurl, fling, launch, throw* tr. (r.) 31
largar *to release, leave* tr. (r.) 30
lastimar *to hurt, damage, offend* tr. (r.) 10
latir *to beat, palpitate, throb, annoy* tr./intr. 133
lavar *to wash* tr. (r.) 10
lavarse *to wash oneself* r. **116**
laxar *to loosen, slacken* tr. (r.) 10
leer *to read* tr./intr. (r.) **117**
legalizar *to legalise* tr. 31
legar *to bequeath, leave* tr. 10
legislar *to legislate* intr. 10
legitimar *to legitimate, prove* tr. 10
levantar *to lift, raise* tr. (r.) 10
liar *to bundle, tie* tr. (r.) 10
liberar *to free, liberate* tr. 10
librar *to draw, issue, save, free* tr./intr. (r.) 10
licenciar *to discharge, release* tr. (r.) 10
licenciarse *to graduate / get a degree* r. 116
lidiar *to fight (bullfight)* tr./intr. 10
ligar *to tie, bind, unite* tr./intr. (r.) 30
lijar *to sandpaper* tr. 10
limar *to polish, file, smooth* tr. 10
limitar *to limit, reduce* tr./intr. (r.) 10
limpiar *to clean, cleanse* tr. (r.) **118**
lindar *to adjoin, border* intr. 10
liquidar *to liquidate, sell off, become liquid* tr. (r.) 10
lisonjear *to flatter, compliment* tr. 10
llamar *to call, name* tr./intr. (r.) 10
llamarse *to be called, be named* r. 116
llamear *to flame, blaze* intr. 10
llegar *to arrive, reach* tr./intr. (r.) **119**
llenar *to fill, fill up* tr./intr. (r.) 10
llevar *to carry, wear, take away* tr./intr. (r.) 10
llorar *to cry, weep* tr./intr. **120**
lloriquear *to cry constantly, whine* intr. (r.) 10
llover *to rain* tr./intr. (imp.) **121**
lloviznar *to drizzle* intr. (imp.) 10
localizar *to locate, find* tr. (r.) 31
lograr *to achieve, get, attain, procure* tr. (r.) 10
lubricar *to lubricate* tr. 24
luchar *to fight, strive, struggle, wrestle* intr. 10
lucir *to display, show, exhibit* tr./intr. 45
luir *to redeem* tr. (r.) 110
lujuriar *to lust, be lustful / lecherous* intr. 10
lustrar *to polish; travel, roam* tr./intr. 10

macerar *to macerate, marinate, soak, mortify* tr. (r.) 10
madrugar *to get up early* tr./intr. (r.) 30
madurar *to ripen, become ripe* tr./intr. (r.) 10
magullar *to batter and bruise* tr. (r.) 10
malcriar *to pamper, spoil* tr. 10
maldecir *to curse, damn* tr./intr. (r.) 57
malear *to spoil, ruin* tr. (r.) 10
malgastar *to squander, waste, mis-spend* tr. 10
malograr *to waste, miss, fail* tr. (r.) 10
malquerer *to dislike, hate* tr. 144
malquistar *to excite disputes, alienate* tr. (r.) 10
malsonar *to sound unpleasant* 2
malvar *to corrupt* tr. 10
mamar *to suck* tr./intr. (r.) 10
manar *to run, flow, spring* tr./intr. 10
mancar *to be wanting, maim, go lame* tr./intr. (r.) 24

tr. (r.) 31
naufragar *to be shipwrecked, fail* intr. 30
nausear *to feel sick* intr. 10
navegar *to navigate, sail* tr./intr. 30
necear *to talk nonsense, act foolishly* intr. 10
necesitar *to need, be in need* tr./intr. 10
negar *to refuse, deny* tr./intr. (r.) **130**
negociar *to negotiate* tr./intr. 10
negrear (= negrecer) *to turn black, blacken* intr. 10
neutralizar *to neutralise* tr. (r.) 31
nevar *to snow* tr./intr. (imp.) 33
niñear *to behave in a childish manner* intr. 10
nivelar *to level* tr. (r.) 10
nombrar *to name, appoint* tr. 10
normalizar *to make normal, standardise* tr. (r.) 31
notar *to notice, remark, mark* tr. 10
noticiar *to inform, notify* tr. 10
notificar *to notify* tr. 24
novelar *to write novels, tell lies / fabulous stories* intr. 10
novelizar *to put into a novel, fictionalise* tr. 31
nublar *to cloud, become cloudy* tr. (r.) 10
numerar *to number* tr. 10
nutrir *to nourish* tr. (r.) 133

obedecer *to obey* tr. 47
objetar *to object* tr./intr. 10
oblicuar *to slant* tr./intr. 10
obligar *to compel, force, oblige* tr. (r.) 30
obliterar *to obliterate, erase* tr. 10
obrar *to work, act, be* tr./intr. 10
obscurecer *to darken, get dark, cloud* tr./intr. (r.) 47
obsequiar *to make a fuss of, lavish* tr. 10
observar *to observe, obey* tr. 10
obstaculizar *to hinder, obstruct* tr. 31
obstar *to impede, stand in the way* intr. 10
obstinarse *to persist, be obstinate* r. 116
obstruir *to obstruct* tr. (r.) 110
obtener *to obtain, get* tr. 179
ocasionar *to cause, occasion, provoke* tr. 10
ocluir *to occlude* tr. (r.) 110
ocultar *to hide, conceal* tr. (r.) 10
ocupar *to occupy* tr. 10
ocuparse *to be in charge of / busy with* r. 116
ocurrir *to occur, happen* intr. (r.) (imp.) 133
ocurrirse *to have an idea* r. 133
odiar *to hate, loath* tr. 10
ofender *to offend, be unpleasant, take offence* tr./intr. (r.) 23
ofenderse *to get upset* r. 23
ofrecer *to offer* tr. (r.) 47
ofuscar *to dazzle, blind* 24
oír *to hear* tr./intr. (r.) **131**
ojear *to glance, stare at* tr. 10
oler *to smell* tr./intr. (r.) **132**
olfatear *sniff, scent, smell* tr. 10
oliscar *sniff, smell strong / high* tr./intr. 24
olvidar *to forget* tr. (r.) 10
omitir *to omit, leave out* tr. (r.) 133
ondear *to wave, sway, swing* intr. (r.) 10
ondular *to wind, wave* tr./intr. 10
operar *to operate* tr./intr. (r.) 10
opinar *to have an opinion, think* intr. 10
oponer *to oppose* tr. (r.) 140
opositar *to take part, be a candidate* intr. 10
oprimir *to oppress, press* tr. 133
optar *to choose, opt* tr./intr. 10
orar *to pray, make a speech* intr. 10
ordenar *to order, command, arrange* tr. (r.) 10
ordenarse *to tidy up, put in order* r. 116
organizar *to organise, arrange* tr. (r.) 31
orientar *to orientate, guide* tr. (r.) 10
originar *to originate, arise* tr. (r.) 10
orillar *to settle, approach the shore* tr./intr. 10
orinar *to urinate* tr./intr. (r.) 10
ornar *to adorn* tr. (r.) 10
osar *to dare, venture* intr. 10

oscilar *to oscillate, swing* intr. 10
oscurecer *to darken, obscure* tr. (r.) 47
ostentar *to make a show of, brag about* tr. 10
otorgar *to grant* tr. 30
oxidar *to rust, become oxidised* tr. (r.) 10
oxigenar *to oxygenate* tr. (r.) 10

pacer *to grace, pasture* tr./intr. 47
pacificar *to pacify, negotiate peace* tr./intr. (r.) 24
pactar *to agree, come to an agreement* tr./intr. 10
padecer *to suffer, endure, suffer from* tr./intr. 47
pagar *to pay* tr./intr. (r.) 30
paladear *to savour, taste, relish* tr./intr. (r.) 10
paliar *to palliate, alleviate* tr. 10
palidecer *to pale, grow pale* intr. 47
palmear *to clap; level off* tr./intr. 10
palpar *to feel, touch, grope* tr./intr. 10
parar *to stop* tr./intr. (r.) 10
parecer *to appear, seem* intr. (r.) 47
parecerse *to look like each other, resemble* r. 47
parir *to give birth* tr./intr. 133
parlar *to speak, talk* tr./intr. 10
parlotear *to chatter, prattle* intr. 10
parpadear *to blink, wink* intr. 10
participar *to participate, notify of* tr./intr. 10
partir *to split, leave* tr./intr. (r.) **133**
pasar *to spend time, pass, happen* tr./intr. (r.) 10
pasear *to walk, promenade* tr./intr. (r.) 10
pasmar *to stun, astound, chill, get blight* tr. (r.) 10
patear (= patalear) *to kick, stamp one's feet* tr./intr. 10
patinar *to skate, slide, skid* intr. 10
patrocinar *to sponsor* tr. 10
pausar *to pause, make pauses* tr./intr. 10
pecar *to sin* intr. 24
pedir *to ask, request* tr. **134**
pegar *to hit, stick, glue* tr./intr. (r.) 30
peinarse *to comb* r. 116
pelar *to peal* tr. (r.) 10
pelear *to fight* intr. (r.) 10
penar *to grieve, punish* tr./intr. (r.) 10
pender *to dangle, hang, be pending* intr. 23
penetrar *to penetrate* tr./intr. (r.) 10
pensar *to think* tr./intr. (r.) **135**
percibir *to perceive* tr. 133
perder *to lose* tr./intr. (r.) **136**
perdonar *to excuse, pardon, forgive* tr. 10
perdurar *to last* intr. 10
perecer *to perish, long for* intr. (r.) 47
peregrinar *to go on a pilgrimage* intr. 10
perfeccionar *to perfect* tr. (r.) 10
perfumar *to perfume* tr. (r.) 10
perjudicar *to damage, harm* tr. (r.) 24
permanecer *to remain, stay* intr. 47
permitir *to admit, allow, permit* tr. (r.) 133
permutar *to swap, exchange* tr. 10
perniquebrar *to break one's leg* tr. (r.) 143
perseguir *to persecute* tr. 134
persuadir *to persuade* tr. (r.) 133
pertenecer *to apertain, belong* intr. (r.) 47
perturbar *to disturb, become upset* tr. (r.) 10
pervertir *to pervert* tr. (r.) 108
pesar *to weigh, grieve* tr./intr. (r.) 10
pescar *to fish* tr./intr. 24
pestañear *to blink* intr. 10
piar *to chirp, cheep, peep* intr. 10
picar *to pierce, sting, prick* tr./intr. (r.) 24
pillar *to catch, plunder* tr. 10
pinchar *to prick, jab* tr. 10
pintar *to paint* tr./intr. (r.) 10
pisar *to tread, step on, trample* tr. 10
placer *to gratify, humour, please* tr. 54
plagar *to infest, plague* tr. (r.) 30
planchar *to iron* tr. 10
planear *to plan, design, glide* tr./intr. 10
plantar *to plant* tr. (r.) 10

plasmar *to form, shape, mould* tr. 10
platicar *to talk over, chat, talk* tr./intr. 24
plegar *to fold* tr. (r.) 30, 33
pleitar *to litigate, go to court* intr. 10
poblar *to populate* tr./intr. (r.) **137**
podar *to prune, trim* tr. 10
poder *to be able, can* tr./intr. (r.) **138**
podrir (= pudrir) *to rot* tr. (r.) **139**
polemizar *to engage in controversy* tr. 31
polvorear *to sprinkle, dust, powder* tr. 10
ponderar *to ponder, consider* tr. 10
poner *to put, place* tr. (r.) **140**
ponerse *to put on clothing, become* r. 140
porfiar *to insist, persist* intr. 10
portar *to carry, bear* tr./intr. (r.) 10
posar *to pose, put, lay down* tr./intr. (r.) 10
poseer *to possess, own* tr. (r.) 117
posponer *to postpone* tr. 140
postergar *to postpone* tr. 30
postrar *to prostrate, humble* tr. (r.) 10
postular *to apply for, take part, apply* tr./intr. 10
practicar *to practise* tr. 24
precaver *to prevent, provide against* tr. (r.) 195
preceptuar *to command* tr. 10
preciar *to appraise, value* tr. (r.) 10
precintar *to reinforce* tr. 10
precipitar *to precipitate* tr. (r.) 10
precisar *to specify, need, be necessary* tr./intr. (r.) 10
preconcebir *to preconceive* tr. 134
preconocer *to foresee, know beforehand* tr. 47
predecir *to predict, foretell, forecast* tr. 57
predestinar *to predestine, preordain* tr. 10
predicar *to preach* tr./intr. (r.) 24
predisponer *to predispose* tr. 140
predominar *to predominate, prevail, command* tr./intr. 10
preferir *to prefer* tr. **141**
prefijar *to prefix, prearrange* tr. 10
pregonar *to proclaim, hawk, make public* tr. 10
preguntar *to inquire, ask, question* tr./intr. (r.) 10
prejuzgar *to prejudge* tr. (r.) 30
preludiar *to prelude, clear the ground for* tr./intr. 10
premeditar *to premeditate* tr. 10
premiar *to reward* tr. 10
prendar *to pawn, pledge, become fond of* tr. (r.) 10
prender *to grasp, seize, catch* tr./intr. 23
prensar *to press* tr. 10
preñar *to get pregnant* tr. 10
preocupar *to worry, be concerned* tr. (r.) 10
preparar *to prepare, get ready* tr. (r.) 10
preponderar *to preponderate, prevail* intr. 10
preponer *to put before, prefer* tr. 140
prescribir *to prescribe, lay down, finish* tr./intr. 98
presenciar *to witness, see, be present* tr. 10
presentar *to present, display* tr. (r.) 10
presentir *to have a premonition, predict* tr. 108
preservar *to preserve* tr. 10
presidir *to preside* tr./intr. 133
presionar *to press, urge* tr. 10
prestar *to lend, loan, be good for* tr./intr. (r.) 10
prestigiar *to give credit* tr. 10
presumir *to presume, suppose, show off* tr./intr. 133
presuponer *to presuppose, budget* tr. 140
pretender *to pretend, be after* tr. 23
prevalecer *to prevail* intr. 47
prevaricar *to prevaricate, act dishonestly* intr. 24
prevenir *to prevent, prepare, warn* tr. (r.) 194
prever *to foresee, anticipate* tr. 195
principiar *to begin* tr. 10
pringar *to dip, take part, stain* tr./intr. (r.) 30
privar *to deprive, be in favour* tr./intr. (r.) 10

privatizar *to privatise* tr. 31
probar *to prove, try (on), test* tr./intr. (r.) **142**
proceder *to proceed, continue* intr. 23
procesar *to try, prosecute* tr. 10
proclamar *to proclaim, declare* tr. (r.) 10
procurar *to try, act as an attorney (for)* tr./intr. 10
producir *to produce, cause* tr. (r.) 45
proferir *to utter* tr. 108
profesar *to profess* tr./intr. 10
programar *to program, plan* tr. 10
progresar *to progress, advance* intr. 10
prohibir *to prohibit, forbid* tr. 133
prolongar *to prolong, extend* tr. (r.) 30
prometer *to promise* tr. (r.) 23
promover *to promote* tr. 128
promulgar *to proclaim, announce* tr. 30
pronosticar *to forecast* tr. 24
pronunciar *to pronounce, articulate* tr. (r.) 10
propagar *to propagate, spread* tr. (r.) 30
propender *to lean towards, incline* intr. 23
proponer *to propose* tr. (r.) 140
proporcionar *to provide, furnish* tr. (r.) 10
propulsar *to reject, propel* tr. 10
prorrogar *to delay, postpone* tr. 30
proscribir *to prohibit, banish* tr. 98
proseguir *to follow up, proceed* tr./intr. 134
proteger *to protect* tr./intr. 35
protestar *to protest, object* tr./intr. 10
proveer *to provide, supply* (past participle: **provisto**) tr./intr. (r.) 23
provenir *to originate, come from, proceed* intr. 194
provocar *to provoke, dare, make* tr. 24
publicar *to publish, issue* tr. 24
pugnar *to fight* intr. 10
pujar *to struggle, raise* tr./intr. 10
pulir *to polish* tr. (r.) 133
pulsar *to play, pulse, throb* tr./intr. (r.) 10
puntuar *to score, punctuate* tr. 10
punzar *to prick, puncture, throb* tr./intr. 31

quebrar *to break; smash* tr./intr. (r.) **143**
quedar *to stay, remain* intr. (r.) 10
quejarse *to complain, grumble* r. 116
quemar *to burn, fire, be very hot* tr./intr. (r.) 10
querer *to like, want* tr. **144**
quitar *to release, remove, rob, strip* tr. (r.) 10
quitarse *to take off, withdraw* r. 116

rabiar *to rage, get furious; have rabies* intr. 10
racionar *to ration* tr. 10
radiar *to radio, broadcast, radiate* tr./intr. 10
raer *to wipe out, rub off, scrape, erase* tr. (r.) 26
rajar *to split, crack* tr./intr. (r.) 10
rallar *to grate, vex* tr. 10
rapar *to shave, crop, snatch* tr. (r.) 10
rapiñar *to plunder, pillage* tr. 10
raptar *to abduct, kidnap* tr. 10
rarefacer *to rarefy, become rarefied* tr./intr. 106
rasar *to skim, level* tr. 10
rascar *to scratch, itch* tr./intr. (r.) 24
rasgar *to tear, rip* tr. (r.) 30
raspar *to scrape* tr. 10
rastrear *to track, trace, rake* tr./intr. 10
ratear *to steal, pinch, creep, crawl* tr./intr. (r.) 10
rayar *to line, stripe, cross out, dawn* tr./intr. (r.) 10
razonar *to reason, explain* tr./intr. 10
reaccionar *to react* intr. 10
reactivar *to reactivate* tr. 10
realizar *to realise, fulfil, carry out* tr. 31
realizarse *to become fulfilled, happen* r. 31, 116
reanimar *to reanimate, revive* tr. (r.) 10

reapretar *to press (tight) again* tr. 33
rebajar *to reduce, lower* tr. (r.) 10
rebañar *to finish up, gather up completely* tr. 10
reblandecer *to soften, become soft* tr. (r.) 47
rebosar *to overflow, run over* intr. (r.) 10
rebuznar *to bray* intr. 10
recaer *to fall again* intr. 26
recalcar *to emphasise, list* tr./intr. 24
recalentar *to re-heat, warm up* tr. (r.) 27
recapacitar *to think over* tr. 10
recelar *to suspect, fear* tr./intr. (r.) 10
recentar *to leaven* tr. (r.) 33
rechazar *to reject, repel* tr. 31
recibir *to receive, get, welcome* tr./intr. 133
recibirse *to be admitted, graduate* r. 133
reclamar *to reclaim, claim, protest* tr./intr. 10
reclinar *to recline, lean* tr. (r.) 10
recluir *to confine, seclude, imprison* tr. (r.) 110
reclutar *to round up, recruit* tr. 10
recocer *to over-boil* tr. 34
recoger *to pick, gather, collect* tr. (r.) 35
recomendar *to recommend* tr. (r.) **145**
recompensar *to reward, compensate, recompense* tr. 10
reconciliar *to reconcile* tr. (r.) 10
reconocer *to recognise, acknowledge* tr. (r.) 47
reconstruir *to rebuild, reconstruct* tr. (r.) 110
recontar *to recount* tr. 50
reconvenir *to remonstrate, reprimand* tr. 194
recordar *to remind, remember* tr./intr. (r.) **146**
recorrer *to travel, cross* tr. (r.) 23
recortar *to trim, cut off* tr. (r.) 10
recostar *to lean against* tr. (r.) 53
recrear *to amuse, entertain* tr. (r.) 10
recrecer *to increase, grow* tr./intr. (r.) 54
redactar *to edit, write* tr. 10
reducir *to reduce, cut down* tr. (r.) 45
reelegir *to re-elect* tr. 84
reembolsar *to reimburse, refund* tr. (r.) 10
reenviar *to send back, forward* tr. (r.) 94
referir *to refer, relate* tr. (r.) **147**
refinar *to refine* tr. 10
reflejar *to reverberate, reflect* tr./intr. (r.) 10
reflexionar *to reflect* tr./intr. (r.) 10
reflorecer *to blossom* intr. 47
reformar *to reform, alter, change* tr. 10
reforzar *to reinforce, strengthen* tr. (r.) **148**
refregar *to fray* tr. (r.) 101
regalar *to give gifts, make a present* tr. (r.) 10
regañar *to scold, growl, tell off* tr./intr. (r.) 10
regar *to water, irrigate* tr. (r.) **149**
regatear *to barter, bargain, haggle* tr./intr. (r.) 10
regimentar *to maintain discipline, organise* tr. 33
regir *to rule* tr./intr. 134
registrar *to record, search, examine* tr. (r.) 10
regoldar *to belch* intr. 2
regresar *to return, regress, go back* tr./intr. 10
rehacer *to redo, remake, rally* tr. (r.) 106
rehogar *to cook in batter / oil, stirfry* tr. 30
rehollar *to trample on* tr. 2
rehuir *to avoid, shun, flee, shrink* tr./intr. (r.) 110
rehusar *to refuse, decline* tr. 10
reinstalar *to reinstate* tr. 10
reír *to laugh* tr./intr. (r.) **150**
rejuvenecer *to rejuvenate* tr./intr. (r.) 47
relacionar *to relate* 10
releer *to read again* tr. (r.) 117
rellenar *to fill, stuff, refill* tr. (r.) 10
relucir *to shine* intr. 45
remanecer *to reappear unexpectedly* intr. 47
remansar *to form a pool* tr. 10

reverdecer *to make green, give new vigour* tr. (r.) 47
reverter *to overflow* intr. 196
revertir *to revert* intr. 108
revestir *to reclothe* tr. (r.) 134
revisar *to revise* tr. 10
revivir *to revive, relive* intr. 198
revocar *to revoke, appeal* tr./intr. 24
revolar *to fly again* intr. 199
revolcar *to roll about, trample, floor* tr. 200
revolcarse *to wallow* r. 116, 200
revolver *to revolve, turn, mix* tr. (r.) 201
rezar *to pray* tr./intr. 31
ridiculizar *to ridicule* tr. 31
robar *to rob, steal* tr./intr. (r.) 10
robustecer *to strengthen, become strong* tr. (r.) 47
rociar *to spray, sprinkle* tr./intr. 10
rodar *to roll* tr./intr. **158**
rodear *to detour, surround* tr./intr. 10
roer *to gnaw, worry* tr. 26
rogar *to beg, ask for* tr. **159**
romper *to break, shatter, tear* (past participle: **roto**) tr./intr. (r.) 23
roncar *to snore* intr. 24
ronchar *to crunch, chew* tr./intr. 10
rondar *to patrol, guard* tr./intr. 10
rotar *to rotate* intr. 10
rotular *to label, make a sign / inscription* tr. 10
rozar *to touch, rub* tr./intr. (r.) 31
rubricar *to sign* tr. 24
rumiar *to ruminate, reflect on, meditate* tr. 10
rumorear *to rumour* tr. (r.) 10

saber *to know, know how to* tr./intr. (r.) **160**
saborear *to relish, taste and enjoy* tr. (r.) 10
sacar *to take out, get* tr./intr. (r.) 24
sacrificar *to sacrifice* tr. (r.) 24
sacudir *to shake, jerk, jolt* tr. (r.) 133
salar *to salt, cure* tr. 10
saldar *to settle, liquidate* tr. 10
salir *to go out, leave* intr. (r.) **161**
salpicar *to splash, sprinkle, spatter* tr. 24
salpimentar *to season with salt and pepper* tr. 10
salpresar *to pickle, preserve with salt* tr. 10
saltar *to jump, leap, hop, skip* tr./intr. (r.) 10
saludar *to greet, salute* tr. (r.) 10
salvar *to save* tr./intr. (r.) 10
sanar *to cure, heal* tr./intr. 10
sancionar *to sanction* tr. 10
sangrar *to bleed* tr./intr. 10
saquear *to pillage, sack, loot* tr. 10
satisfacer *to satisfy* tr. (r.) 106
secar *to dry* tr. (r.) 24
sedar *to soothe, quiet, allay* tr. 10
seducir *to seduce, entice* tr. 45
segar *to mow, cut* tr./intr. **162**
seguir *to follow, continue* tr./intr. (r.) 79, 134
sellar *to seal* tr. (r.) 10
sembrar *to sow* tr. **163**
semejar *to resemble, look like* intr. (r.) 10
sementar *to scatter (seed)* tr. 33
sentar *to sit, suit, fit* tr. (r.) 164
sentarse *to sit down* r. **164**
sentir *to feel, regret* tr./intr. (r.) **165**
señalar *to point, signal, indicate* tr. (r.) 10
separar *to separate, detach* tr. (r.) 10
sepultar *to bury* tr. (r.) 10
ser *to be* intr. (aux.) **166**
serrar *to saw* tr. 33
servir *to serve* tr./intr. (r.) **167**
silbar *to whistle, hiss* tr. 10
simular *to feign, simulate* tr. 10
sintonizar *to synchronise, tune in* tr./intr. 31
sisar *to thieve, filch, take in* tr. 10
situar *to put, situate, locate* tr. (r.) **168**
sobar *to rub, slap, knead* tr. 10
sobrar *to be in excess, be left over* tr./intr. 10
sobregirar *to overdraw* tr. 10
sobreponer *to superimpose, overcome* tr. 140
sobresalir *to project, excel, stand out* tr. 161
sobresolar *to resole* tr. 2
sobrevenir *to supervene, follow,*

happen suddenly intr. 194
socorrer *to help, aid, assist* tr. 23
sofocar *to smother, suffocate, choke* tr. (r.) 24
solar *to sole, pave* tr. 2
soldar *to weald* tr. (r.) 2
soler *to be in the habit of* intr. **169**
solicitar *to solicit, request, apply* tr. 10
sollozar *to sob, cry, whimper* intr. 31
soltar *to loosen, undo, let go of* tr. (r.) **170**
solucionar *to solve* tr. 10
solventar *to settle a debt* tr. 10
someter *to subdue, submit, surrender* tr. (r.) 23
sonar *to ring, sound* tr./intr. (r.) **171**
sonarse *to blow one's nose* r. 116, 171
sonreír *to smile* intr. (r.) 150
soñar *to dream* tr./intr. **172**
sopapear *to slap, box* tr. 10
soplar *to blow, blow out* tr./intr. (r.) 10
soportar *to support, endure* tr. 10
sorber *to sip, suck* tr. 23
sorprender *to surprise, astonish* tr. (r.) 23
sorregar *to irrigate* tr. 33
sortear *to sort, raffle, dodge* tr. 10
sosegar *to tranquilise* tr./intr. (r.) 33
sospechar *to suspect* tr./intr. 10
sostener *to sustain, support, maintain, uphold* tr. (r.) 179
soterrar *to bury, hide* tr. 33
suavizar *to ease, soften, smooth* tr. (r.) 31
subarrendar *to sublet, sublease* tr. 33
subastar *to auction* tr. 10
subir *to go up, rise, climb* tr./intr. (r.) **173**
subrayar *to underline, underscore* tr. 10
subscribirse *to subscribe, agree to* r. 98
substituir *to substitute, reduce* tr. 110
substraer *to take away, remove* tr. 188
subvencionar *to subsidise* tr. 10
subvertir *to subvert, disturb* tr. 108
suceder *to happen* intr. (r.) 23
sudar *to sweat, perspire* tr./intr. 10
sufrir *to suffer, endure, bear up, undergo* tr./intr. 133
sugerir *to suggest, hint* tr. **174**
sujetar *to subdue, subject, hold* tr. (r.) 10
sumar *to add, sum* tr. (r.) 10
sumergir *to submerge, plunge, immerse, sink* tr. (r.) 52
superar *to exceed, surpass, overcome* tr. (r.) 10
suponer *to suppose, assume, have authority* tr./intr. (r.) 140
suprimir *to suppress, omit, eliminate* tr. (r.) 133
surgir *to surge, appear, spout* intr. 52
surtir *to stock, supply, gush* tr./intr. 133
suspender *to suspend, hang* tr. (r.) 23
suspirar *to sigh* tr. 10
susurrar *to whisper, murmur* intr. 10

tachar *to cross out* tr. 10
tajar *to slice, chop, cut, trim* tr. 10
talar *to fell, cut down* tr. 10
tambalear *to stagger* intr. (r.) 10
tañer *to pluck, play strings* tr./intr. 23
tapar *to cover, hide* tr. (r.) **175**
tardar *to take a long time* intr. (r.) 10
tartamudear *to stammer, stutter* intr. 10
teclear *to type, run one's fingers over the keys* tr./intr. 10
tejer *to weave* tr. 23
telefonear *to telephone* tr./intr. 10
telegrafiar *to telegraph, cable* tr./intr. 10
teleguiar *to guide by remote control* tr. 10
temblar *to tremble, shake* intr. (r.) **176**
temer *to fear, dread* tr./intr. (r.) **177**
tender *to spread out, lay* tr./intr. (r.) **178**
tener *to have, possess* tr./intr. (r.) **179**
tentar *to touch, try* tr. (r.) **180**
teñir *to dye, stain* tr. (r.) **181**

terminar *to end, finish, terminate* tr./intr. (r.) 10
testar *to make a will or testament; erase* tr./intr. 10
tirar *to draw, pull, throw* tr./intr. (r.) 10
tocar *to touch, play* tr./intr. (r.) **182**
tolerar *to tolerate* tr. 10
tomar *to take, have* tr./intr. (r.) **183**
tontear *to be foolish, flirt* intr. 10
torcer *to twist, turn* tr./intr. (r.) **184**
toser *to cough* intr. 23
tostar *to toast, tan, roast* tr. (r.) **185**
trabajar *to work* tr./intr. (r.) **186**
trabar *to join, lock, get entangled* tr./intr. (r.) 10
traducir *to translate* tr. **187**
traer *to bring* tr. (r.) **188**
tragar *to swallow* tr./intr. (r.) 30
traicionar *to betray* tr. 10
trajinar *to bustle about, rush around* tr./intr. (r.) 10
tramitar *to negotiate, transact* tr. 10
trancar *to lock, stride* tr./intr. 24
tranquilizar *to tranquilise, calm down, quieten down* tr. (r.) 31
transferir *to transfer, postpone* tr. **189**
transformar *to become, transform* tr. (r.) 10
transfregar *to rub together* tr. 101
transigir *to compromise, tolerate* intr. 52
transitar *to pass, travel* intr. 10
translucir *to be translucid, become clear, conjecture* tr. 45
transmitir *to transmit* tr. 133
transponer *to transfer* tr. 140
transportar *to transport* tr. (r.) 10
trascender *to transcend* tr./intr. 136
trascolar *to percolate* tr. (r.) 36
trascordarse *to remember incorrectly, forget* r. 2, 116
trasegar *to pour over, decant* tr. 162
trasferir *to transfer, defer* tr. 108
trasladarse *to move, transfer* tr. (r.) 116
traslucir *to be translucid, become obvious* tr. (r.) 45
trasmontar *to go over mountains* tr./intr. 10
trasmudar *to transmute* tr. 129
trasoír *to hear incorrectly* tr. 131
trasoñar *to make schemes, imagine wrongly* tr. 172
traspasar *to transfix, pierce* tr. (r.) 10
trasquilar *to shear, clip* tr. 10
trastornar *to turn upside down, disturb* tr. 10
trasvolar *to fly across* tr. 199
tratar *to try, treat, deal with, handle* tr./intr. (r.) 10
travesar *to cross* tr. (r.) 33
trazar *to sketch, trace, draw* tr. 31
trenzar *to braid, plait* tr. (r.) 31
trepar *to climb, clamber* tr./intr. (r.) 10
tributar *to pay taxes, render* tr. 10
tricotar *to knit* tr. 10
trillar *to thresh, thrash, use frequently* tr. 10
trinar *to trill, warble, fume* intr. 10
trinchar *to carve, slice, arrange* tr. 10
triplicar *to treble* tr. 24
triscar *to mix up, set, consume* tr./intr. (r.) 24
triturar *to grind, crush* tr. 10
triunfar *to triumph* intr. 10
trizar *to tear to pieces* tr. 31
trocar *to barter, exchange* tr. (r.) 24
trocear *to cut into bits* tr. 10
trompicar *to trip, stumble* tr./intr. 24
tronar *to thunder, shoot* tr./intr. (r.) **190**
tronchar *to split, crack* tr. (r.) 10
tronzar *to slice, break into chunks* tr. 31
tropezar *to stumble, trip* intr. (r.) 31, 33
trotar *to trot* intr. 10
tullir *to cripple, disable, excrete* tr./intr. (r.) 133
tumbar *to fall down, lie down* tr./intr. (r.) 10
tumultar *to stir up, cause disorder* tr. (r.) 10
tundir *to thrash* tr. 133
turbar *to disturb, upset, perturb* tr./intr. (r.) 10
tutearse *to talk with familiarity using*